D1374596

The European Peasantry

L'exploitation familiale traditionale caracterisée par une confusion, en son sein, de l'activité économique, du destin familial et du droit de prorieté.

Revue française de l'agriculture, 1965

What is your greatest need for the coming decade? More land for the family.

Brindisi, 1966

Sûr de l'appui de la masse paysanne un combat de plus en plus dur pour obtenir une politique de révalorisation des prix agricoles et par voie de conséquence l'arrêt de l'exode rural et le salut de l'exploitation familiale libre.

Le Comité de Guéret, 1967

Everybody knows that the so-called peasant question will be put quite differently once the percentage of rural population is no longer 56, as at present, but say 30 or 20 per cent, as in industrially developed countries.

E. Kardelj, 1962

On ne remédiera pas aux maux du libéralisme économique par le maintien artificiel des structures artisanales, precapitalistes, sous-productives. Mieux vaut chercher à concilier technocratie et democratie, lier les avantages techniques de la grande exploitation avec les bénéfices économiques d'une suppression de la sous-consommation et les agréments sociaux d'une gestion requérant la participation active de chaque adherent.

R. Dumont, 1956

The European Peasantry

THE FINAL PHASE

S. H. Franklin

Associate Professor
Department of Geography
Victoria University of Wellington, New Zealand

METHUEN & CO, LTD
11 New Fetter Lane, London EC4

First published 1969

Printed and bound in Great Britain
by The Camelot Press Ltd, London and Southampton
SBN 416 12370 8

Distributed in the USA
By Barnes & Noble Inc

Contents

Plates (following page xvi)

Figures

Tables

Preface and Acknowledgements

My interest in the peasantry arose out of a sense of wonderment at how so large a body of people could pursue a way of life so foreign to the urban existence to which I was born, and it arose also out of a sense of discomfort when faced with essentially folklorist explanations of this existence. It was stimulated by reading two memorable books: Jacques Weulersse's, *Les Paysans de Syrie et du Proche-Orient*, a book which first led me to suspect that on the whole French geographers were preferable to others; and Doreen Warriner's *The Economics of Peasant Farming*. I would like to acknowledge the kindly advice and assistance Dr Warriner has always offered me when I have visited Britain. Distance prevented me from discussing with her my work during its final stages, and I shall always regret this.

On the whole I have never found distance from Europe to be a particular hindrance to undertaking this study. Library facilities are good in New Zealand, and I suspect somewhat better than those of most large provincial centres in England. Certainly whenever I have been in England I have always been left with the impression that, psychologically speaking, the Channel presents a barrier for the English as great as the physical barrier which the Pacific and the Atlantic together have presented to me. Nevertheless had it not been for the financial assistance of northern hemisphere foundations, field work would have been impossible, and the whole project would never have got off the ground. I am deeply grateful to the Rockefeller Foundation for their support of a fellowship in 1959. I am indebted to the Deutscher Akademischer Austauschdienst for financing my stay in Germany in 1963. And I wish to thank also the University of Manchester for granting me a Simon Research Fellowship in 1965–6. Their generosity and hospitality made it a very happy period.

I am widely indebted to a large number of scholars and officials, mostly on the Continent, for the time, the documents, the advice and assistance they so freely granted me. Let me record here my sincere appreciation of their help. Plate 14 is reproduced by the kind permission of the Ente per la Riforma Fondiaria in Puglia, Lucania and Molise.

The encouragement and sympathy which I have always received from my colleagues at Victoria University of Wellington I value greatly. I would like to mention in particular, Dr J. Williams, the former Vice-

Chancellor, K. M. Buchanan, the Head of the Department of Geography, and the Deans of the Faculties. An especial acknowledgement must be reserved for my departmental colleague, Euan McQueen, who has so generously given his time to comment on the style and composition of the drafts. I was most fortunate to have the assistance of two charming cartographers, Mrs Barbara Winchester and Miss Robin Somervell; to be able to draw upon the photographic expertise and patience of Mrs Jean Benfield, and latterly Mr J. S. Murphy. I was blessed to have such an efficient and accurate typist as Mrs Lorna Guerin. The Editorial Board of *Pacific Viewpoint* has kindly allowed me to reproduce the Gosheim diagrams.

Without the family economy, little would have been achieved. My parents looked after our three children whenever my wife and I were on the Continent. To know that our children were happily living with their generous grandparents freed us both of intolerable worries. My wife accompanied me throughout our long journeys; for her companionship and help I shall always be grateful.

As for the errors and omissions, inaccuracies due to rounding apart – they are all exclusively mine.

Introduction

In the post-war era the question of the future, or the fate, of peasant farming in Europe has been placed in a context quite different to the one within which the issue had been debated in Europe during the inter-war period. Then general economic stagnation had been a threat and at times a reality. Industrial expansion was erratic and not general. Consumption levels were slow to rise; autarkic economic policies prevailed; and if the economies of the western countries suffered because of the cyclical characteristics of the capitalist economy, the overwhelmingly agrarian economies of eastern Europe displayed in an aggravated form features which have since been recognized as typical of a colonial or dependent economy. The transition to the post-war context was obscured initially by the destructive and disorganizing effects of the war itself. The absolute shortage of food, the destruction of buildings, equipment and livestock ensured that during the first years of peace the production of food, the rebuilding of assets and often the provision of employment assumed prime importance in the minds of the administrators and the peasants themselves. Successively, however, most economies entered a phase of industrial expansion which became sustained as the '50s progressed. The threat of economic stagnation disappeared, the demand for industrial labour appeared to be insatiable, and in the unrelaxing search for new markets – in the West, that is – industry made available to the rural populations the machines, the materials and the consumption goods created by modern science and technology. The demand for food rose and shifts in preferences occurred with the rising living standards of the urban dwellers. As the interdependences of an expanding and diversifying economy multiplied some reassessment of the function of peasant farming in an expanding industrial society became unavoidable. The reassessment was neither immediate or voluntary. Until the end of the '50s historic attitudes prevailed both in the East and the West. Subsequently opinions began to evolve and attitudes to modify, largely under the pressure of events. The process is far from complete, only a few general principles have been evolved, and a host of ambiguities remain unresolved. It is with this reassessment – the events and developments that have promoted it, the problems which have been created, the policies that have been formulated to cope with a very dynamic situation – that the book is largely concerned.

In those countries which wholly collectivized their agriculture the reassessment was uncompromising, total and apparently final. I do not believe, however, that the collectivized peasantry has become a quite separate issue from the study of the peasantry that possesses individual holdings. From what I know and have seen of the collectivized countries I think it would be extremely valuable to apply the concept of the peasant economy to the study of these collectivized peasantry at their present and immediately past stage of development. The *chef d'entreprise* with his individual plot of land may be regarded as a very particular type of peasant who is required to provide off-farm labour to the socialist sector, without any assurance of the rate at which the work will be remunerated. The euthanasia of the remnants of the peasant economy in the collective system appears to be dependent upon the progressive improvement in both the level of and security of remuneration, as well as an increase in the relative importance of the income from the socialist sector. In Russia, certainly, significant changes in these respects appear imminent. To be competitive with the private sector the collectives must also solve the problems associated with intensive and livestock farming systems in the context of large-scale organizations. But if the collectivized peasantry during the last decade or so has not been a wholly separate issue, it has been a highly particular and specialized issue which it has not been practical to discuss. In this volume, therefore, the 'East' or Eastern Europe, refers only to Yugoslavia and Poland, which having rejected wholesale collectivization, have been forced to make a reassessment of the future of their peasantry within a framework not unlike that adopted by the West. By excluding the collectivized peasantry of Eastern Europe a greater degree of unity has been achieved in what is a rather complex subject.

The initial chapter provides a short explanation of the peasant productive system or peasant economy. For want of such a concept I had to construct my own and in doing so settled upon the labour commitment of the enterprise as the decisive factor. By adopting Gerth and Mills' use of 'orders' and 'spheres of activation' I was able to add a valuable sociological content to the idea of a peasant economy and created for myself a tool that enabled me to bring some order into the often contradictory and paradoxical situation so characteristic of the peasantry in the contemporary era. My 'theory' proved to be remarkably similar to Chayanov's theory of peasant economy, as I learnt from the English translation first published in 1966; though, in fact, he uses neither the concept of labour commitment nor the concept of kinship and economic orders. What is significant, however, is that looking at the same phenomenon generations apart we produced a similar sort of explanation. I am aware of what atrocities may be committed, and at what length, in the social sciences in the name of theory.

Consequently the theoretical section is brief and contains only what is necessary to an understanding of the general features of present-day peasant society – the principal topic of the first chapter.

General issues are returned to in the final chapter, but they are of a different sort. The conclusion is concerned with the future of the peasantry: what likely effect present socio-economic structures will have upon the evolution of peasant society in the next decade or two. What contribution the worker-peasant class and rural industrialization will make towards the raising of rural living standards. How permeating the influence of vertical integration will be. And, finally, what implications European experience of the past two decades has for the formulation of agrarian programmes in less developed areas.

By contrast the chapters devoted to individual countries – they constitute almost four-fifths of the book – are much more detailed, and concentrate upon the diversities which are so characteristic of the European peasantry at its present stage of development. There is nothing more injurious to the understanding of rural life than that durable and popular fiction, the peasant stereotype. These chapters may contribute towards his demise. They can be treated as separate essays; and though there is a reason for their order, it should not deter anyone from choosing those sections which interest him most in whatever order he prefers.

Four fundamental topics, however, are developed in each of the regional chapters: The socio-economic structure of the peasantry, which is basic to any understanding of the contemporary situation; the regional context within which these structures are evolving. The economic performance of the peasantry both in an absolute and relative sense; and, finally the formulation and implementation, and the ambiguities, of agrarian policies which reflect the influence of these three factors. Naturally each country lends itself to the elaboration of more specific topics, and this creates a degree of variety. Income parity and the worker-peasant class are subjects treated best in detail in a German context. In the case of France, the formulation of a structural policy deserves special attention. Land reform has been a prominent feature of the Mezzogiorno in the last fifteen years, and the relations between the peasant and socialist sectors have been a distinctive feature of agrarian affairs in both Yugoslavia and Poland. One naturally regrets the absence of any detailed reference to other countries, but the main lessons of Dutch and Danish experience are utilized in the conclusion, and the detailed study of the Cassa's programme for the Mezzogiorno is highly relevant to any discussion of agrarian development in Spain, Portugal and Greece.

The analysis of peasant social structures is never an easy matter, mainly because the basic statistics one uses for this purpose refer to agrarian structures and not socio-economic structures. In Europe the long-standing practice has been for the administrations to collect figures which refer to farms or holdings. But the ancient and honoured custom has been to use these figures as if they referred to people. Thus farms of less than five or eight or ten hectares, depending upon the country, have usually been called small peasant farms and the people associated with them have been classified as the small peasantry. In the post-war world the degree of correspondence between the agrarian and socio-economic structures has been diminishing as the socio-economic differentiation of the peasantry has taken place. I feel certain that this lack of correspondence will be a source of confusion for many readers, and I doubt if the conservative habits of most census takers will ever change rapidly enough to catch up with the processes which are under way in the rural areas. More accurate analyses are provided by the sample surveys conducted by rural sociologists, but there are not nearly enough of them. The small peasant class, numerically always the most important of the classes, has borne the brunt of the post-war changes. It is helpful when reading about them to remember that usually this class contains a group of marginal and viable full-time farms; a group of farms worked by elderly people, many of whom belong to the marginal group; and a group of part-time and worker-peasant farms. The labour force within each class of holdings varies according to whether it is composed mainly of males or females, and whether they are occupied full or part-time. Some labour may be supplied by hired workers, male or female, on either a full or part-time basis. The occupational character of the family which resides upon the farm may be simple or complex. As a whole the family may spend all of its time engaged in working on their own holding. It is not uncommon, however, for one or more members to work, part-time, on other persons' farms. It has become very common in the post-war period for part of the family, including the chef himself, to work full-time in the non-agricultural sector; and there are instances where all members of the family are engaged outside agriculture. When dealing with socio-economic structures one is concerned principally with the general character of the holding, the composition of the labour force, the occupational structure of the family; prime importance always being attached to the economic behaviour and socio-economic character of the *chef d'entreprise* himself.

Whenever possible I have resisted using a foreign term if a suitable English one exists; but I have not converted hectares (ha) to acres, quintaux to bushels, densities per square kilometre (km^2) to densities per square mile, and I have preferred to use the precise continental term, milliard – one thousand million; and all this will be good practice for those Anglo-Saxon populations intent on joining Europe. Some words, structural and restructuring – for instance – have been given rather unusual connotations, but this is inevitable. The phenomena they describe are absent from British life. One French term, however, proved to be indispensable. It is still a common occurrence to find in the rural areas of Europe a person, male or female, who may or may not be the proprietor of the land, who may be part owner and part tenant of a number of non-contiguous strips of land that constitute the holding, or exploitation, who directs the agricultural work either in the capacity of a full-time operative or as a part-time factory worker or farm worker; who is not necessarily a proprietor or owner occupier, but who is in fact the *chef d'entreprise* and usually the *chef de famille*, in short the chef, the central figure of this study.*

The study of the peasantry involves one in something more than the study of agricultural economics, or systems of land use, or marketing practices or any one of the relevant specialism. To study the peasantry is to become involved in a wide range of issues, in politics, in regional planning, in social change, in economic development and so on, for the simple reason that the peasantry are one of the major classes of European society. Their evolution and future touches many of the profound material and immaterial aspects of European civilization – as the British have come to understand because of their desire to enter the Common Market, and as the New Zealanders have learnt to their dismay.

* A Glossary of special terms, initials of organizations, etc., will be found at the end of this book.

1. The eternal order of the fields: Boll, Kreis Hechingen, Baden-Württemberg, summer 1959.

2. A Polish family lifting sugar beet near Kalisz, October 1966.

3. Land reform peasants, near Grossetto, the Maremma, 1959.

4. (*a*). The feminization of the labour force in a worker peasant community. Gosheim, Kreis Tuttlingen, Baden-Württemberg, 1959.

4 (*b*). The persistence of handicrafts among the aged, near Mladenovac, Yugoslavia, 1966.

5 and 6. Market day near Szydlowiec, October 1966.

7. Autumn ploughing near Bochina, Cracow, 1966. Three families are at work within this confined space.

8. Old persons' holding, Bavaria, 1959.

9. Small peasant farm, Schlossau, Kreis Buchen, Baden-Württemberg, 1959.

10. Small peasant farm near Radom, Poland, 1966.

11. Investment in farm dwellings south of Cracow, 1966.

12. Tractorization of an Auvergne farm, 1959.

13. A capitalist farm, Bavaria, 1959.

14. Promise of a new order: bureaucrat, technocrat and braccianti.

15. *Origins:* the cassali of San Cataldo, Potenza, 1959.

16. *Assignees:* a two generation family near Policoro, Metaponto, 1959. (The two young men are temporary workers hired for the tobacco harvest.)

17. *Achievement:* podere in the Maremma, 1959.

18. *Failure:* abandoned poderi near Scanzano, Lucania, 1966.

19. *Waste:* irrigated land in the valley of the Bradano, farmed extensively by capitalistic entrepreneurs who have received the backing of the Cassa.

20. *Initiation:* recent industrial growth in Egesheim (pop. 409, 1961), a worker-peasant settlement. Kreis Tuttlingen, Baden-Württemberg, 1963.

21. *Fulfilment:* the Hermle factory at Gosheim, 1963.

22. Investment in the future, the new middle school, Gosheim, 1963.

23. Vocational deprivation in the Auvergne.

24. A cultural heritage to be preserved: Argentat in the region of Limousin, France.

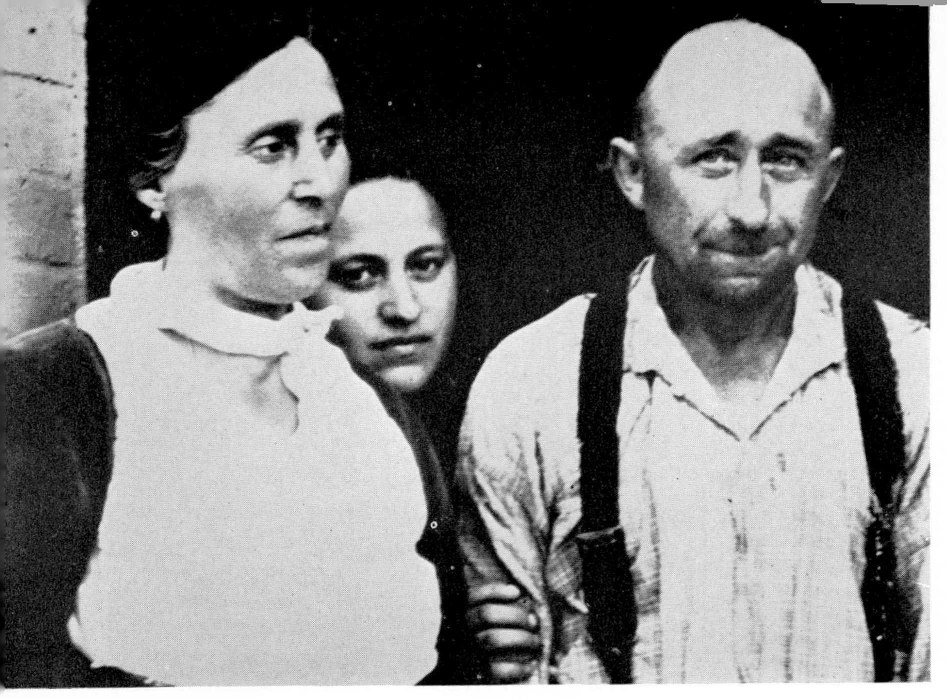

25 (*a*). *Peasants:* Dignity, innocence, resignation.

25 (*b*). *Worker peasants:* Wealth, mobility and leisure, Gosheim.

1 PEASANTS: concept and context

The term 'peasant' is one of those major, indispensable, useful, and therefore imprecise and hard to define words, like capitalism and socialism. Its content is primarily economic, but as with the other two terms, certain sociological associations or implications are very strong: and some ideological attachments appear to be indissoluble. Peasant in fact is a prejudicial word – people tend to have very fixed ideas which they hold uncritically about what constitutes a peasant; and a great deal of confusion is created by seeking to establish an unnatural degree of precision for this convenient and general, but inexact, term. The problem of definition, which cannot be wholly avoided, can however be reduced to manageable proportions and almost circumvented by first considering the different, but not unrelated, contexts within which the word is most frequently used.

At a high level of abstraction the peasantry can be dealt with in the context of a peasant system of production, or peasant economy.[1] One of the enduring and essential – in fact – revolutionary characteristics of the capitalist system of production is the labour commitment of the entrepreneur. With the introduction of the capitalist system labour became a commodity, like any other commodity to be purchased or dispensed with, hired or sacked, according to the needs of the firm and the state of the market. For the peasant *chef d'entreprise* such freedom of action can never exist. His labour force consists mainly of his kith and kin; his wife, his children and their dependants, his elderly parents. To hire and fire them according to the dictates of some external regulatory mechanism would be at once, inhuman, impractical and irrational. Inhuman because only in exceptional circumstances are alternative employment opportunities ever generally available. Impractical because members of the labour force, as members of the family are entitled to a share in the ownership of the means of production; because historically the enterprise is the sum of the labours of the generations. Irrational because the objectives of the enterprise are primarily genealogical and only secondarily economic; because the aim of the chef is to maximize the input of labour rather than maximize profit or some other indicator of efficiency.* In contrast to the capitalist entrepreneur, the peasant chef's labour commitment may be deemed to be total. Peasant society has therefore always been a great creator of work

[1] Franklin (1965). * See note at end of this chapter.

and employment, with varying degrees of under-utilization of labour arising out of particular combinations of technology, eco-system and social order. Its historic significance stems from this commitment, which underlies its capacity, demonstrated throughout the centuries, to colonize, to ameliorate, to support and to persist.

This commitment is derived from the general institutional characteristics of the peasant family enterprise – the second context in which the term has meaning. Throughout all aspects of peasant life those things which belong to the kinship order – family, status, marriage and death, are inextricably mixed with those things that belong to the economic order: occupation, inheritance and property. The one man instructs his sons in the rigours of social behaviour in the role of father and as *chef d'entreprise* he teaches them the imperatives of good agronomic practice. The personal and family crises of birth, death and marriage, the biological cycle of the family, involve and affect the future, the profitability, the productivity, in areas of *Realteilung*, where the land is shared out amongst the heirs, the very physical composition of the farm, even the appearance of the landscape itself. As the capitalist system of production has come to dominance a growing separation of the kinship from the economic order has prevailed without becoming final. Family firms, where the head of the household, because of that kinship status, remains an inefficient and tradition bound *chef d'entreprise*, are not unknown in the capitalist world, in big as well as small businesses; neither is nepotism. But what is regarded as normal, even praiseworthy and divine in structure in the peasant world, is questioned by and held repugnant to the advanced capitalist and nascent socialist world. Amongst the great mass of the proletariat the industrial functions of the family have been almost completely extinguished, the status of *chef d'entreprise* has disappeared from most families, and in working hours the separation between the kinship order and the economic order is almost total. Still, as Chayanov recognized, the peasant type of enterprise is not a solely rural phenomenon,[2] it can be found in the towns too, especially in the underdeveloped world. The addition of a number of features derived from the nature of agricultural activity lends certain distinctive qualities to the peasant farm enterprise, and makes the peasant family holding a particular, but most common form of peasant enterprise, as well as being the principal institution of the peasant productive system.

There have been eras when the peasant enterprise was the prevalent institution, and the peasant system was the predominant mode of production. In this context the peasantry have become strongly associated with a certain stage of economic development and here the greatest degree of confusion about the meaning of the term arises, often because of an un-

[2] Chayanov (1966): 90.

recognized change in the level of abstraction. At a high level of abstraction it is very convenient to equate the period when the peasant economy was the dominant mode of production with a certain stage of economic development. Theories dealing with economic growth in a labour surplus economy do in fact use the peasant economic system as a datum. It is a change in the level of abstraction, however, to utilize one historical or regional type of peasant society and to equate it with a general stage of economic development. The 'pop' variety of economic history and anthropology runs perilously close to doing this with its 'all time – all space' Peasant-Traditional Society: Stage of Economic Growth combination, that is based on such a vertiginous telescoping of history and such a homogenized version of geography. The product of this type of thinking is not so much a model of peasant society as a stereotype. This volume is concerned with the stage of growth context in a rather particular way. The whole of Europe has now reached the stage where the peasant economy is either no longer the predominant mode of production, and in some countries has not been for decades, or it has reached the point of losing its pre-eminence. What we are witnessing in Europe is the functioning of the peasant economy at a stage of development that is neo-capitalist in the West and which has passed beyond the period of primitive socialist accumulation in the East. Many of the paradoxical features of contemporary peasant life are related to the exposure or creation of contradictions within the kinship-economic orders of the peasant enterprise arising out of its incorporation within these predominantly non-peasant systems.

Of very real significance to an understanding of the contemporary peasantry are the phases of economic development experienced by the post-war economies, socialist as well as capitalist; especially, the sustained growth of industrial employment and the expansion of urban demand for agricultural produce. The first has been instrumental in encouraging and maintaining the flow of labour out of the agricultural sector; the second has exposed the area of productive activity in the peasant economy – the processing of produce and the organization of marketing – most accessible to the penetration of capitalist or socialist modes of production. In all probability it is from this salient that the peasant economy will be finally overrun and demolished. At the moment, however, the essential traits of the peasant productive system and peasant family enterprise reveal themselves as remarkably durable. The outflow of labour has changed the general character of the labour force; hired temporary or permanent labour is increasingly difficult to obtain both in the East and the West; but the effect has been to strengthen the familial character of the labour force amongst that sector of the peasantry seeking to maintain or establish itself as a mechanized and modernized 'middle' peasantry. Increased opportunities for employment have allowed the chefs of the small and dwarf holdings to meet their labour commitment by following, in a new sphere, the old practice of expanding the families' economic horizons by taking up off-farm non-agricultural work. The initial period of capitalist expansion associated with the destruction of rural based industries – with the 'agriculturalization' of the countryside – has been replaced with a period of re-industrialization under the auspices of neo-capitalism and socialism. Ultimately this process ought to result in the destruction of part of the peasant economy through the incorporation of the worker-peasants within the ranks of the industrial proletariat, especially if the gap between industrial and agricultural earnings continues to show no tendency to decrease. In most countries, however, the process has still a long way to go. Most recently, during the phase of post-war food and accommodation shortages the peasant household has displayed its strengths rather than weaknesses by revealing once again its historic capacity to function as the secure and productive basis of a binary economy. The war and immediate post-war years also enhanced the residual or security function of the family enterprise, which the needs of old age have always ensured would be one of its prime functions. Poland and Yugoslavia at present are not wealthy enough to offer an alternative and attractive system of old age security to country people, and only in recent years have the neo-capitalist economies of France and Federal Germany accepted general responsibility for the burden. This is another reason for the persistence of the peasant economy in the general context of a non-peasant system.

Imperceptibly, inevitably, the introduction of 'stage' and 'phase' to the argument has brought the discussion closer to the fourth context in which the peasantry may be discussed, the particular historical and geographical context, where the degree of social stratification and differentiation that exists in these far from sack-of-potato-like communities becomes most apparent. At this lowest level of abstraction the prejudicial character of the word peasant comes most strongly to the fore. Many English speaking people have a 'folklorist' or 'feudal' concept of the peasant which at its worst degrades the word to the level of a pejorative and renders it useless except in comic strips. Is a man who possesses a tractor, views television, joins an activist rural group, one is often asked, still a peasant? Not, the answer must be, in the sense of the mid-nineteenth-century concept of the peasant, any more than a present-day Ford operative or capitalist manager still resemble their last century counterparts. The condition of the peasantry like the condition of the working class has changed remarkably; and as always, the geographical diversity of that condition remains quite considerable. But in the context of 'peasant economy' or 'peasant enterprise' these post-war peasants remain 'true' peasants. They have acquired modern technologies, machinery and expertise, but they have retained their labour commitment, and have been strongly influenced by it in their search for the optimal combination of resources. The labour commitment has been retained because it is derived from the institutional character of the family enterprise. When that changes then the labour commitment will no longer exist, and the farm operators will no longer, in any meaningful sense, still be peasants.

Currently peasant families in Federal Germany are far smaller than they were in pre-revolutionary Russia; but as in Chayanov's era the biological cycle and generational ascent or decline of the family still influences the organization and development of the farm. Instead of having to find work for a large number of children at a low level of technology, the present-day chef has to find work for a smaller number of dependants but at a much higher capital-man ratio and much higher level of personal expectation – hence the frantic quest for more land, the over-capitalization of under-sized holdings, the trend towards intensive livestock farming. The modern chef operates in a quite different socio-economic context to the chef of the Stolypin era and his condition is accordingly different, but his objectives and actions still derive their logic from the nature of the peasant economy and the peasant enterprise. And when, as in some parts of France, demographic history has produced holdings without heirs, farms without families, then the enterprise falls apart. The peasant economy cannot exist without the mass of its labourers, whereas, and this suggests a further evolution in the nature of its labour commitment, the capitalist system will not persist without the mass of its consumers. One further reason why, ultimately, the peasant economy in the West has to go: as an economy it is not designed to engender a mass of high level consumers. In Poland, however, the provision of employment for a large part of the population has been recognized as the most important function of agriculture for a long time to come. At that country's level of development the chef's labour commitment is positively useful, peasant agriculture is not a burden on society, and hence its dissolution will be delayed.

During the last two decades the peasantry have sought in a variety of ways to satisfy the imperatives of their old system in circumstances which have proved to be increasingly and radically different from previous ones. Each phase in the development of the capitalist and socialist systems appears to intensify two trends. In the industrial field labour is rendered more homogeneous and mobile at increasingly higher levels of proficiency and with greater subdivision and specialization of the manufacturing processes. In the sphere of daily existence the separation of the kinship and the economic order ever widens, until the very future of the family appears to be jeopardized. The peasant economic system is built around the family and its perpetuation, the immobility of and lack of specialization of labour, a considerable interpenetration of economic and social roles. It is difficult to suppress the conviction that the new system will demolish the old one for all time; that an atmosphere of finality hangs about the present phase. Inevitable outcomes, however, are the fruits of historical perspective. Both in the East and the West the 'dirigists' already hold opinions about the eventual form rural society will attain when present trends finally work themselves out. Though the residual function of the peasant holding is stressed for the immediate future in Poland, for a later date a Dutch-like solution is envisaged by some critics; and the socialist transformation of the countryside has not been abandoned as an objective in either Poland or Yugoslavia. An American-like solution exercises an ever increasing appeal amongst the transatlantic minded technocrats of the West. But in their particular regional contexts both solutions are positively ambiguous. Before they are achieved a lot of things must happen in the rural world and many of them are contingent upon other changes, political as well as economic, at the national level. During the past two decades, in what has been a fundamentally contradictory situation, the peasantry have fought strenuously to preserve and improve their standing; and there is every reason to suppose they will continue to do this for the next generation or two. Generation, not decade, for this is the time interval in which changes are completed in peasant societies.

The post-war peasantry

During the war and immediate post-war years peasant life reverted to a much more autarkic existence and the residual functions of the peasant enterprise were most prominent. Food was at a premium, the supply of manufactured goods had dwindled, outlying regions took advantage of their isolation and became once more the foyers for that mixture of armed national resistance, banditry and insurrection which has been a regular feature of peasant political existence. But in a remarkably short period of time all this changed, and changed it seems for ever. Peasant society was caught up in a phase of economic and technological development which has resulted in a profound restructuring of rural life, and what promises to be a final divorce from the existence of the preceding centuries.

One principal effect of the post-war economic expansion has been to revitalize, accelerate and give new direction to the differentiation of the peasantry. The small peasant class has been divided into a group of commuting, part-time, worker-peasants' holdings and a group of old persons' holdings where the failing powers of the chef combine with the inadequate acreage of the farm to place the unit in the class of uneconomic, marginal, or as fashion insists, non-viable holdings. To this group belong also the small and sometimes medium peasant farms suffering from isolation and hampered by the environmental disadvantages, as well as the common problems of capital shortages and the vocational inadequacies of the chef. But within the small peasant class highly intensive holdings succeed very well when favourably placed to serve the demands of the adjacent or accessible, growing and richer urban markets; whilst there are others struggling to enter the ascending category of middle family properties, actively mechanizing and more dependent than ever upon family labour because of the rising costs of hired workers. As a group the peasant-capitalist farms are of limited importance. In the West higher labour charges have borne heavily upon their costings and forced them to mechanize, and become more dependent upon family labour, or better qualified, better paid permanent rather than temporarily hired workers. In the East the group has been virtually denied an existence. Rising labour costs have not hindered the expansion of the large-scale farm in either its capitalist or socialist form. This renewed or newly acquired strength of the capitalist farm in the West, in the Paris Basin, the north Italian plain, in Lucania, of the socialist farm in the Regained Territories of Poland, the Vojvodina in Yugoslavia, is one of the more remarkable features of the post-war agrarian scene. In the East the socialist farm has been used, with varying degrees of success, as a means of promoting the productivity and technical standards of the peasant sector, as a means of incorporating, even absorbing it within the collective sector. In the West the widely contrasting conditions between the capitalist and peasant sector have weakened the political solidarity of the agricultural community, and with the introduction of the Common Agricultural Policy, three or four regions, basically capitalist in organization, have been given the opportunity to emerge as the principal poles of agrarian development. Above all the affinities between the large-scale productive and the large-scale marketing sectors in both the East and the West are jeopardizing the future of peasant farming by highlighting its deficiencies. Already in France, and in the Commission of the E.E.C., some agricultural economists are reconsidering the future of the hired agricultural labour force, the probable emergence of a highly qualified, better paid, group of workers more suited to the needs of an expanding and a more productive large-scale sector. In the East the future of large-scale farming has rarely been questioned. Certainly in the technological and dynamic context of the second half of the century the developments in the large-scale sector cannot fail to have an immediate bearing upon the development of the peasantry.

Yet these last two decades will always be remembered as a period when more and more peasants, particularly in what used to be known as the backward areas of Southern and Eastern Europe, acquired the freehold of their properties or were promoted socially from the level of day labourer to that of *chef d'entreprise*. In those countries which collectivized this process was brought to an abrupt halt. But in Yugoslavia, Poland and in Southern Italy, much has been done by the state, perhaps reluctantly at times, to establish the small and middle peasant community that was the ideal of many interwar agrarian reformers. In Italy the transfer of land to peasant hands by private transactions has been another factor. Paradoxically, the period when they gained access to the land was also the period when amongst the progressive elements of the French peasantry, for the first time in centuries, doubt was thrown upon the necessity of owning land, upon the advisability of using limited capital resources to acquire the freehold, when novel and more productive alternatives for investment were appearing. At the very period when the strength of the landowning peasantry reached a maximum, industrial society provided the first glimpse of an alternative source of security which for centuries the peasantry had striven to assure by means of the ownership of land. Except in those countries which have ruthlessly collectivized, all this effort has burdened future generations with the cost of structural reform, with the costs of eradicating one of the largest archaeological monuments of contemporary Europe: the parcellated, in places pulverized, patterns of field, strip and property.

Every aspect of peasant life, of farm organization and practice were in one respect or another brought into question by the new dynamic state of the economies. Inheritance customs and the immense capital burden they impose upon the incoming chef were subjected to increasing criticism. These practices had already been modified in some areas, because of altered demographic circumstances in the south-west of France, where the indivision of property and dowry were the rule; because of greater and more attractive employment opportunities in industry in parts of Baden-Württemberg, where parishes formerly practising subdivision converted to the indivision of properties.[3] Peasant daughters discovered factory workers with regular and rising incomes to be quite attractive as spouses, economically speaking, and an increasing number were able to acquire an unheard of degree of independence by working in shops, offices and factories. As a basis of livelihood and security the family property lost a little of its former importance, but new circumstances revealed unsuspected potentialities. Greater opportunities for economic promotion in urban areas meant that more heirs wished to finance their education or city dwellings with the money drawn from their inheritance. Improved circu-

[3] Bourdieu (1962) and Röhm (1957).

lation gave some rural properties an enhanced urban value as building or housing sites. In Poland the position of the urban migrants was regarded as a contradiction of social justice: they have, 'received payments in lieu of land from their families amounting, collectively, to many thousand million zlotys', and they 'obtained, at public expense, their whole training, a place to work, and sooner or later housing, virtually without financial sacrifices of their own. As often as not family settlements reduce the farm's productive capacity and considerably lower the owner's standard of living.'[4]

The tractor, that emblem of modernization, revealed the constraints of the field size, the extravagance of the strip system, most of all the interdependence of investment, amortization, costs, net loss or gain. As many writers have pointed out, the tractor was the catalyst for the peasant's introduction to the world of book-keeping, co-operation, planning, ultimately linear programming. If it revealed a new world, motorization also brought into doubt many precepts belonging to the old. It conspired with many other innovations to focus attention upon the relation of the kinship and the economic orders within the peasant enterprise, and to expose the contradictions inherent in the relationship within the context of an economic system no longer peasant. The participants in the drama naturally realized and saw these contradictions in personal terms. In his desire to purchase a tractor the chef was more influenced by his role as a member of the labour force than by his role of entrepreneur. Economically the purchase was often unwarranted and the consequence was indebtedness which the productivity of the farm, even mechanized, could not support. Modernization was often the basis for a conflict between the generations, the status of the father as head of the household apparently degraded because of his inadequacies as *chef d'entreprise*. The educational sphere of activity which belonged to him as chef and father appeared to be subverted by the new avenues for vulgarization. The many sided character of farm activities, its polycultural practices, had its roots in pre-industrial society when agriculture was largely self-sufficient. In the industrial world the practices received justification from the use of the risk spreading argument and from the autarkic policies of the warring national states.[5] Polycultural practices also suited admirably the chef's labour commitment and consequently his marketing decisions were based on the imperatives of his economy rather than the laws of the market. The increasing scale and capitalization of the agricultural processing industries, the diminution in importance of the farm in relation to the preceding and subsequent links in the whole chain of production, are now creating a situation where the chef must decide at the beginning of the agricultural cycle what he

[4] Polish Perspectives (1963): 10, 57. [5] Van Deenen (1964): 48.

plans to produce for the market rather than taking the customary post-harvest decisions, when the chances of climate and the needs of the family specify what is available for sale. The innovation is not the marketing of produce by the peasant sector; it is the determination of the whole organization and planning of the farm according to the dictates of a highly organized supply and marketing sector. Specialization in cropping and livestock practices now bring the chef in direct conflict with the labour commitment of the old order.

The family, the status of sons, particularly the ascriptive character of roles, the status of women – the least-known section of the whole rural population, the whole kinship order, has been subjected to change as the economic order of peasant life has experienced new pressures. The function of the contemporary peasant family is very much influenced by its position within the agrarian structure. Amongst the worker-peasant class, in the East and the West, the family is ceasing to be an exclusively production unit and is gradually becoming an income earning unit, a process which greatly affects intra-family relations and family authority.[6] Amongst the middle peasantry, however, the family retains its exclusive qualities as a production unit. Part-time farming, and migration in some regions, have been responsible for a considerable feminization of the agricultural labour force,[7] the males performing the mechanized after five o'clock or weekend work. Attitudes towards the freedom and status of women may have become more enlightened in rural areas, but they still work enormously long hours in the kitchen and the fields, whilst a home shared with in-laws remains the bane of many young brides. The variety of circumstances and strata is too great, the information too limited for one to generalize about the quality or character of peasant family life, except for one thing: universally the urban model of family existence, urban aspirations and mores, appear to be the preferred standards or objectives of the farming populations.

The rural community is no longer the semi-closed, restricted community of the past. It has been opened to urban and supra-national influences by modern communications. It has been diversified by the settlement of exogenous non-farming strata in some areas, by the emergence of an indigenous commuting population in others. As a basis for collective or co-operative action it has not been as influential as at one time was expected. The classes which were the principal vehicles for the transmission of knowledge, attitudes and authority, have in the East been eliminated or their power greatly reduced, as in the West, by the appearance of new elements associated with the modern technologies. In the West some of the older elements have hindered the emergence of a new peasantry, whereas some have assisted, even promoted their development. In the East the

[6] Bicanic (1956): 87–8. [7] Barberis (1963).

slowness with which new and mutually satisfactory links between the local community and the central authorities have emerged has retarded their evolution. Migration has sculptured the demographic pyramid to a variety of shapes, distorting the sex-ratio, the hierarchies, the attitudes of the old community, and creating new associations between the villages of the Mezzogiorno and Milan, Turin, Stuttgart, even Gosheim; between Bosnia and Zagreb; between the rural areas of Poland and the new industrial towns, where out of a total urban population of sixteen million inhabitants, nine million were either born in the countryside or are children of families which have recently moved to the towns from the villages.[8]

Polish sociological surveys, amongst others, have revealed the influence exerted by the conditions of rural life upon the attitude of the migrants towards the town life and upon their objectives once they become part of the urban milieu.[9] Liberation from physical strain and fatigue and the monotony of thankless day-long drudgery was regarded as a principal benefit of migration; and rather than factory work, occupations in the bureaucracy, the tertiary services and petty trade and business, which provided a certain status with a minimum of physical effort were originally the preferred objectives of the immigrants. Similar attitudes were expressed by French migrants when they were interviewed.* There can be no doubt that sheer physical effort – work – is the central physiological, psychological, sociological and economic as well as statistical fact of peasant existence. As the data presented below in the chapter on Federal Germany reveals, in a very real sense the peasant farm is an exposition of human labour; the plight and personal suffering of those involved captured in this *crie de coeur* of a young peasant girl, 'Toute mon énergie, je l'avais mobilisée dans ce seul but: accomplir cette somme considérable de gestes quotidiens: mon travail.'[11]

If low living standards, low incomes, personal frustration, the absence of hope and prospects, unmitigated routine and drudgery, the conflict of

[8] Turski (1967): 4, 15. [9] Turski (1967): 4, 16.

* Vincienne's survey, like Barbichon's, stresses the nuances in the immigrants' attitudes and objectives.[10] Some of Vincienne's respondents, the majority of whom has resided in the town for ten or more years, stressed the loss of managerial independence involved by city work: in the town it is the boss who commands; one receives orders, one has to obey, even when worn out you are obliged to work; whereas in the country they have more liberty as well as having more work. Her survey stressed that the concept of security had been given a different interpretation in the towns. Regular wages were a mark of the security offered by urban existence, the risks of harvest were seen as a measure of the insecurity of rural life; attitudes which reflected the influence of status and occupation, length of residence, etc. Both articles underlined the need to apply rural socio-economic stratifications to migration studies.

[10] Vincienne (1965) and Barbichon (1964)

[11] Debatisse (1963): 27.

the generations, a sense of inferiority, have been amongst the factors pushing the young and hired hands off the land, a group of other factors has restrained the chefs and the prospective *chefs d'entreprise*. If work is the central fact of peasant existence, then security, and a certain independence, have been its essential recompense. It is instructive to put oneself in the position of adviser to a young German peasant of twenty years of age, with the prospect of assuming the management of his parents' five hectare farm at the age of forty; and then choose any decade during the last fifty years when one would have argued that his long-term prospects were better elsewhere than in agriculture, bearing in mind the major periods of food shortages and inflation as well as the chronic unemployment; also that with each generation of chefs there comes a time of life when a change of occupation is not feasible. For some sections of the rural population, secular trends, the generational rhythm of change amongst the peasantry, the nature of the capitalist system itself, ideologies, political and personal interests have restrained migration, even promoted the survival of peasant society. In the welfare state, however, the urban proletariat has achieved, for a variety of reasons and in a variety of ways, a degree of security and a perennial, if at times nominal, share in the rising national product. Prospects for the young, outside of agriculture, are better than they have ever been, even if the infrastructure necessary to their transition leaves much to be desired, and is often non-existent. Against the myths and realities of a better urban existence the card of rural security is no longer the trump it was, not quite the restraint to migration. Nevertheless as a category the *chefs d'entreprise* rather than abandon farming have sought to obtain from the wealthier industrial state, particularly in the West, an increasing amount of welfaristic support, a recognition of their right to a share in the rising national income, a degree of security comparable with that of the industrial worker combined with an entrepreneurial independence totally lost to the mass of unskilled and skilled, even managerial classes, of the industrial sector. The less affluent economies of the East cannot support similar demands in their present state, but the peasantries have received the benefits of better prices, and in Yugoslavia, their claim to social and cultural services is acknowledged. For Kardelj, the peasant question is no longer the problem of the development of agriculture, but a social problem.[12]

The period when the relative economic and demographic importance of the peasantry has declined quite rapidly has been a period when if their political pull has not increased, governments, nevertheless, have been very sensitive to peasant issues. Both in the East and the West agrarian matters have been very pertinent, at the macro and micro level, to a number of policies associated with economic growth and national development:

[12] Kardelj (1962): 182.

trade balances, labour supply, the cost of living, the qualitative improvement of diets, the increase of national product, the rate of growth of national income itself. In the East the drive for collectivization exacerbated an already sensitive issue and the centralized structure of the regimes imposed severe limitations upon any political expression of peasant attitudes, and still does. It is in this sphere of political organization, activity and expression that one of the absolute distinctions between peasant life in the East and the West persists and where a degree of reform and innovation appears unavoidable, because in Poland and Yugoslavia the peasant populations will not disappear for decades. Despite inadequate means of communication between the peasantry and politicians in the East, in general throughout Europe, the state has been charged with the burden of solving the problems of the peasantry. The greater articulation of peasant needs and the more specifically economic nature of their problems implies that the state-peasant relationship is going to be closer, more permanent and politically more influential in an industrialized society than it ever was in the largely agrarian societies. The peasantry of Poland and Yugoslavia may reject the state instigated programme of collectivization, but they look to the same state for the provision of artificial insemination programmes, contractual agreements for the production of certain crops, and the propagation of new cropping systems. In Southern Italy the progressive involvement of the State in peasant affairs began with the land reform and has expanded into a whole agrarian plan for the South. The peasant movement in France has not hesitated to ask the state to interfere with private property rights and the law of contract when the changes have suited their ambitions. The experiences of their leaders have led them to recommend the reformation of parliamentary government by the addition of a Chamber of Economic Organizations and Social Bodies.[13] Since the appearance of Levi's *Christ Stopped at Eboli*, regionalism has exerted a growing appeal on sections of the peasant movement. The evolving character of peasant society is having precisely the same effects upon the nature of the state as developments in the industrial sector are, involving it increasingly in the economic and daily affairs of the nation. Despite the prominence of individualistic ideologies amongst peasant parties this ought to occasion little surprise. What is happening should not be visualized so much as peasant society being absorbed by industrial civilization. It should be seen as a system which is fundamentally autonomistic having to give way to one that is fundamentally collectivist. In the circumstances the peasantry have no alternative but to participate and integrate; and, having lost the defences natural to an autonomous existence, acquire those suited to a collective one.

[13] Debatisse (1966–7): 15–18.

Whatever their relative standing with regard to the urban and factory populations, throughout peasant Europe there has been an undoubted rise in consumption levels and levels of living. The productivity of farming and the marketable surplus have increased as the inputs of capital and knowledge have risen; so has the productivity of labour. This has been at the basis of the increased purchasing power, which has often been used to purchase a type or quality of good non-existent before the war. Plastics and artificial fibres, in their own way, have contributed towards an improved working life and sense of individuality amongst the women, as the tractor did amongst the men. Wherever one goes in Europe there are visible signs of improvement, even in so short a period as 1959–66. As evidence one can cite: the clothing of the Sunday worshippers as they stride back to their homesteads, the contents of the carts moving homewards after market day, the additions to the dwellings in Poland. The mopeds tucked away off the road beyond Grassano, the plastic ware in the hills above Potenza, the quality and cheapness of the ready to wear clothes in the open markets of Lucania in the Mezzogiorno. The television sets in Alsace, the car in Germany; but more often it is the capital improvements that attract one's attention in the West. From the tables in the statistical yearbooks one can read off the progressive improvement of hygienic, domestic and cultural standards. Regional differences persist, in fact are accentuated by the process of growth itself. A very considerable, and according to German evidence, growing dispersion of incomes is apparent amongst farms belonging to the same category. These regional and economic disparities render even more suspect the simple stratification of peasant groups based on the increasingly inadequate data for agrarian structures. Compared with the past things are generally much better, but as Niehaus reminds us, comparisons are drawn between classes not generations.[14] In terms of annual holidays, access to institutes of higher education, in terms of the consumption of semi-durable goods, the peasant population rank somewhere near the bottom of the social scale. Hence the agitation concerning the relative standing of the different social categories, the sense of disgruntlement with official policy, the recriminatory quality of much peasant literature, the sense of inferiority about rural and village life.

Every writer agrees that the old sort of village life with its inbred and introverted qualities, with is communal participation in work and festivals, is fast disappearing, as are the last remnants of traditional peasant culture, particularly under the impact of the mass media. But at the same time old practices and institutions are being adapted and metamorphosed to meet the emerging conditions of peasant life. In Germany and France some

[14] Niehaus (1954): 54.

arms of the church have associated themselves with the defence of or revitalization of the peasantry. In its propaganda to stimulate co-operative action the French Ministry of Agriculture cites ancient practices to initiate rather than to provide working models. The co-operative is being revived and experimented with in the East and the West, basically to suit it to the new scale of capital resources and managerial standards necessary for its successful integration within the more complex structure of the agricultural processing industries. Increasingly involved in national affairs the peasant movements, in the West, concern themselves with projects far beyond the immediate concern of their members. Events like the Rome Treaty have elevated their vision to a supranational level, and already the peasant leaders have taken their problems to the bureaus of the E.E.C. Commission rather than to the lobbies of their national ministries. The political and humanistic leanings of their leaders have related the problem of their farm surpluses to the context of a starving Third World.

At the historical and geographical level it is clear that the particular socio-economic context within which the peasant economy functions is nearly as important to determining the condition of peasant life as are the characteristics of the peasant enterprise and economy. Nevertheless these concepts remain analytically useful for they bring some coherence into a highly diverse and variegated situation in which the flexibilities of peasant society are as apparent as the rigidities.

A definition

Two recent definitions of the peasantry have followed a similar approach to the question adopted in this volume, and the results are almost indistinguishable. For Tepicht,[15] peasant agriculture signifies a definite type of productive forces (a large V, a small C, with a particularly small C of industrial origin),* a specific structure of production (weak integration in the social division of labour, lack of specialization), and a particular form of productive relations (identification of the farm with the household). Shanin,[16] influenced by Russian and Polish writers, enlarges: The family farm is the basic unit of peasant ownership, production, consumption and social life. The individual, the family and the farm appear as one indivisible whole. The family's social structure determines the division of labour, status and social prestige. Peasant property is at least *de facto* family property. The kinship group remains the basis of social relations. My own emphasis has been placed upon what I regard as the most decisive element of all, the labour commitment of the chef, the basis of the peasant productive system, arising from the interpenetration of the

[15] Tepicht (1966): 44.
[16] Shanin (1966).

* In Marxist usage, C for Capital and V for Labour.

economic and kinship orders in the peasant enterprise. Both Shanin and I agree, independently, upon the importance of the peasant household's residual function, which combined with the labour commitment of the enterprise ensures that a minimum of work, and therefore income, will be available in some degree for as many as possible, in the very worst of circumstances. In times of crisis they 'are able to maintain their existence by increased effort, lowering their own consumption and particularly by withdrawing from market relations'.[17] 'This function is as significant to the State as to the individual chef and his family. Because in providing them with a minimum of security it allows the burden of general poverty to be shifted to and dispersed throughout the rural areas amongst the less articulate and unorganized peasantry.'[18] The disappearance of general poverty in the industrial society means that the residual function of the peasant enterprise is no longer of such great importance to the state, which is now more inclined to regard the peasantry as a source of industrial labour. Neither is it of such importance to the peasantry themselves, who to share in the increasing wealth of society must link their enterprise with the preceding and subsequent sectors of the whole agricultural industry, abandon their autonomous form of existence and in doing so enter another, perhaps final, phase in the century-old crisis of peasant existence.

A magnitude

How many peasants remain in continental Europe, excluding the U.S.S.R., can be determined only approximately. One has to decide who is and who isn't a peasant, and how to classify the collectivized agricultural populations of the Eastern countries; and then one has to try to make the categories within which the statistical information is presented conform to one's needs. Statisticians quite rightly prefer notions like rural population and agricultural labour force to those like peasant. But even an agricultural labour force, as will become clear in the following chapters, is not easily defined. There are problems associated with permanent and temporary workers – particularly the females, part-time workers, and degrees of under-employment. One convenient practice is to restrict the enumeration to males between 15 and 64. This has its own drawbacks. It underrates the number of old men who hang on in farming. It refers to about only half the number of people who at some time or other go out and work in the fields. It includes men in the capitalist as well in the peasant sector, men in fishing and forestry. But it does provide one of the best bases for international comparisons. At the beginning of this decade in continental Europe the total active male population aged 15–64 numbered about 104 million; the number of active males in agriculture, forestry and fishing,

[17] Shanin (1966): 7. [18] Franklin (1962): 23.

was about twenty-nine million, and they were divided into four major concentrations: the biggest, about eight million, was in the E.E.C. Iberia and Greece with about six million came next followed by Yugoslavia and Poland with five million. In the collectivized agriculture of the East something less than seven million males were occupied. With these broad magnitudes in mind we may now turn to the very diverse situations and trends within the particular countries which are hidden behind these general totals.

A note on the chef's labour commitment

The results of van Deenen's survey[19] published in 1964 allow one to demonstrate graphically the existence of the chef's labour commitment. Take the case of a holding with three labour units in Fig 1.1. If the farm is between 10 and 20 ha, the amount of labour applied annually per

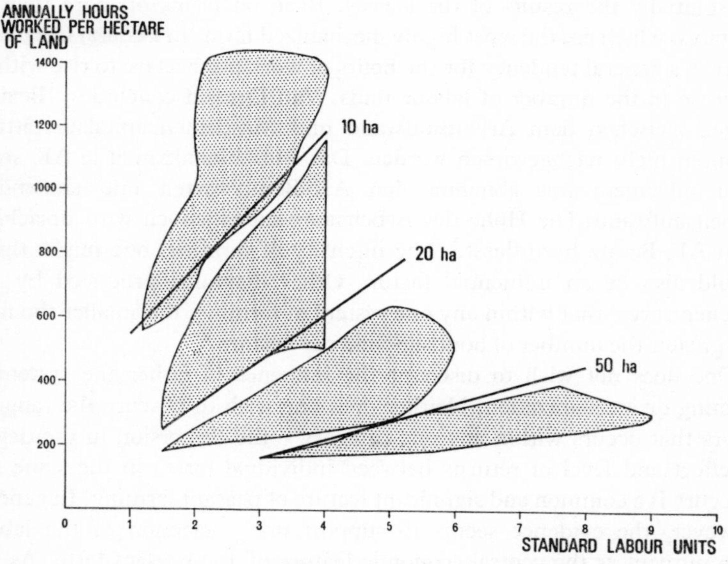

Fig. 1.1. Labour commitment of the peasant holding

hectare may vary from approximately 500 to 900 hours. If the farm is between 20 and 50 ha the amount will vary from between 200 and 400 hours. If it is less than 10 ha it may vary from as much as 900 to 1,400 hours. For row crop farms the average figures are shown in Table 1.1.

Three points should be noted. First, a range of hours exists for each category of farm size; but, secondly, as the size of farm decreases the modal number of hours worked per hectare increases for any given number

[19] van Deenen (1964).

TABLE 1.1 *Hours worked in relation to farm size*

Size of Farm (ha)	*Total Hours of Agri. work*	*S.L.U.s*	*Agri. work per S.L.U. hours*	*Hours per ha*
5–10	7,331	2·45	2,992	931
10–20	8,947	2·95	3,033	645
20–50	11,319	3·76	3,010	410
50 +	15,807	5·45	2,900	218

of labour units. Thirdly, within any one size category, say the 10–20 class, as the number of labour units increases there is a general tendency for the number of hours applied per hectare to increase. This tendency is one of the factors which discounts mechanization as a prime factor influencing substantially the results of the survey. Even on farms of more than 50 hectares, which are the most highly mechanized farms in Federal Germany, there is a general tendency for the hours of work per hectare to rise with an increase in the number of labour units. Van Deenen concludes, 'Beziehungen zwischen dem Arbeitsaufwand und Maschinenkapitalausstattung konnten nicht nachgewiesen werden. Das Maschinenkapital je AK steigt zwar allgemein mit abnehmenden AK-Besatzwerten und sinkendem Arbeitsaufwand. Die Höhe des Arbeitsaufwandes jedoch wird ürsachlich vom AK-Besatz beeinflusst.' The intensity of farming, one might think, would also be an influential factor. Other diagrams produced by van Deenen reveal that within any one system of farming, the smaller the farm the greater the number of hours applied per hectare.

One does not wish to discount the influence of either the system of farming or mechanization. Neither does one wish to obscure the range in hours that occurs within any one category – the dispersion in the degree of effort and level of returns between individual farms in the same size category is a common and significant feature of peasant farming. In general, however, the evidence seems to support one's selection of the labour commitment as the central economic feature of the peasant farm. As van Deenen puts it, 'Der effektive Arbeitszeitaufwand . . . wird weniger vom "notwendigen" Arbeitsbedarf sondern mehr von den verfügbaren Arbeitskräften bestimmt.'

The chef's labour supply is conditioned primarily by the size of his family and the phase reached in its biological cycle.* Because of the close

* Variations in the size of one farm's labour force according to the biological cycle of the family through one generation are illustrated below (Table 1.2). All the figures refer to standard labour units (after Priebe). Chayanov (1966) includes more detailed examples. See also Röhm (1961).

relationship between the kinship and economic orders in the peasant economy, he is committed to that labour supply. He must find work for it either by enlarging the economic horizons of the enterprise – through a development of the binary economy – or by extending, through purchase or leasehold, the size of the holding; or by finding work on the holding,

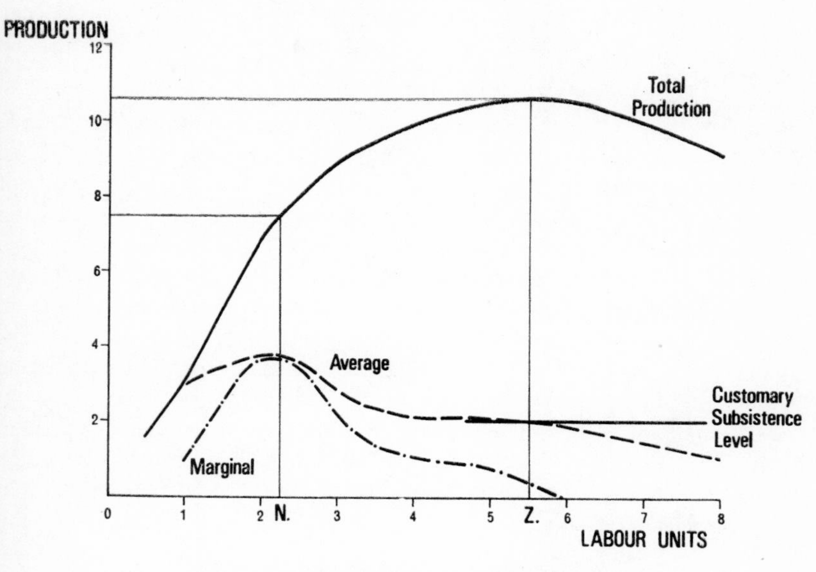

Fig. 1.2. Labour inputs and productivity

whether or not it can be justified 'economically'. Unlike the capitalist or socialist chef, in general, he cannot sack that labour if its productivity is too low. At a given level of technology when there is no possibility of increasing the size of the holding, the chef must be content with the

TABLE 1.2 *Labour Units*

Family cycle	*Chef*	*Wife*	*Son*	*Son*	*Daughter*	*Grand-parent*	*Daughter-in-law*	*Total S.L.U.*
Marriage	1	0·8				0·5		2·3
1st Pregnancy	1	—				0·5		1·5
2nd Pregnancy	1	—				0·5		1·5
3rd Pregnancy	1	—				—		1·0
Children 14–16	1	0·8	0·5	0·5	0·5	—		3·3
Children over 18	1	0·8	1	1	0·8			4·6
Son's marriage	1	0·8	1	1	0·8		0·8	5·4

maximum output rather than the highest return per unit of labour. Content with a position nearer Z than N in Fig. 1.2. It always being understood that, given the general absence of economic accounting amongst peasant farmers, they have only the roughest of ideas concerning the productivity of their labour inputs.

2 BAUERN: worker-peasants and family farms in Federal Germany

The illusion of the ever present past is easily maintained in the German countryside. From the ramparts of Burg Hohenzollern, at the edge of the Swabian Jura, the near-by villages look like models prepared for an economic history seminar. Three great eras of rural history are still discernible, Bloch-like, in the landscape: the tribal settlement of the early middle ages with its associated system of strip farming. The feudal period – the castle looking down on the church tower, the church tower superior to the house tops of the commoners. The Agricultural Revolution which abolished the three-field system and gave to the strips – which still remain – the variegated pattern they now display as harvest time approaches. Fifteen centuries in one glance.

The castle itself is, of course, a nineteenth-century imitation of a Gothic past. The village of Boll, which the castle overlooks, is attached by a vein to the major artery of circulation that puts its inhabitants within twenty minutes of the mechanical industries of Balingen. In fact 38 per cent of the work force are *Pendlern*,* 29 per cent are employed in manufacturing industries, mostly in Balingen. Only 28 per cent of the population earn their living from agriculture (in this respect Boll is about average in comparison with adjacent villages), and 62 per cent of the agricultural labour force is composed of women.

That legerdemain landscape reveals the past and hides the present and future. Yet, in another sense, it is the very continuity with the past that makes the German countryside one of the most up to date, progressive and vital in the whole world. In contrast to the French countryside the rural areas of Western Germany are hardly less densely populated than they were a century ago. Concentration of population has occurred, but to a far lesser degree and with far less destructive effect on rural institutions and communities than in other countries. The process of 'agriculturalization,' which in other lands meant the narrowing of the rural community's

* A Pendler (pl. Pendlern) is someone who resides in one settlement and works in another, moving daily or weekly, like a pendulum, between residence and work place. In respect to any given settlement, an Auspendler is a resident who moves out to his work place; an Einpendler is a non-resident who works in the settlement.

economic horizon as its manufacturing activities and artisanal classes were destroyed by the industrial development of the urban centres, was consciously resisted in many parts of Germany. By largely maintaining the historic binary character of peasant society the Germans have been able to preserve their rural communities and to create a very advanced type, which without delay one must add, owes its existence to certain peculiar German traits that render imitation very difficult. Nevertheless, the lesson to be learnt from the German example is of general interest. The West German rural communities remain vital today because in the past they remained populated, and because they remained populated they could industrialize. But a vital rural community is not synonymous with a vital peasant society. The West German peasantry has experienced the crisis that has afflicted all other European peasant groups. Its situation is as paradoxical and contradictory as any other. Where it distinguishes itself is in the partial solution it has found to these problems, via the creation of the part-time, and especially the worker-peasant, class, which are continuing to serve as the medium by which the transition from a peasant to a capitalist society is performed without a wholesale de-rooting of the rural population or a disruption of the rural community. At the same time this process is creating an economic space in the agricultural sector in which a middle and large peasant class is attempting to establish itself.

Four principal types of farm exist in Federal Germany: the capitalist farm, the middle and large peasant holding, the small marginal peasant holding and the part-time farm. The capitalist farms control 10 per cent of the agricultural land – often very fertile land. Economically they are significant, but sociologically they are of no great importance. The middle and large family farms are of significance both socially and economically, for they contain almost two-thirds of the agricultural area and employ 43 per cent of the total labour force expressed in standard labour units (SLU). The small marginal farms of less than 10 ha and the part-time holdings, which fall into the same size category contain, even to the present day, 29 per cent of the agricultural land and provide employment for 52 per cent of the farm labour force (Tables 2.1 and 2.2). Their importance does not need to be stressed.

The post-war period has witnessed a very considerable, but on first glance rather deceptive decline in the number of holdings and the number of people dependent upon the land. These changes have continued, even accelerated, the long-term trend in the diminution of agriculture's importance at the national level. Its contribution to the national income is now proportionately smaller than at any previous time. No longer is it a major source of employment. The vastly increased volume of national income makes the task of financing the reconstruction of agriculture all the less burdensome. On the national level, because of these changes, agriculture no longer constitutes a major problem. At the sectoral level, however, these changes have left the agrarian structure fundamentally unaltered. During the period 1949–66, the total number of holdings declined by a quarter; the figure fell from 1·93 million holdings to 1·43 million. The gross figures, however, hide two divergent trends; the decline was registered solely amongst the small and part-time holdings (−577,000), whilst the capitalist (+1,200) and the middle and large peasant holdings (+60,200) registered an increase. According to the figures presented by Gerda Drews, this pattern has persisted since the mid-

TABLE 2.1 *Distribution of labour force by size of farm, standard labour units*

Type	*Size (hectares)*	*1956–7 '000s*	*%*	*1963–4 '000s*	*%*	*1956–7 = 100*
Capitalist	50 +	153	5	102	5	67
Large peasant	20–50	409	13½	334	15	82
Middle peasant	10–20	651	22	608	28	93
Small peasant & part-time	0·5–10	1,784	59½	1,151	52	65
Total		2,997	100	2,195	100	73
Small peasant & part-time	5–10	728	24	497	23	68
	2–5	624	21	380	17	61
	0·5–2	432	14	274	12	63

Source: *Grüner Bericht* (1965): 186.

TABLE 2.2 *Evolution of Federal German agrarian structure, 1949–64*

Type	*Size hectares*	*Numbers '000s* 1949	*Numbers '000s* 1964	*% of Holdings* 1949	*% of Holdings* 1964	*% of Agricultural land* 1949	*% of Agricultural land* 1964
Capitalist	50 +	15·8	16·8	0·8	1·1	10·3	10·5
Large peasant	20–50	112·7	126·4	5·8	8·7	24·0	28·5
Middle peasant	10–20	256·9	295·8	13·2	19·7	26·2	31·8
Small peasant & part-time	5–10	404·5	308·1	20·8	20·6	21·1	17·2
	2–5	555·1	343·2	28·5	22·9	13·6	8·7
Part-time	0·5–2	602·6	403·8	30·9	27·0	4·8	3·3
		1,947·6	1,494·1	100·0	100·0	100·0	100·0

Source: *Grüner Bericht* (1965): 34–5.

30s.[1] Farms in the 2–10 ha class have declined in number whilst the middle and large peasant holdings have increased, and the capitalist holdings have varied only slightly in number. It is the labour character of the holdings, and the nature of their capital composition, rather than their structure which has been undergoing change.

The motorization of farming

The extensive motorization of farming which has occurred during the post-war period is representative of the changing capital composition of the farms and the greatly increased amount of capital provided per worker. Motorization is not synonymous with mechanization and a lot of the investment has in fact been directed to the mechanization of routine farm work. However, the tractor has come to symbolize the whole process of innovation; and the progress of motorization is more easily followed.

In the post-war period farms of every size have acquired tractors, and the total tractor park has increased tenfold. Practically every farm of 10 or more ha now has a tractor and many of the small ones also possess a machine. In fact 44 per cent of the tractor park is in the less than 10 ha category. In general it would be true to say that the middle and large peasant and the capitalist farms are in the process of arranging themselves into the one or two tractor farm category; and all farmers, irrespective of size, are caught up in the process of motorization – but not for identical reasons.

In the small peasant and part-time class of 10 ha or less, females are supplying the bulk of the labour, particularly the full-time labour. The function of motorization in these circumstances is to supplement the labour of the males of the family whose full-time occupation is now increasingly found outside of agriculture. The tractor is permitting the small farm to persist as a part-time family enterprise. To put it another way – on these farms the chef is forced to depend almost entirely upon his family for his labour supply. On these farms the family supplies 95 per cent of the labour force, and the proportion supplied by hired labour which has never been considerable has halved in recent years. Because the farm is of an insufficient size to warrant the full-time employment of the chef himself, he turns over the bulk of the full-time work to the women of the family. He does the work they cannot readily perform as a 'five o'clock' job. Without the tractor the reorganization of the family labour would be impossible. Hence the rationale of motorization in this category derives from the rationale of the part-time holding.

In the middle and large peasant class the rationale is quite different. The intention here is to maintain the farm as a full-time enterprise, if possible to render it economic. The machine allows the family to work a

[1] Drews (1965): 232.

somewhat larger area of land and to operate at a larger scale with increased labour productivity. Family labour supplies 81 per cent of the labour needs in these two categories, and 71 per cent is supplied as full-time family labour. The amount of labour supplied by hired persons has dropped from 28 per cent in 1957/8 to 19 per cent in 1962/3. Motorization has had to compensate for this. The tractor performs an important psychological role in these conditions, for it not only reduces the burden of physical labour but raises the vocational status of farming; a worthy consideration where the young of the family are concerned.

An investigation by Bergmann referring to the conditions of the mid-'50s explained the function and attraction of modernization within the context of the family farm, and at the same time revealed its limitations.[2]

His data showed that motorization reduced the farmer's labour requirements and raised his productivity. For example, on a row crops and cereals type of farm the replacement of draught animals by a tractor reduced labour requirements as follows:

TABLE 2.3 *Motorization and reduction of labour required*

	Size of farm		
	6 ha	*12 ha*	*24 ha*
Reduction of labour requirement	31%	6%	13%
Raised returns per unit of labour	35%	6%	11%

Motorization also increased the area of land which the family was able to use, by one-third if the family rated 1·3 standard labour units, by one-fifth if it rated 2·5 S.L.U. But in terms of establishing viable family farms the changes were not all that significant for they amounted to the creation of a 10 ha farm in the first instance; and a 24 ha farm in the second instance. Furthermore the capital charges involved in the conversion were considerable. The replacement of one standard unit of labour entailed a capital expenditure of 43,000 DM on a 12 ha farm and 31,000 DM on a 24 ha farm – equivalent to anything from eight to two and a half times the family's net income. These rates in the middle and large peasant farms were much higher than in the small peasant and capitalist farms, because motorization involves a more thoroughgoing reorganization of the farm at that scale.

On the small peasant farm the costs of substituting tractors for animal and human labour were low and no major reorganization of the enterprise

[2] Bergmann (1958).

was called for. The reduction in labour requirements as the figures demonstrate was considerable as were the increases in labour productivity. Thus there is a considerable rationale behind the motorization of the small farm. For the large peasant and capitalistic farms motorization continues an established trend, counters the increasing costs of hired labour, and the gains in productivity are considerable. But on the family sized units the changes are costlier and the gains smaller.

Viable farming is not generally speaking an outcome of motorization. The effect is to cut one's losses rather than increase one's surplus. To motorize is to reduce one's losses by 28 per cent on a 12 ha farm, by 43 per cent on a 24 ha farm. Only on the very largest of farms or the most intensively farmed of holdings does motorization turn loss to a profit.

The labour force in agriculture

Increasing inputs of capital and knowledge have been matched by decreasing inputs of labour. In standard labour units Federal Germany's agriculture employed in 1965/6 only half the labour force employed in 1950/1. In that year the numbers of permanently employed stood at 5·1 million persons, about the same figure as in 1939, and the part-time labour force amounted to 1·6 million persons. In 1965/6 when persons engaged on holdings of 0·5–2 ha that produced less than 1,000 DM of goods for the market were excluded from the statistics, an amendment that exaggerates somewhat the decline in the labour force, the permanently employed numbered 2·6 million, the part-timers, 0·5 million. These gross figures tend to obscure the selective manner in which this decline has occurred, according to the status of the labour in one case, according to the socio-economic character of the holding in another. In terms of numbers of persons (not standard units), the total labour force has declined by 49 per cent. The permanent and the part-time family labour forces have declined by 48 and 16 per cent respectively, whereas the percentage decline in the permanent hired labour force has been 72, and in the part-time hired labour force 61. Rising wages and employment opportunities elsewhere have made hired labour a costly and scarce commodity. As a whole German farming is more dependent than ever upon family members for its labour force, and somewhat more dependent than previously upon part-time family labour. When attention is directed to the different types of farm (Table 2.4) it becomes very apparent that practically no change in the size of the permanent family labour force in the large peasant and capitalistic holdings has occurred, and that both types of holdings are now more dependent upon part-time family labour than in the immediate post-war years. On the medium peasant holdings the permanent family labour force has decreased by 12 per cent only, and the part-time family labour force has tended to increase particularly amongst the males. In this class of holding it would appear three divergent trends exist. Some marginal holdings have gone out of production, others have become part-time holdings, but the majority are seeking to establish or maintain themselves as full-time family units. The drop in the numbers of employed in all categories – family, hired, permanent and part-time – is most marked in the small peasant and part-time class of farms. But it is obvious that a

TABLE 2.4 *Labour character of holdings, 1949–1965/6 (thousands)*

		Full-time Family labour		*Part-time Family labour*		*Full-time Hired labour*		*Part-time Hired labour**		
Holdings	*Year*	*Total*	*Males*	*Total*	*Males*	*Total*	*Males*	*Total*	*Males*	*Females*
Small and part-time <10 ha	1949	2,661	1,237	1,513	746	290	164	167	61	106
	1956	2,358	869	1,390	892	135	73	247	104	143
	1965/6	1,098	341	779	560	59	34	77	36	41
Medium peasant 10–20 ha	1949	872	410	122	19	244	148	119	35	84
	1956	811	400	95	44	99	60	139	49	90
	1965/6	763	367	153	66	29	17	39	17	22
Large peasant 20–50 ha	1949	381	182	45	7	304	195	105	34	71
	1956	352	176	33	14	178	116	113	40	73
	1965/6	387	191	55	27	58	41	38	19	19
Capitalist >50 ha	1949	41	19	5	1	204	148	59	15	44
	1956	37	19	4	2	135	95	41	41	27
	1965/6	39	20	6	3	67	51	11	6	5
Totals	1949	3,955	1,848	1,685	773	1,042	655	450	145	305
	1956	3,559	1,464	1,523	952	547	344	540	234	333
	1965/6	2,287	919	993	678	213	143	165	78	87

* Figures are for 1957/8.

Sources: 1949 *Statistisches Handbuch*, Landwirtschaft und Ernährung. 164 Sonderheft. Berichte über Landwirtschaft 1956. 1956 and 1965/6 *Grüner Bericht*.

principal reason for the decline in the permanently employed family labour force is to be sought in the rapid reduction of the number of holdings in this class; a factor which has had little influence on the size of the family labour force in the middle and large peasant class.

The amount of labour utilized per hectare has declined with the migration out of farming and the increase of mechanization. Since the early '50s the density of labour has fallen by 39 per cent on farms of less than 5 ha and by 42 per cent on those of more than five. On the medium peasant farms the number of S.L.U. per 100 ha is now at 13·7 compared with 17·5 in 1956–7. In the large peasant class it is 8·8; on the capitalist farms, 6·4.

Small peasant farms of 5 to 10 hectares now return a figure of 20·5 cf. 27·1 in 1956–7; but on the smallest ones the figure ranges from 31·2 upwards to 60, even 80. As the total output of farming has been increasing, this decline in the density of labour means that the productivity of labour, as well as the productivity of the land, has risen – but not, as we shall see, sufficiently to give labour, and management, an acceptable level of income.

Federal aid and private investment

Under the general heading of rendering agriculture more efficient, and more capable of dealing with the competitive conditions that will emerge as the Common Agricultural Policy of the E.E.C. takes effect, agrarian policy in the Federal Republic has to deal with three separate issues arising from the evolving structure of the farming community. The first issue is the creation of a modernized and viable group of family farms recruited from the large and middle peasant range; the improvement of efficiency on the capitalist farms is a subsidiary aspect of this issue and one which the limitations upon space prevent us from discussing. The second issue is concerned with the treatment of the positively non-viable group of small peasant farms, many of which are operated by elderly persons. The third issue concerns the evolution of the part-time farm.

Federal policy does not for political reasons positively emphasize these separate issues, or the particular needs of the various socio-economic groups; the approach tends to be a general one. Here it accords with the views of Herr Rehwinkel, the leader of the Peasants Union, who is equally disinclined to draw distinctions. For instance he regards, for the purposes of electoral strength, the worker-peasant as an integral part of the peasant movement.* Nevertheless certain aspects of policy cannot avoid having a greater significance for some sections of the farming community than others. The expenditure to improve the income of the farming population benefits most sections of the farming community, though not equally, and most can in some measure benefit from the amounts set aside to provide cheap credit. However, the money provided for the improvement of the agrarian structure and the working and living conditions in agriculture is largely an investment in the future of the middle and large peasant farms.

Two set of federal expenditure accounts are published annually, the total budgetary appropriations for agriculture (3,799 million DM, 1965), which include the sums set aside for the Green Plan (3,289 million DM,

* In response to the question put to him in 1965 by one of the editorial staff from *Wirtschaftsdienst*, that the farmers unions – in all countries – must be opposed to rural depopulation because this would weaken the political influence of their organizations, which is indeed very strong, Herr Rehwinkel replied: 'I will not deny that this may also be one of the reasons why we take as strong a stand in favour of the part-time farmer as for the larger farming interests.'

1965); the biggest single item accounting for the difference being the expenditure for stockpiling, which is another way of supporting incomes. An analysis of the Green Plan disbursements, at least up until 1965, is a sufficient indication of the nature and volume of state aid to agriculture and its variations. About 40 per cent of the expenditure has in most years been directed towards the improvement of the agrarian structure, the other 60 per cent has been directed towards raising incomes.

The rural habitat, whose embellishment has been the devoted task of the pre-industrialist generations, has left a heavy charge upon the present ones; so that in one way and another the expenditure upon structural reformation has been absorbed largely by the re-ordering of the environmental conditions of rural life. The expenditure upon individual items, however, has varied significantly through the course of time. At the beginning of the period (1957) almost a quarter of the expenditure was upon the improvement and realignment of rural roads, whose broken and inadequate surfaces and insufficient or inappropriate densities had, together with the parcellation of the fields, been a cause of so much wasted time. A further 36 per cent of the monies was directed to the extraction (*Aussiedlung*) of farm houses and buildings from overgrown villages, which often were no longer agricultural in function, and their re-establishment on the outskirts of the community with their fields grouped and closer at hand. Included within this expenditure was the improvement of farm building suited to a rationalized farming system (*Aufstockung*). Eleven per cent went towards the provision of better water supplies, a prerequisite for high standard dairy farming. An equivalent proportion was directed to a continuance of the centuries old drainage and ditching of the fields, their protection from waterlogging, their amelioration during droughts, and the provision of controlled irrigation works for the better meadows.

In more recent years the relocation of farms, their improvement and also that of the roads have retained their importance. The provision of good water supplies has received the same allotment of money, but its share in the total outlay has fallen proportionately. As an item of expenditure drainage has disappeared. Its place has been taken by field consolidation (*Flurbereinigung*) which currently absorbs nearly 300 million DM annually. Since 1945 3·7 million hectares have been consolidated; under the Green Plan between 200,000 and 300,000 hectares have been treated annually at a cost per hectare that varies from *c.* 1,300 DM in normal circumstances to as much as 2,600 DM when they are difficult. At the beginning of the '60s 2·7 million ha of land, never before consolidated, were considered to be urgently in need of attention, as was a further 0·6 million ha already once consolidated. Two novel items have appeared more recently in the accounts, both highly interesting innovations, indicative of a growing concern with something more than *Raumordnung*. Since 1960 appropriations for 'problem' or 'backward' regions, where small farms are very common, have risen from 10 to 110 million DM. Equally impressive is the increase in financial aid to the old, via the pensions scheme, which has risen almost eighteenfold since 1959 and now amounts to 535 million DM. This expenditure has had an immediate influence upon the income of the older generations, and combined with the 210 million DM provided for the sickness and accident benefits it has assisted in improving the social status of the rural populations. At the same time by accelerating the movement of the old out of farming it is speeding the transference of control to younger men, thereby contributing to the structural reform of agriculture.

The major portion of the Green Plan disbursements have been made with the intention of raising farm incomes, principally by reducing the price of fertilizers and the costs of benzine, by improving the quality of milk and other products, by providing cheap credit and tax remission. These support measures it is calculated raised net incomes by as little as 8 and as much as 24 per cent, according to the size and cropping system of the holding. Certainly those holdings with a greater degree of commercialized production have benefited most. Since the mid-'50s direct federal aid to farming has risen from 455 million DM to 1,944 million DM. As the financial arrangements of the Common Agricultural Policy have been determined they have required some modification of the aids to incomes, particularly as common prices have been set for milk and other products. At the same time it has been necessary to provide financial aid for novel items, like the improvement of market structures, particularly by investing in agricultural processing plants, and specific investment programmes for individual holdings in recognition of the increasingly competitive conditions which the Market will induce. Fundamentally these changes and additions have not altered the character of the Green Plan; rather they have extended and improved the scope of its activities.

These federal expenditures are dwarfed by those undertaken by the farmers themselves to improve their incomes and productivity. Between 1950 and 1960 the total value of food production, in current prices, rose by 80 per cent. Current expenditure rose by 84 per cent but capital expenditure increased by 335 per cent and depreciation by 125 per cent. The surplus, from which the incomes of the family labourers and chefs together with the returns for management and reserves are drawn, rose by only 31 per cent. Expressed in constant prices the picture is much the same. The surplus increased by 16 per cent only, capital expenditure rose by 180 per cent, current expenditure by 73 per cent.

Three-quarters of the total value of German agricultural production is currently attributable to livestock production, and since the end of the war the stress has been on developing this sector. The proportion of current costs attributable to expenditure on animals and animal foodstuffs has almost doubled during the '50s and now with 27 per cent of the total constitutes the largest single item on the bill (Table 2.5). General trends in the pattern of output will confirm the importance of this type of expenditure, whilst the maintenance of the productivity of land renders the outlays upon fertilizers and pesticides indispensable. Forty per cent of farm costs are determined by either the nature of farming itself or by the prevailing structure of output. Admittedly economies can be made by a more scientific use of fertilizers and feeding stuffs, which would raise returns per unit of expenditure. But it is hard to believe that the solvency of German farming will ever depend upon these matters.

TABLE 2.5 *Current costs and capital charges in the '50s (millions DM)*

Current costs	*1950/1*	%	*1960/1*	%	*Percentage increase*
Salaries of hired workers and Social Security payments	1,475	24	1,812	16	23
Fertilizers and pesticides	730	12	1,510	13	107
Feedstuffs and animals	914	15	3,056	27	234
Maintenance of buildings and machinery	1,553	25	2,160	19	39
Fuel and power	285	4	866	8	204
Taxes	499	8	439	4	-12
Interest	185	3	731	6	295
General costs	564	9	841	7	49
	6,205	100	11,415	100	84
Capital costs					
New buildings	165		920		457
New machinery	725		2,650		265
Grand total	7,095		14,985		
Depreciation*	1951/2		1958/9		
Buildings	460		480		
Machinery	360		1,260		

* Taken from Plate and Woermann, Table 5a *Agrarwirtschaft* Sonderheft 14.
Source: 1950/1 *Statist. Jahrb.* Ernährung, Landwirtschaft und Forsten 1960. 1960–1 *Agrarwirtschaft*, February 1963: 45.

The wages of hired workers are an important item of costs too, 16 per cent of total charges; but the percentage has been declining (it was 24 per cent in 1951) and will in all likelihood continue to decline until it levels off as the hired labour force adjusts itself to the new farming structure. And then it will be questionable whether hired labour and its rates of remuneration will affect the majority of farmers. Proportionally less was spent on the maintenance of buildings and machinery in 1960–1 (19 per cent) than in 1950–1 (25 per cent), but together with outlays on fuel and power over one-quarter of current expenditure is now associated with the mechanization of farming. The costs of interest repayments have increased fourfold in step with the increase in borrowings of short, medium and long term credit. In all 3·6 milliard DM. were spent in 1960/1 on the repair and maintenance of buildings and machinery, the provision of fuel and power and the servicing of debts arising out of this expanded investment. An additional 1·8 or 1·7 milliard DM was charged as depreciation. Without a doubt this is the section of the costs bill where economies have to be made if the surplus is to increase.

Reviewing the whole trend of capital and current expenditure in the '50s it would not be inaccurate to summarize it by saying that of all the measures, private and federal, adopted to improve the economic standing of the rural community, first place has been assigned to the mechanization of farming. In 1960/1 2·65 milliard DM was invested in machinery; a further 1·68 milliard DM was spent upon its repair and maintenance. These sums can be compared with the 1·3 milliard DM spent upon fertilizer and the 2·1 milliard DM expended on animal feeding stuff. They can also be set against the total federal aid to agriculture for that year: 2·5 milliard DM. In fact it is highly instructive to compare the total expenditures under these various headings for the '50s.

TABLE 2.6 *1950/1–1959/60*

	Milliard DMs	
Total expenditure on:		*Sub-totals*
New machines and new materials	13·65	
Repair and maintenance of machinery	14·22	*27·87*
Fertilizers	10·33	
Animal feeding stuffs	14·13	*24·46*
Federal Aid to Agriculture under the Green Plans 1956–62	9·58	*9·58*

Parity income

To assess the effectiveness of Federal aid to agriculture and, incidentally, the results of private investment, the German authorities have undertaken a sampling of farm accounts, the results of which are published regularly and in considerable detail in the Green Reports.* One of the most useful concepts used is that of *Arbeitseinkommen*, the amount left to remunerate labour and management after costs, including a charge for capital, have been subtracted from gross income. When charges for non-family labour are subtracted from *Arbeitseinkommen*, the sum remaining to the members of the family, again for their labour and management, is known as *Roheinkommen*, or family income. The results are usually expressed in terms of marks per standard labour unit (DM/S.L.U.).

It is the expressed intention of the Federal government to seek to provide the farmer with an income equivalent to that earned by an industrial worker of comparable skill. Originally comparison was made with the earnings of workers resident in moderately sized urban centres in regions where the percentage of the labour force in non-agricultural activities neither exceeded 70 nor fell below 30 per cent. The aim was to avoid the influence of the higher wage levels of the major industrial areas. Since 1964/5 the high levels of employment and the high demand for labour throughout all regions have rendered the distinction meaningless, and this has had the effect of raising the level of the equivalent income and retarding the attainment of parity.

The equivalent income is known as the *Vergleichslohn* (parity wage or parity income), and it is possible, without failing to recognize the over-generalization that is unavoidable with this sort of analysis, to measure the comparative performance of the agricultural sector over time. Essentially one is attempting to discover the degree to which agriculture is offering its labour force a return for its efforts comparable to that which it might obtain in the industrial sector. And for all the crudity and inadequacy of the data the results leave no doubt that the leeway is still considerable; in part, of course, owing to the constant increase in the parity income dependent as it is on the rising level of industrial wages, which in Germany have shown some correspondence to a rising level of productivity.

Table 2.7 attempts to summarize a considerable mass of data relevant to the issue. It reveals that in 1963/4 the majority of farms, irrespective of the type of farming system, still could not match the parity income, and hence must be classed as marginal. This data deals only in averages and the variations around the mean are known to be considerable. We shall discuss this matter in a moment. But to round off this first impression we

* The German title is: Bericht der Bundesregierung über die Lage der Landwirtschaft (Grüner Bericht). This annual publication also contains the Green Plan: Massnahmen der Bundesregierung (Grüner Plan). The German Ministry of Agriculture, for its part, issues annually a more detailed record of the sample farm accounts: Landwirtschaftliche Buchführungsergebnisse.

TABLE 2.7 *Achieved earnings as a percentage of parity income 1963–4*

Type of farm		*Capitalist*			*Large*			*Middle*			*Small peasan*		
*Farming system**		H	G	F	H	G	F	H	G	F	H	G	F
North Germany	98 +	*	*		*								
	90–97					*		*					
	80–89								*		*		
	70–79						*						*
	60–69			*						*		*	
South Germany	98 +	*	*		*								
	90–97												
	80–89							*					
	70–79			*		*			*				
	60–69						*			*	*		
	50–59											*	*

* H Based on row crops
G Based on cereals
F Based on fodder crops and grass

shall cite Kötter and van Deenen's attempt to map by *Kreis* (the Germa county) the standard size of farm that would give a family income (*Rohein kommen*) of 12,000 DM; i.e. provide a farming unit of 2 S.L.U. with a income that was already only 86 per cent of the 1964 parity income. Their map displayed very few areas where holdings of less than 12 h could achieve this standard, and they were concentrated in the riches areas of Rhine Pfalz, North Rhine-Westphalia and Lower Saxony. Ove most of the Federal Republic a 20 ha holding was the minimum size c farm which could provide the desired standard of income: which is to sa there is a prima facie case for considering only 10 per cent of Germa farms to be economic.

The adoption of a new *Vergleichslohn* since 1964–5 has had the effect c worsening the relative standing of agricultural earnings. The disregard c regional differences in industrial wage levels meant the parity income wa raised from 7,475 DM to 8,466 DM, a 13 per cent increase; and by 1965– it had risen to a figure of 9,217 DM. This has had the effect of increasin the difference between the parity income and the achieved or attaine income for all farms from 22 per cent under the previous method of cal culation to 33 per cent under the new one. It meant for the class of capitali farms that the 16 per cent excess of achieved income over parity incom was turned into a 19 per cent deficiency. In the large peasant sector th

[3] Kötter and van Deenen (1961).

disparity was increased, on average, from 12 to 32 per cent; whilst in the small and medium peasant class the disparity rose from 29 to 37 per cent.

To sum up: in the past decade the full-time family holding has become both the model for the centre of the agrarian structure, and the dominant mode of exploitation in post-war German agriculture. The small peasant and the part-time holding constitutes the other pole of development in the evolution of the agrarian sector, and it has become the model for the development of the tail of the agrarian structure. Farming has rid itself of a large number of marginal enterprises. The character of the labour inputs has altered and the amounts in varying degrees have been reduced. In all parts of the farm structure, and particularly in the head and middle, capital has been replacing labour and the *chefs d'entreprise* have sought to raise the productivity of both labour and land through this investment. The most marked success has been achieved in the field of increasing output and yields. The costs have been considerable and the surplus has been slow to rise. Only because of the marked migration from agriculture has the per capita surplus risen. Even so, the rise has not been sufficient

TABLE 2.8 *Socio-economic character of Federal German labour force, 1964–5*

Derivation of income	*Capitalist*	*Large peasant*	*Medium peasant*		*Small peasant & part-time farmers < 10 ha*				
	> 50 ha	*20–50 ha*	*10–20 ha*		*Total*	*Small peasant 5–10 ha*		*Part-time and worker peasant*	
Full-time holding	17,000	135,000	240,000		119,000	95,000		24,000	
Part-time holding*			42,000		280,000	142,000		138,000	
Worker-peasant holding†			9,000		608,000	56,000		552,000	
Population 1960 Millions	0·68		1·4		4·6	1·5		3·1	
Labour force '000s	*M*	*F*	*M*	*F*		*M*	*F*	*M*‡	*F*‡
Family – full-time	210	214	375	404		243	357	133	434
– part-time	29	29	84	65		172	76	372	135
Hired – full-time	107	39	20	13		12	9	23	17
– part-time	30	33	21	28		14	17	22	26
S.L.U. '000s	314	121	394	188		291	163	247	207

* Bulk of income is derived from the farm.
† Off-farm earnings are the main source of income.
‡ Excluding the labour force of holdings in the 0·5–2 ha which produce less than 1,000 DM annually for commercial use, i.e. the labour force of approximately 298,000 holdings controlling 300,000 ha of land.
Source: *Grüner Bericht* 1967: 39 and 185, and 1965: 188.

to give the majority of workers anything like the desired level of return. This is particularly discouraging for the middle and large peasant concerns which are obviously seeking to obtain most of their livelihood from farming, unlike the part-time enterprises.

By 1960 something like six and a half million people were still dependent in some degree upon agriculture as a source of livelihood. For about half of them off-farm earnings provided a greater share of total income than that produced on the farm, and the great majority of people possessing holdings supplemented their income from non-farm sources. For a large proportion of men associated with the part-time holdings farm work is now a secondary matter but along with household chores it absorbed most of the working day for the majority of their wives and some of their daughters. By the '60s about 600,000 worker-peasant enterprises remained in existence, the single largest socio-economic category in the German countryside. Another 300,000 small, frequently marginal, units completed the part-time category. The other principal class, the full-time family farms numbered nearly 500,000 (Table 2.8). The particular evolution of these two categories will occupy us for the rest of the chapter.

The middle and large peasant units: family farms of the future?

For centuries it has been the custom in Germany to assimilate the available labour supply of the family and the draught power of the farm to the conventionally established living levels of the region and to express it all in one single concept: the *Ackernährung*, a measure of how much land is needed to support a family in full-time farming. The concept is still widely used in the rural areas as any inquiry will soon demonstrate. The practice has been adopted by agricultural economists themselves, so that in the professional shorthand of the early '50s the 10 ha farm and the family farm were synonymous. With considerable confidence and some emphasis Priebe could write in 1954: the family containing between 1·5 and 2 standard labour units is the core about which the peasant family enterprise is crystallizing; according to the techniques and levels of intensiveness adopted, the size averages out at about 10 ha.[4] But as the '50s progressed more and more doubt was thrown on the validity of using area as a measure, and more prominence was given to specific economic criteria, especially to return per unit of labour. By the early '60s therefore, Priebe was attempting to define a family farm in terms of gross income and returns per unit of labour, assuming always that in standard labour units the labour force would be near to 2.[5] The family farm was now synonymous with the 2 S.L.U. unit, which, in Kötter's words had become the 'archimedische Punkt'[6] (Plimsoll line) against which all future consideration of struc-

[4] Priebe (1954): 141. [5] Priebe (1961): 53–65. [6] Kötter (1960): 1–12.

tural reorganization, mechanization, and investment had to be aligned.

The 2 S.L.U. farm derives its rationale from the demographic evolution of the agricultural population in the past century. In pre-industrial times, Kötter points out, some members of peasant families were forced to remain single to prevent an uneconomic subdivision of the property.[7] This gave the farm a relatively abundant supply of labour, largely unmarried. The practice was in a sense made acceptable because culturally people were accustomed to everyone not having the same chances. In industrial society the reverse attitude prevails and the greater wealth and more diversified employment opportunities now afford most people a better chance of marriage. The presence of a relatively large number of unmarried individuals in peasant families is becoming increasingly rare and the labour character of the enterprise has altered accordingly. In future the labour force is most likely to be confined to those who are married or those who have the chance of marriage: as a rule, the married couple, perhaps with one of their elders, or one of their offspring, and later his wife. Only a marked revolution in the social character of the rural areas, Kötter concludes, can reduce the labour force below this level. An alternative evolution, the re-emergence of capitalist farming, appears to be prohibited by the same demographic and social forces that have helped to produce the 2 S.L.U. farm. The large peasant farms and estates that used to be dependent on additional and unmarried hired labour have little chance of increasing their importance in the prevailing labour conditions. Especially as it is known that two-thirds of the agricultural labourers have to change their occupation when they wish to marry.

The economic performance of the family farms has improved considerably during the '50s. Gross income per ha has risen by just over 60 per cent, whilst the net income per worker has increased by 119 per cent in the 10–20 ha class and by 158 per cent in the 20–50 ha class. When these results are considered in relation to the desired level of income, the parity income, it becomes apparent that only on the largest and most intensive of farms are the desired results being obtained. In 1964–5 only the row crop farms in the north were exceeding the parity income per worker, and it was the bigger and more intensive farms that held the best relative standing (Table 2.9). Of equal interest and significance are the facts that over time the intensive farms are improving their relative standing more rapidly than the other types of farm; and that in regional terms, too, disparities appear to be increasing. For instance in the 10–20 ha class the row crop farms (North Germany) improved their relative standing to the parity income by 42 points between 1956/7 and 1964/5, whereas the wheat and fodder crop farms improved their standing by only 17 and 13 points.

[7] Kötter (1960).

TABLE 2.9 *Achieved incomes per worker, 1956–7 and 1964–5* (in DM per S.L.U.)*

	10–20 ha				*20–50 ha*			
	1956/7		*1964/5*		*1956/7*		*1964/5*	
NORTHERN GERMANY								
Parity income	4,223	100	7,433	100	4,223	100	7,433	100
Achieved income								
Row crops	2,756	65	7,952	107	3,084	73	8,739	117
Wheat	2,728	65	6,192	82	2,951	70	6,722	90
Fodder	2,448	58	5,296	71	2,311	55	5,212	70
SOUTHERN GERMANY								
Parity income	4,129	100	7,489	100	4,129	100	7,489	100
Achieved income								
Row crops	2,824	68	5,771	77	2,998	73	6,986	93
Wheat	2,434	59	4,575	61	2,621	64	5,265	70
Fodder	2,220	54	5,391	72	2,463	60	5,100	68

* N.B. This and the following table use the parity income for 1964/5 as established under the old method. (See page 33).
Source: *Grüner Bericht* (1965): 109.

A similar trend was observable for Southern Germany, but when a comparison is made between the two regions (Table 2.10), the improvements in achieved income of the southern regions have fallen behind the northern ones.

TABLE 2.10 *Achieved income per worker, South Germany. (North Germany = 100)*

	10–20 ha		*20–50 ha*	
	1956/7	*1964/5*	*1956/7*	*1964/5*
Row Crops	103	73	97	80
Wheat Farms	89	74	89	78
Fodder Farms	91	102	106	98

Source: as Table 2.9.

The authors of the 'Green Reports' have themselves become aware of these trends. In the 1966 Report they wrote: 'It is quite clear that in the last few years the bigger and more intensively farmed enterprises, those using the best land, have displayed a greater increase in the net income per worker than the other categories.'[8] Moreover they were able to demonstrate

[8] *Grüner Bericht* (1966): 92.

for the 10–20 ha class of farms that the deviation from the mean farm income per worker is increasing over time for all types of farming systems and in all regions. The factors influencing these trends are manifold, but it is possible to illustrate with statistics the character of the two most important: the effect of the system of farming and the role of widely differing managerial capacities. Within the context of family farming, the more intensive farming systems undoubtedly make the best use of the factors of production on land of approximately the same fertility. Since most of the fertile land is used more intensively the cumulative effect is to create a large advantage for the intensive farms. This explains the better performance of the intensive types of farming in the past few years. To explain why greater deviations from the mean income are appearing within even the intensive farming systems one has to fall back on the enormously large range of managerial abilities which is known to exist within all farming systems but which remains largely uninvestigated.[9]

Table 2.11 sets out the average economic returns for three groups of Hessian farms within the same size class 10–20 ha, working land of comparable fertility. The divergence in return per unit of labour is very striking. For row crop farms it was 4,049 DM, for wheat and row crop farms, 3,390 DM, for fodder crop farms 3,075 DM; a range of 32 per cent. The

TABLE 2.11 *Economic returns for 10–20 ha farms Hessen, 1961–2*

	Row crops	*Wheat – Row crops*	*Fodder*
No. of farms in group	15	94	13
Average size of farm ha	15	14	18
Land valuation DM/ha	1,340	1,070	1,140
Livestock units per 100 ha	96·7	101	110·5
Labour per 100 ha	16·2	14·1	13·3
Capital DM/ha	7,212	5,908	5,666
Cereal yields quintals/ha	34·7	25·3	25·8
Milk yields kg/cow	3,478	3,274	3,275
Gross income DM/ha	2,283	1,825	1,790
from cultivation	581	193	90
from livestock	1,412	1,296	1,386
Costs DM/ha. Materials, labour and depreciation	2,181	1,830	1,862
Net gain DM/ha	+102	−5	−72
Capital per labour unit DM	44,158	41,901	42,601
Machinery per labour unit DM	11,648	9,043	6,947
Income per unit of labour DM	4,049	3,390	3,075

Source: *Landwirtschaftliche Buchfürhungsergebnisse* 1961/2 and 1962/3.

[9] Scholz (1960).

intensity of land use appears to be the principal factor influencing the returns. Generally the row crop farms are more capitalized, their yields are the best, whereas the fodder crop farms appear to carry too much labour and are consequently under-mechanized. Given the labour return per ha which these farms returned, all of them would have to be over 20 hectares in order to attain the level of the current parity income.

Work and the peasant family

Much more is known about the economics than the sociology of the family sized farm. For this sort of information one is dependent upon the occasional monograph, often excellent but limited in scope, issued by one of the agricultural institutes, and above all upon the unique sample survey of 755 farms published in 1964:[10] The work force of the majority of the farming families included in the survey consisted of two or three generations In the 10–20 ha class only 2 per cent were of one generation; in all the remaining classes no more than 5 per cent of the families were of one generation. Two important consequences arose from this fundamental characteristic. Firstly, the majority of farms were managed by middle-aged or old persons. With the exception of the over 50 ha class of farms, half the *chefs d'entreprise* were of more than 50 years of age, and 70 per cent of more than 40 years, beyond the limit when vocational retraining is really practical. For their vocation the majority had only the preparation of an unsupplemented *Volkschule* (primary) education, and this was true also of their heirs, though the conditions modified sensibly in the large farm category, where again in contradiction to the general trends 40·5 per cent of the *chefs d'entreprise* were between 30–39 years of age. Secondly, the majority of farms have at their disposal a potentially large labour force which in most cases is well utilized both in the sense of the full or part-time employment of most members of the family and in the sense of the large number of hours of work contributed by some family members. At the time the survey was undertaken, 1959/60, it is noteworthy that the family sized farms had a labour force 20–45 per cent in excess of standard two-man unit.

The majority of families included in the sample were dependent upon agriculture as the sole source of income; in the 10–20 ha class 73·5 per cent, in the 20–50 ha class 86·1 per cent. For a small percentage of families the *chefs d'entreprise* undertook seasonally non-agricultural work. But a fifth (22·8 per cent) of the 10–20 ha families and 12·8 per cent of the 20–50 ha families derived some income from family members fully occupied in non-farming activities. The average family consisted of either 3–4 or 5–6 persons. Children under 14 represented between one-fifth and one-third

[10] van Deenen, *et al.* (1964).

of the family, the remainder were able-bodied males and females, the basis of the labour force. In terms of standard labour units on the 10–20 ha farms, full-time males contributed 52·5 per cent of the labour force, full-time females, 18·3 per cent. Males full and part-time contributed 57 per cent, females 35·5 per cent, non-family labour 2·5 per cent, seasonal labour a significant 4·9 per cent.

These figures require elaboration. It is as important to regard farm work from the viewpoint of its timing as from the viewpoint of its volume or proficiency. The utilization of seasonal labour on even the 10–20 ha farms underlines that at certain periods, harvest or haymaking, the demands of the agricultural cycle exhaust the potential of the family labour force. The availability of the female members of the family is equally important on these occasions. Between a quarter and a third of the cultivation of row crops, whatever the type of farming, is the responsibility of the women; for muck spreading they are useful too. Traditionally, milking and the care of the *basse cour* have been their domains. The women not only allow a greater degree of flexibility in the arrangement of the work schedule, they enlarge the scope of economic activities. In addition they run the home and attend to the wants of the family. Since so much income in peasant households is received in kind there are good grounds, as the Bonn investigators recognized, for taking a more economic view of this labour than is customary with the household chores of the city housewife.

A peasant's wife *averages over the whole year* a working week of between 71 and 77 hours. This time is split between household duties and farm work which takes about a third of the hours. The men confine themselves predominantly to farm work, but one would hesitate to say they always undertook the heaviest labours. Their total hours worked ranged from 3,158 (60 hours per week) to 3,443 (66 hours per week) on the family-sized farms. On the over 50 ha farms the hours of work were much shorter, 2,563–3,247, and somewhat shorter on the 5–10 ha farms. In a double sense the peasant family farm is truly an exposition of labour: because of the amount of time devoted to each piece of land; because of large measure in which the individual's existence is absorbed by work. A working year of 3,500 hours is equivalent to 60 per cent of a person's total waking life. Work, then, in all its economic, sociological, managerial and psychological ramifications dominates the future of the peasant family farm, as in fact it has conditioned its evolution. Only on the largest of farms, over 50 ha, did the working year of the *chef d'entreprise* approach that prevailing in the industrial sector in 1959 (2,100 hours) – and then it was at least some 10 per cent greater. Overtime raised the industrial working year (and industrial wages correspondingly) to an average of 2,300 hours, almost erasing the difference. On the 10–20 ha farms the working year of the *chef d'entreprise* was 40–50 per cent longer than the basic industrial year. The chef's wife supplied an additional 1,350–1,740 hours of farm work on average, equivalent to 66–77 per cent of the basic industrial year, so that jointly they supplied two full industrial years as a minimum. By comparison the agricultural work performed by the farmer's wife on the larger farms varied from 382–773 hours; in any case it was well below the levels obtaining on the family enterprises. When the total input of labour, and the composition of that labour is considered (Table 2.12) it becomes apparent how much of the labour input of the family farm goes virtually uncosted by the chef, in strong contrast to what occurs on the capitalist farms.

Here one meets the double problem associated with family farming. Because the chef does not have to meet a wages bill he is less conscious of the need to use that labour economically. Additionally the status of that labour confuses an economic issue by introducing sociological and psychological considerations, particularly in the case of the wife. Owing to the insufficient scale of operation, to maximize income the chef finds uses for his wife's time almost to the limits of her physical capacity – the data in the van Deenen survey supports this assertion; and she being in many cases a joint owner through her dowry, has a psychological attitude quite different to that of a wage labourer. The labour of other family members is not exploited quite as fully, but on 10–20 ha farms, male members employed full-time average between 2,500 and 2,800 hours a year, whilst the females average on farm work alone between 1,200 and 1,500 hours per annum. Their total working year, including house and farm work ranges from 2,800 to 3,100 hours. All this family labour suffers from the disadvantage of having in general received very little vocational training. It may be inexpensive but it is also not very efficient. One must acknowledge the totally different basis upon which the peasant family enterprise is predicated, but within the context of an industrial society's frame of reference family labour receives a ridiculously low hourly rate of remuneration. In 1959 hourly rates of earnings (for all types of labour) on farms of over 50 ha averaged out about 17 per cent below the average hourly rates for industrial workers in not highly industrialized areas; on the 10–20 ha farms average hourly earnings were between 33 and 45 per cent below these levels, though it must be understood the range between individual farms is considerable and the estimates themselves are very gross.

According to a small, tantalizing, survey conducted in 1959, long hours of work were recognized as the principal disadvantage of farming life by the peasants themselves.[11] The origin and cause of these long hours is, however, without a simple explanation. Müller found amongst the people

[11] Müller, J. O. (1964).

TABLE 2.12 *Composition of labour input on family and capitalist farms, 1959–60*

Type	*10–20 ha*					*50 + ha*			
	Man & wife	*Other family*	*Total family*	*Hired*	*Hours*	*Man & wife*	*Total family*	*Hired*	*Hours*
	Percentages					*Percentages*			
Row crops	46·9	39·4	86·3	13·7	8,947	19·0	33·3	66·7	15,807
Row crops – Wheat	55·6	37·2	92·8	7·2	8,451	12·0	14·9	85·1	25,894
Row crops – Wheat-Fodder	57·3	36·3	93·5	6·5	8,185	22·0	35·2	64·8	15,841
Fodder	66·4	27·1	93·5	6·5	7,585	29·2	54·5	45·5	13,001

Source: van Deenen (1964): 38.

he investigated that mechanization had speeded up some farming operations, but the length of the working week remained unaltered because the time saved was utilized to intensify the farming and to extend the arable area of the farm. An adaptation that cannot be related to any economic criteria like cost and benefit because practically all of the farmers included in the survey neither planned their operations according to any economic criteria nor maintained adequate book-keeping systems; though in the context of the family enterprise it is obvious why these changes were made. Prevailing social norms appeared to the investigators to determine the length of the working week; a thesis consistent with the evidence adduced, which on reflection does not constitute an explanation. For this one must resort to the data provided in the van Deenen survey – already discussed in Chapter 1 – which demonstrates that the size of the family labour force determines the total input of labour, or alternatively, total labour input = total volume of family labour.

We have returned once more to the rationale of the family enterprise: work is income, an equation easily transmuted to a social norm through the psychological processes of internalizing work as a value stripped of any economic meaning. In accordance with this process the majority of the chefs included in the Müller survey proclaimed themselves satisfied with their work and occupation, because of the results and the freedom afforded. But for them, results meant physical results – seeing things grow, having healthy cows, the harvest – not monetary returns. And freedom was equated in most cases with freedom from supervision, of the sort a factory worker is subjected to, by the foreman, the stop watch and the conveyor belt, not entrepreneurial freedom, to plan, project and develop. Again the ambiguity of the peasant's existence is to the forefront, in all its aspects summed up in the quite unrealistic comment of one respondent: I'm a free man, and we don't have to get up in the morning like the factory workers. (Ich bin ein freier Herr, wir müssen nichts morgens raus wie der Fabrikarbeiter.)[12]

From the material provided by the Müller survey one can compose a portrait of the typical German *chef d'entreprise*: a hard working man, unperturbed by the duress of his labours unless suffering from sickness or war injuries, operating by the rule of thumb, happy to be associated in his daily tasks with his kind rather than strangers, and content with his work, its results and his status because they were all evaluated within a self referential and self enforcing context; beset, nevertheless with a disturbing realization of the insufficient monetary return and, significantly, prepared to invert old standards and judge his present condition against those prevailing in the working class. A cartoon that would have to be modified,

[12] Müller, J. O. (1964): 197.

but not substantially, to incorporate the variations created by the influence of industrialization in the community or the aspirations, and better educational advantages associated with youth.

The future of the family farm

The family farm seems destined to become the centrepiece of the future farming structure. The trend towards the standardization of the 2 S.L.U. unit during the recent decade is most striking. In all there are 375,500 full-time farms in the medium and large peasant class and there are an additional 94,640 full-time farms in the 5–10 ha class. Some of these may become part-time enterprises, others may develop into valid family concerns. For the next decade it will be both convenient and safe to place a round figure of half a million on the size of the family farming sector. Paradoxically during the very period when the proposals to ensure its economic substance were implemented, as the measure of viability was given economic rather than physical content, as observers became aware of the implications of the parity policy in a prosperous and highly productive industrial economy, any certainty concerning the future of the family farm, perhaps more accurately, any surety concerning the final lineaments which the family enterprise might assume, were dispersed. By 1966 the confidence in the future of the family farm which had been so evident to the author in 1959 had begun to disappear in some quarters. Undoubtedly a remarkably fluid and unprecedented situation exists at present in German agriculture. As Kötter recognized, the structural problem in agriculture has acquired a pre-eminently dynamic character.[13]

Two factors will hinder the emergence of a satisfactory and valid form of family farming in the next two decades: the inability to achieve income parity in terms of hourly rates, even though it might be achieved in terms of volume; the inadequate rate at which land for the enlargement of family holdings will become available, which in its turn will lessen the chances of attaining the desired volume of income. Only through a reduction of the number of 10–20 ha holdings will this obstacle be removed, and this seems to be a most unlikely contingency because of the existing demographic character of the farming population.

The prospects of the middle and large peasant farms obtaining a parity income at a comparable hourly rate of earnings remains remote. Van Deenen's survey of 1959 reveals that the average total time spent on agricultural work ranges from 7,585 to 8,947 hours on middle peasant farms and from 8,648 to 11,319 hours on large peasant farms. One may strike an average of 8,600 hours. Let us assume that with an input of 8,600 hours parity income per unit of labour is achieved. However, if the farm

[13] Kötter (1960): 11.

is worked by two standard labour units, this means each labour unit must work an impossible 4,600 hours to earn the same income that a factory worker would acquire with the expenditure of 2,400 hours of effort. A total input of 8,600 hours represents the efforts of 3·6 not 2 standard labour units. The per capita earnings are accordingly reduced, and the rate of hourly earnings will be far below that of the industrial sector. This, incidentally, cannot be attributed to the greater degree of capital per worker in the manufacturing sector. Capital per man runs out higher in the peasant family farm, though it is necessary to add, the composition of that capital is different to its composition in the industrial sector.

If one makes the further assumption that the earnings for a two-man unit shall be at parity with industrial earnings, and if one accepts on the basis of the nature of farm work a 15 per cent reduction in hourly rate of earnings on the farm, so that the rate is 3.20 DM on the farm and 3.75 DM in the factory, then: the numbers of hours expended per ha will be as follows: column A; and should be compared with the figures for the actual input of time per ha collected in the van Deenen survey, column B. For a long time to come agricultural workers appear to be condemned to very much lower rates of remuneration.

	A		*B*
Size of Farm	*hrs/ha*	*van Deenen farm size*	*hrs/ha*
20	234	10–20	529–645
30	157		
40	117	20–50	352–410
50	94	50 +	149–218

Only through a most extraordinary and therefore improbable evolution of the German agrarian structure is sufficient land for the stocking up of existing holdings likely to come forth at a rate adequate to the needs of the family farms, which must seek to operate at a larger scale in order to be economic.

During the sixteen year period 1949–65, 500,000 ha of farm land went out of production. The area of land farmed by the 0·5–10 ha and 100 + categories declined by 1,800,000 ha. A net 1,300,000 ha of land was acquired by holdings in the 10–100 ha category, as follows: 10–20 ha: 585,000 ha; 20–50 ha: 605,000 ha; 50–100 ha: 110,000 ha. On average each farm in these categories increased, respectively, by 2·0, 4·5 and 8·0 hectares. For the next fifteen years the prospects are about the same.

Assuming again that a loss of 500,000 ha of agricultural land is borne by the less than 10 ha class, that 1·5 million hectares of land is transferred from this class to the 10–100 ha categories, by 1980/1 the 0·5–10 ha class will retain a total of only 1·6 million hectares compared with 3·6 million ha in 1965 and 5·3 million ha in 1949. Assuming no increase in the number of 10–20 ha and 20–50 ha farms the redistribution of this 1·5 million ha of land will produce an average increase of 2·5 ha on the 10–20 ha farms and a 5·6 ha increase on the 20–50 ha farms.

To produce an average increase in area per farm which would begin to exert some considerable influence upon the chances of attaining parity income would require something like the abolition of every farm of less than 10 ha during the next fifteen years and the commencement of a substantial decline in the number of medium peasant holdings. This, however, is highly unlikely for demographic reasons. As Table 2.13 indicates, on family sized holdings the majority of chefs are between 25 and

TABLE 2.13 *Demographic characteristics of family sized farms, 1965*

Full-time farms	*Age group*		*Size of holding* 10–20 ha	20–30 ha	30–50 ha
Full-time *chefs d'enterprise* (male) as percentage of total chefs	25–60		80·2	81·7	80·6
	25–45		45·5	46·3	50·6
Total of full and part-time chefs (males and females)	55–70 +	Thous.	99·0	30·1	13·9
Total of full and part-time male dependants	20–45	Thous.	89·6	32·1	17·8

Source: Statistisches Bundesamt.

60 years of age, and nearly half are between 25 and 45. Most of them are committed to farming for the rest of their working life. They are unlikely to give up the holding during the next fifteen years except for reasons of age. When one enumerates the total of chefs, males and females, who are likely to quit farming because of their age during the next fifteen years, and compares that number with the number of male family dependants of an age at which they are likely to be committed to farming as a career, as future *chefs d'entreprise*, then the rate at which existing chefs are likely to be replaced appears to be very high. The data drives one to the conclusion that little change can be expected in the family farming sector until established demographic conditions have run their course. Kinship and the two generation structure of the family are going to influence the agrarian structure for some time to come.

German commentators have come to recognize this predial and structural issue as one of the most critical factors affecting the future of farming. They acknowledge that so far little has been done to deal with the matter, and what legislation exists is unsatisfactory.[14] But as we shall see, French experience reveals it is no easy matter to initiate and implement legislation when such sensitive issues are involved. It seems inevitable that the next decade or two will be the era of the family holding–at considerable cost, no doubt, to the tax-payer and the consumer. The family unit will dominate socially and economically through its possession of the bulk of the agricultural land and the majority of the farming population. These decades will not, however, be a period of stability. The biological cycle of the family, the persistence of the kin group as a necessary feature of farm and labour organization will entail the majority of family farms in carrying a little too much labour, exerting a depressive effect upon their income potential. Combined with the effects of the Common Agricultural Policy this should stimulate the *chefs d'entreprise* to seek an amelioration of their condition through the adoption of technical and managerial reforms to which, no doubt, the Federal Government will contribute massively. The overall effect can only be an acceleration of the process of differentiation that is already evident. In all probability a group of more competitive, somewhat larger farms, run by younger, better trained men, capable of pushing through the enlargement of their properties will emerge alongside a larger marginal group of farms, whose chefs, lacking the necessary attributes, will eventually drop out of farming at some critical point in the cycle and history of their family. The dynamic situation which has charaterized German agriculture during the past decade will not dissipate itself in the next. Instead of being dominated by the small and marginal farm problem, in future the literature will be concerned largely with the problems of the family sized unit. And as the realization spreads that a diminution of the numbers of family sized farms is an absolute condition for the establishment of viable farming – perhaps, at the same time, arguments in favour of the advantages and possibilities of capitalist farming will receive more favourable attention.

The small farm problem and the worker-peasant community

Ten years ago the small peasant farm issue dominated agrarian affairs in Germany. Numerically the small farms constituted the largest of all groups in the farm population and numerically articles on the small peasant and worker-peasant communities occupied a large part of the literature. Much of what was written at the time is now of historical interest only. But because of the very considerable effect which the evolu-

[14] Hiss (1966).

tion of these communities has had upon the nature and future of the whole rural community, and because that evolution is not yet complete, the small farm issue deserves a particular place in any analysis of the German agrarian structure. Once again the available demographic data is useful for revealing the diverse elements and trends that exist within the general grouping of the small farms (Table 2.14).

TABLE 2.14 *Small peasant and part-time farms, 1964–5, socio-economic classification of their chefs d'entreprise (thousands)*

Size ha	*Total*	*Old people*	*War widows*	*Full-time small peasants*	*Worker peasants*	*Others*
2–5	317·4	105·7	27·2	40·6	138.7	5·2
5–7·5	162·6	43·8	11·2	55·0	48·8	3·8
7·5–10	127·0	29·5	6·9	66·7	22·1	1·8
2–10	607·0	179·0	45·3	162·3	209·6	10·8

Source: Preliminary Results of Agricultural Labour Force Census 1964/5 (Photocopy).
Old People: Males and Females over 60 years of age.
War Widows: Females aged 35–60.
Small peasants and worker peasants: Males aged 25–60.
Others: Males less than 25 years of age, females less than 35 years of age.

Four main socio-economic groups are present in the small farm category: the war widows, the elderly, the worker-peasants and the full-time operators. The majority of the old people's farms, whether full-time farms or not, were of less than 5 ha. They fulfilled the traditional role of providing security for the declining years. The farms managed by war widows are the product of a terrible phase of history. Mostly they were of less than 7·5 ha though they existed in the 10–20 ha group also. In time presumably they will be taken over by younger men as full or part-time enterprises, or go out of operation. Just over a half of the small farm chefs between 25 and 60 years of age belonged to the worker-peasant class (they were particularly well represented in the 2–5 ha as well as the 0·5–2 ha categories); the remainder ran full-time holdings.

During the past fifteen years the small farms have borne the brunt of the changes modifying the agrarian structure. As a class these farms are on the decline, but they still account for 70 per cent of all holdings over 0·5 ha, they control 29 per cent of the agricultural area, and most significant of all, they still provide employment of one sort or another for about half the labour force, measured in standard units. For the next decade or two their requirements will influence policy making almost as much as the needs of the emerging family-sized farms. Three separate issues will be involved.

First, the exodus of the older people from agriculture, their welfare and security in the immediate future, the retirement of their land from agriculture or its transference to expanding family sized enterprises. Secondly, the improvement of the social and economic conditions on the undersized family concerns, when it is practicable; alternatively the elimination of these unprofitable units. Thirdly, the future role of the part-time farm, to which category many of the undersized family units are most likely to gravitate.

The elderly farmers

Birth, marriage and death, each of these events jeopardize the property and provide the occasion or opportunity for its continuance and transmission. The bestowal of the property rights upon the heir or heirs, their assumption of these rights, the protection of the elders' residual claims, have constituted the drama of peasant life for centuries. Greater life expectancy has made the problems of old age all the more pressing in rural areas. The need for security is probably no greater than in the past but it has to be provided for a longer period of time.

To provide more security in old age and as a means of releasing more land to the property market, the Federal Government introduced in 1957 a pension for all full-time farmers; and most successfully according to the available evidence. Since that date there has been a very large increase in the frequency of chefs handing over the farm at 65 years of age,[15] and in a double sense peasant life has assimilated to industrial standards: by accepting 65 as the retirement age, by participating in the apparatus of the welfare state. The van Deenen-Mrohs sample revealed about a quarter of the chefs for which the legislation was designed had contracted into longer established health and old age pension schemes before 1957. Under the new legislation pensions were made available to all chefs, their wives, widows or widowers who possessed or had once possessed family sized holdings. In effect the lower limit was approximately three hectares. Consequently only 5 per cent of the chefs possessing farms of less than 2 ha and 21 per cent of those with farms between 2 and 5 ha were contributing to the fund. Over 5 ha the proportion rose to 73 per cent and over 10 ha to 92 per cent. The legislation does not therefore meet the needs of the aged on the very small properties, some of whom it is true may benefit from industrial schemes once having been factory workers. It is designed to accelerate the departure of the aged from the land by entitling a chef to receive a pension if he gives up farming after his fiftieth year. He is not forced to sell the property; a leasing of the land for a period that does not terminate before his 74th year is considered to fulfil the requirements. He

[15] van Deenen and Mrohs (1965): Darstellung 3.

need not part with the whole or lease the whole of his property, provided what he relinquishes meets the minimum size considered adequate to support family farming, and provided what he retains does not exceed this minimum by more than 25 per cent.[16] These minimums are established regionally by the fifteen agricultural pension offices (*Landwirtschaftliche Alterskassen*). As a whole the legislation is intelligent in design and progressive in outlook.

The full-time operators

Small peasant farmers are afforded the same sort of federal assistance to improve their incomes and structures as middle and large peasant farmers. They appear to do as well as any other group so far as direct help is concerned. Their receipts per hectare are generally above the averages for the other groups. The structural reforms, with a certain degree of inevitability because of the higher costs associated with the smaller farms, tend to benefit more frequently the larger peasant and capitalist concerns. More small farms than big farms are involved in field consolidation but in recent years only about 16 per cent of the farms benefiting from relocation have been in the small peasant class. Relocation is a costly business. In 1964 total costs per farm averaged out at 170,760 DM for farms of less than 5 ha. For 10–15 ha farms the costs were higher but not excessively so – 27 per cent. Similarly the middle-sized farms benefit most from land stocking-up schemes – schemes costly to implement (6–9 thousand DM per hectare), few in number, limited in extent, but indicative of the small structural changes that are being effected.*

The small peasant farm displays all the disadvantages and limitations of the middle peasant farm plus the additional handicaps of sometimes being located in distant or environmentally poor regions. A very wide range of incomes exists within the group, even within the same village.[17] Federal aid has hardly improved their standing with respect to the industrial parity income, and where there has been some slight improvement, in the intensive farms of Lower Saxony and Rhine Westphalia, this has been counterbalanced by increasing regional disparities. The small farms of the south are worse off relative to those in the north and their position relative to the parity income has deteriorated in the last few years. Like the middle-sized family properties the small peasant farms will be subjected as a group to increasing differentiation in the coming years and they will be amongst the first to experience the depredation of their numbers.

[16] Soziale Sicherung in der Bundesrepublik Deutschland (1964): 80–4.

* For details and illustrations see: Die Verbesserung der Agrarstruktur in der Bundesrepublik Deutschland 1964–5.

[17] Rolfes (1954): 14–22.

It is impossible to forecast how many chefs will struggle to establish valid family units, how many will choose to join the ranks of the part-time category; how much federal pressure will be applied to hasten the exodus, how much feather-bedding will be provided to satisfy the demands of pressure groups. In the 5–10 ha category no doubt those with full-time farms will attempt to increase their scale of operation and create family-sized units, thus adding to existing problems of the viable family unit. It is most noticeable that on small full-time holdings the proportion of chefs between the ages 25–55 increases with the size of the farm, as does the ratio of the male succession group to the older chef group. Both facts indicate that as the size of farm increases so does the chance of a successor being available to take over on the retirement or death of the present chef (Table 2.15).

TABLE 2.15 *Male full-time chefs d'entreprise working full-time holdings (Percentages)*

Years	*2–5* ha	*5–7* ha	*7·5–10* ha	*10–20* ha	*20–30* ha
25–55	38·3	49·9	61·7	64·8	67·3
55–70 +	61·1	49·0	37·2	33·3	31·3

The part-time farmers

For the small farm operator who chooses to enter the class of part-time farmer rather than strive to establish a valid family unit, there are a number of models available for him to copy.

The first is a very traditional form in a modern setting with up-to-date trappings. The chef has two businesses: the farm and the inn, the farm and a transport business or building concern. They remain joint family affairs like the peasant holding, with the daughters helping in the kitchen or the bar whilst the sons are haymaking or driving. The second form is also traditional, but the enterprise is less likely to function as a joint family concern, because the chef has a second occupation, bürgermeister, post office official, rather than a second business. In circumstances like these one will often find that the duties of office detract from the farm work, so that it falls largely upon the shoulders of the chef's wife and perhaps a middle-aged sister or sister-in-law. The young daughter, for her part, may hardly participate in the agricultural work, and neither may the son. She may work in an office in a near by town, commuting daily. He may be a *Fernpendler*, who has moved further afield and who returns home at irregular intervals, particularly when the work load on the farm reaches a maximum. The property maintains a certain cohesion within the family, even in these circumstances. The son may plan to return to the village and take up part-time farming when his parents age. Both daughters and sons often acquire building sites for their future homes as part of their inheritance. Given the rising price of building land in Germany and the many opportunities for residing in a village and working in a nearby town, these are real advantages, and in this manner the family farm eases for some of its members the transition from one sort of life to another without a de-rooting of the population who are quitting the agricultural sector.

When the chef himself takes up regular full-time employment and becomes a five o'clock farmer, an *Arbeiter-Bauer* (worker-peasant), performing the heavy farm work with the aid of a tractor in the evenings and at the weekends, then a critical stage in the evolution of the peasant economy, which acquires a binary character, has been reached, and the merger with industrial society is one step closer. If the chef in the course of time becomes an industrial entrepreneur on his own account – this is not infrequent – but works the farm and factory with family labour, some traces of the peasant economy remain. If he becomes an employer of wage labour for his factory, the transition to a capitalist economy may be said to be complete. His retention of the farm in these circumstances is of little economic significance, but it does become one more obstacle in the path of predial reform.

Part-time farming, when the agricultural side is subordinate to the chef's other business interests, or when the chef is occupied most of his time in a factory is common throughout the whole of Western Germany. The 1960 Agricultural Census provides one with the total number of *chefs d'entreprise* for holdings of more than 0·5 ha. It classifies those chefs for whom farming is a secondary matter into two groups: those drawing income from rent, pensions and similar sources – the elderly part-time farmers (221,000) – and those (459,000) with businesses or other occupations. The latter represented 28½ per cent of all chefs. In the Saar, a small and highly industrialized district, the percentage reached its highest, 46; but generally speaking in every *Länder* 2 to 3 out of every 10 chefs were worker-peasants. For more circumscribed areas, the *Regierungsbezirke*, higher proportions were returned: 4 out of every 10 in Kassel, Wiesbaden, and North Baden for example, and nowhere did the proportion fall below 10 per cent. Schwaben, in Bavaria, had the lowest rate of 13 per cent. Hessen and Baden-Württemburg had more than a proportional representation of worker-peasant enterprises; jointly they accounted for one-third of the total.

The most immediate agrarian effects of the increase in part-time farming in the post-war period have been the decline in the number of milch cows on worker-peasant holdings* especially in localities where women can find employment easily, and the appearance of *Sozialebrache* – land left fallow for socio-economic not agronomic reasons. The geographer Hartke first drew attention to it[18] and though the agricultural economists regarded it as of rather secondary importance[19] 'social fallow' has become a common if not major practice. By 1957, for instance, 0·5 per cent of the total agricultural land in Hessen was under *Sozialebrache*, 5,200 hectares in all. In certain *Landkreis* the proportion rose to 4 per cent and in some parishes almost 50 per cent.[20] For Naurod, an overwhelmingly worker-peasant and *Auspendler* village near Wiesbaden, Beckhoff records the proportion of land under 'social fallow' as rising from 7 to 10 per cent of the total agricultural area between 1953 and 1962.[21] The supply of land available for renting has increased with the growth of part-time farming, but the existence of *Sozialebrache* suggests that either it cannot find a market, or that it is not being offered on the market. The lowest rents occur in the principal areas of part-time farming which argues for supply exceeding demand.[22] The land to be rented is offered in the form of a multitude of small and separate strips which hinders the rational operation of a part owned-part leased property. In the absence of any co-ordinating institutions and together with the varied personal exigencies of the small property owners the present unregulated situation is likely to persist for some time to come.

In the mid-'30s, in the early post-war period, the participation of the family enterprise in a binary economy was still regarded by agrarian writers, as it had been almost from the beginning, as a secondary, even impermanent feature of peasant life. When the necessity arose, as in times of massive industrial unemployment for instance, it was thought the worker-peasants could withdraw from the industrial sector to concentrate their activities upon the farm. This was the famous 'Puffer' or cushion argument.† The current view regards the arrangement as a more permanent feature of the agricultural landscape; the peasantry, it is thought, will continue to participate for a long period of time in both sectors. Much less rarely has this type of part-time farming been regarded as a decisive step towards the abandonment of agriculture. Yet the constant rise in industrial wages is persistently reducing the proportionate contribution of

* Between 1959–65 the number of holdings of less than 10 ha declined by 23 per cent; those with milch cows declined by 31 per cent.

[18] Hartke (1956).
[19] Kötter (1953): 38.
[20] Hessen im Wandel (1960): 109.
[21] Beckhoff (1963): 192–6.
[22] Röhm (1959): 805–33.

† In diesem Sinne würden Nebenerwerbsbetriebe sozusagen einen Landpuffer darstellen, denn erfahungs gemäss werden sie in Konjunkturzeiten extensiv, in wirtschaftlichen Krisenzeiten intensiv genutzt. (Kuhnen 1959.)

the farming sector to the family income, so that the income differential between factory operatives with and without small holdings is fast disappearing.

Many writers in the post-war period have cited as evidence for the permanency of part-time farming the investment of factory earnings in agricultural holdings; also the slight increase in the size of the part-time holding, a feature not unaffected by speculation in building sites. But the general trend has been for the number of holdings in this class to decline and in the coming decades an acceleration of the outflow seems more than ever likely. By entering the factory doors the chef opens himself and his family to the influence of foreign attitudes, standards and practices, each possessing a certain cachet in the modern world against which traditional attitudes towards work and its returns must inevitably be compared. How long it will take for them to erode old attitudes no one knows, but erode they must and with that erosion will come the abandonment of farming, and later perhaps the disposal of the property.

The worker-peasants

By its very nature the worker-peasant class fits neatly into none of the customary divisions which the social sciences have imposed upon reality. Few investigators have recognized this; in the treatment of the subject they have been confined by the limits of their own discipline. Some have stressed the historical, others the geographical aspects.[23] A few, Linde and Hesse in particular, have dealt with the worker-peasant primarily as a feature of the evolution and the increasingly complex nature of the rural community. Agrarian economists have recognized the class as an important feature of the rural social structures (Röhm and Kuhnen), as a means of transition to an industrial form of society (Priebe), but their very orientation has led them naturally to disregard the industrial side of the activity and to stress the agrarian aspect and its significance for the evolution of agriculture. Consequently the worker-peasant family as a socio-economic type, remains largely uninvestigated. Never to my knowledge has an attempt been made to analyse the phenomenon of the worker-peasant family within the context of the theory of the peasant economy.

The derivation of income, or the supplementation of income, from off-farm sources is a common feature of the peasant economy. When it is obtained by working as a temporary labourer or a domestic for other peasant families, or when it is derived from artisanal or commercial activities in the village, off-farm employment has more effect upon the social than the economic character of both the community and the family. It is an influential factor in the social stratification of the village

[23] Stockmann (1934) and Hoffman (1935).

community and a basis for the aggrandizement of certain families and the relative decline of others. However the appearance of employment opportunities related to the penetration of capitalist, or for that matter socialist, manufacturing is of far greater significance and more permanent in effect. Not only does it introduce the technology and mores of industrial society, and enlarge the occupational opportunities of the individual, it also promotes the division of labour in an economy characterized by very little division of labour; above all, it associates the farming population with the sector in which productivity and hence earnings are more rapidly increasing. Ultimately it produces a situation in which the rationale of the peasant economy is destroyed. Though, it must be added, only in very recent times and in a relatively few areas has this situation been reached.

The peasantry have commonly entered the capitalist system of production as employees commuting to nearby small towns, or as workers in the branch factory of a large firm which has been located in their native village. In both cases a ceiling is placed upon the social promotion of all but a few. They are most unlikely to reach the level of the entrepreneurial class, and at best may only reach the level of the skilled operative and the foreman. Their status is not much different from that of the members of the working class, though their possession of land obscures this until the rise in industrial wages has reduced the contribution of the farm to negligible proportions. What is more, territorial ties, family and religious relationships tend to prevail over occupational associations. Only through individual promotion and geographic mobility are they severed. As a mass phenomenon the worker-peasant class remains part of the socio-economic life of the rural and farming community, and only slowly, through its different experiences and the divergent attitudes which result, does it become an agent of change. Only when a certain stage of economic development has been reached does the worker-peasant class become the catalyst for the abandonment of farming. Even then it is reluctant to cut all ties with the land, so that the structural predial problems remain largely unsolved.

When the worker-peasant class is given the chance to become part of the entrepreneurial class, then the impact of industrialization upon village life is far more disturbing. A new element is introduced into the matrix of the social structure: an indigenous class of capitalists and factory owners. Old kinship ties, if originally they were useful in promoting industrialization, cannot be expected to withstand the strain of increasing differentiation according to wealth and education. In the post-war period the increasing demand for labour has often led to the introduction of a second foreign element: a proletariat, composed of exogenous, landless people with no ties or associations in the village. The cumulative effect of such changes can be illustrated from the case of Gosheim, originally a small peasant, then

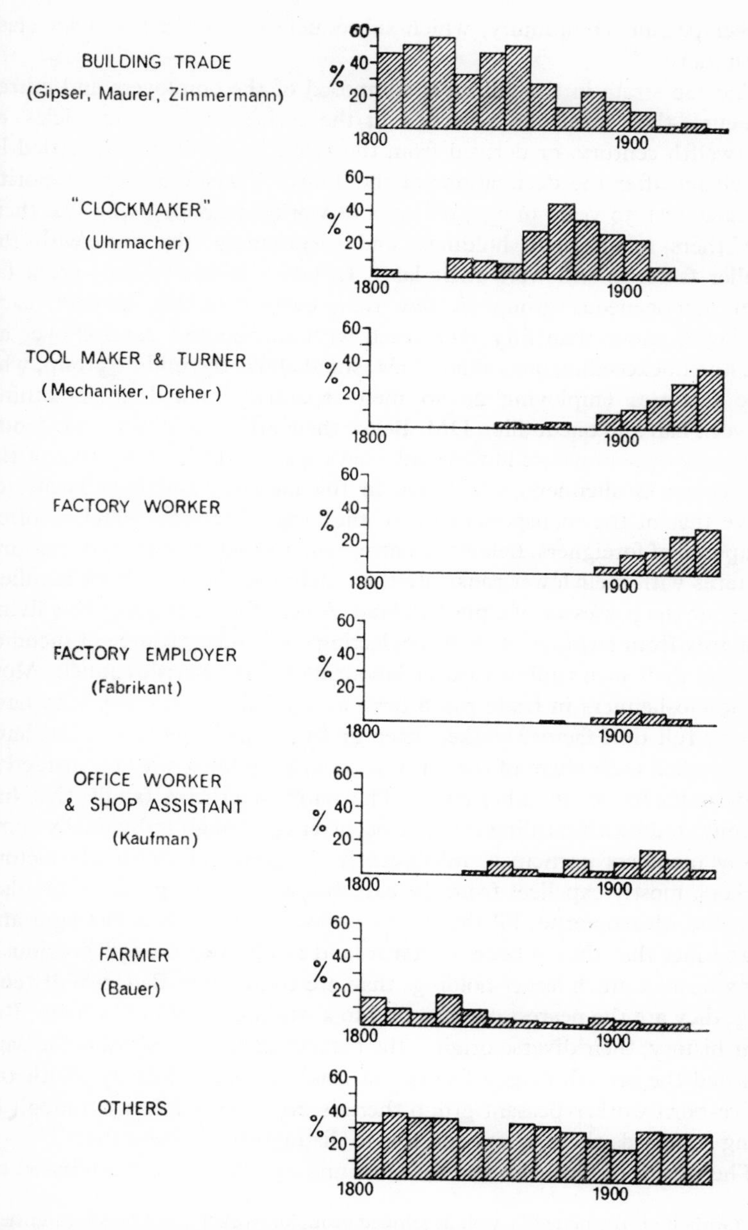

Fig. 2.1. Part-time occupations of chefs d'entreprise–chefs de famille born 1800–1940. Gosheim, Baden-Württemberg

worker-peasant community, which subsequently produced its own class of capitalists.*

The top strata in the village is composed of the employers and entrepreneurs, their surnames recorded in the earliest village chronicles of the twelfth century, or derived from the group of families that settled in the village after the decimations of the Thirty Years War. The majority are now over 50 years of age, the sons of worker-peasants, who like their forefathers retain small holdings, and surprisingly, the ones with the smaller factories still work their land. In terms of status, they are a far from homogeneous group. A few rich, even powerful, owners, each employing more than fifty men, each with undisputed control over an investment exceeding one million DM, stand above the middle group, who have factories employing 20–50 men separately valued at something between half and one million DM. Below them are a more numerous group of factory owners whose lowest ranks have a status little above that of the indigenous Gosheimers, who work in the factories and own farms, or above that of the managerial staff of the larger factories, which is often composed of foreigners. Below the entrepreneurs and, as indicated, merging in status with their lower ranks are the remaining Gosheim born families, everyone the possessor of a piece of land. A very few of them make a living primarily from farming, without neglecting a secondary source of income: working their own timber yard or labouring for the parish council. Most of the Gosheimers in trade run a farm as a sideline and many who have become full-time factory workers keep up five o'clock farming. A few have relinquished their share of the farm, accepting building sites for attractive modern homes as an inheritance. The native Gosheim family that has nothing to do with farming is a rare occurrence, though individually some family members participate infrequently. In terms of status the factory workers, mostly expellees from the east, but including a group of families from the Mezzogiorno, fill the lowest ranks. Distinguished in origin and by the fact that they possess no farm land at all even though previously many farmed much larger holdings than are common in Baden-Württemberg, they are the nearest one can find to a working class in Gosheim. But their history, their diverse origins, the recency of their establishment have retarded the growth of any feelings of class or class solidarity. With the native-born worker-peasant group there is even less solidarity, though in living standards there is less and less to distinguish between them.

The wealth of Gosheim and the surrounding villages has been based on

* Gosheim is the node of a well developed group of worker-peasant communities, in Baden-Württemberg; located on the edge of the Jura between Rottweil and Tuttlingen. In 1933 it had a population of 978. In recent years the figure has surpassed 2,500 (Franklin 1964).

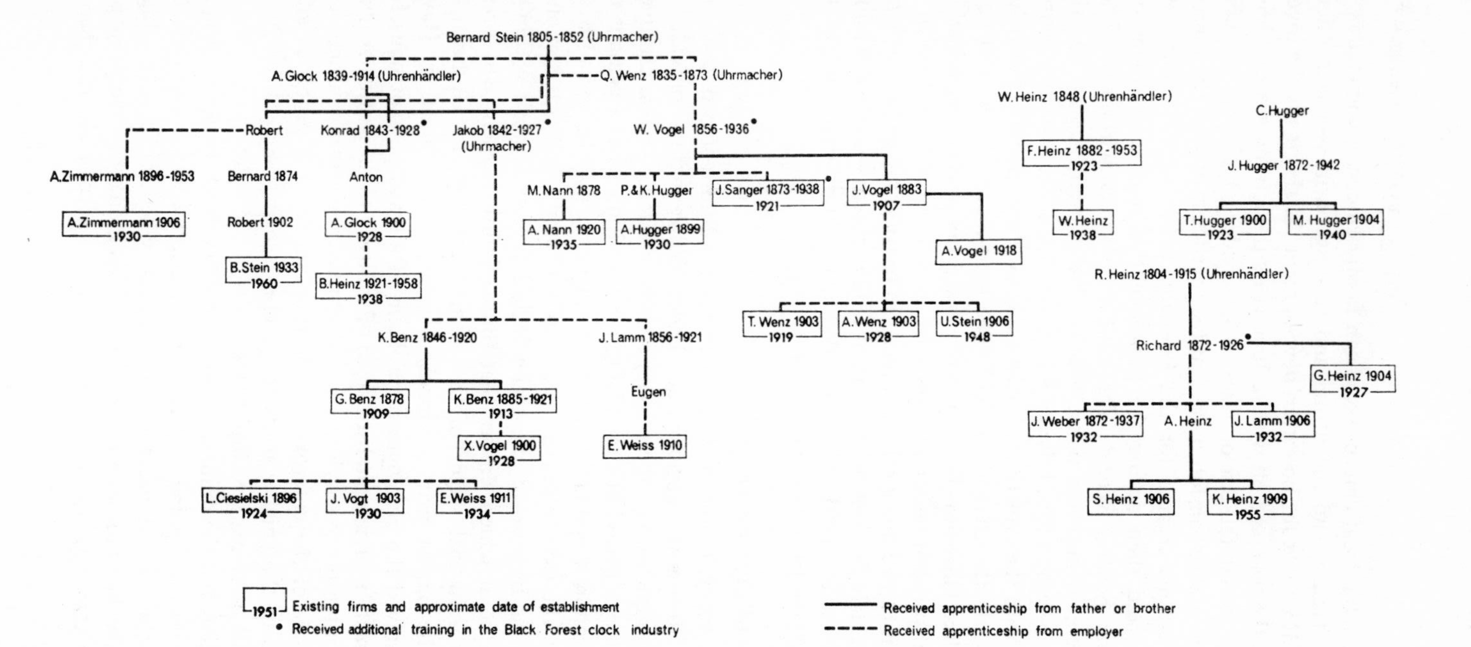

Fig. 2.2. The apprenticeship of Gosheim entrepreneurs (c. 1850–1950)

very considerable local enterprise, cheap family labour, a commodity no longer in existence, and the fitting and turning business which offered particular advantages for bootstrap development. In the 1930s the investment on a lathe was paid off within three years though the working life of the machine lasted for ten or more. This made a high rate of capital accumulation and expansion quite feasible, particularly with the buoyant market conditions created for the Gosheim products, first during the Great War, and then during the period of the Nazi rearmament programme, the Second World War, and the Wunderwirtschaft. These products, screws, nuts and bolts, spindles shafts, ratchets, cogs and time pieces, were required by all the growth industries of the twentieth century and to stay with the growth industries some Gosheim manufacturers have entered already the electronics field. The auto-didactic industrialization of villages like Gosheim (Fig. 2.2) has worked because for organizational reasons the worker-peasant families have been able to participate in the development of technologically advanced industries, turning to their own advantage certain features of the peasant family system – cheap disciplined labour, coherence and loyalty, extended obligations – without, to this stage, disrupting their own community.

The future of the worker-peasant

Success, however, has created problems for the future at two levels, one industrial, the other sociological. Baden-Württemburg provides an excellent example of how the peasant and the capitalist system can live in symbiosis for a period of time easing the transition from a peasant to a capitalist economic system. Though the transition may be spread over a long period, the worker-peasant community is only a half-way station. It cannot persist because of the technological forces at work within the capitalist system which ensure that the capitalist element will prevail within the industrial sector of the binary economy. In Gosheim, for instance, the largest firm is already planning for automation. Having originally solved the employment problem of a small peasant household by the adaptation of a capitalistic form of industry to its particular needs, now, in its attempts to survive as a competitive capitalist organization, the industrial side of the enterprise is creating employment problems anew. The future of the smaller firms in general is being jeopardized by the strength and more massive capital resources of the large.

Automation and the diminution in wage differentials between rural and urban localities are going to have a general influence on the industrial future of the worker-peasant communities whether they are highly industrialized like Gosheim or, as is more common, they are principally *Auspendler* communities. It is too early to be precise about either the nanner in which they will be affected or how successfully they will respond o the changes. But one thing ought to be clear. Any economic difficulties which may arise cannot at this late stage be overcome by a resort to or lependence upon the agricultural part of the binary economy. In earlier lecades this might have been feasible, indeed it was often the intention ehind the creation of the part-time holding. The contribution of the gricultural sector was then relatively much larger. The part-time holding rovided security. On the basis of its residual function a family income, ather than an individual income, was accumulated from diverse sources. But the disproportion between the contribution from the industrial and gricultural parts has grown so great that a change of disposition has ecome impossible. The part-time holding provided also a physical base, shelter, which alleviated the worker-peasant of the costs of rehousing as e became incorporated in the industrial system. Increasingly the farm has een retained not for the security of income it afforded but because modern neans of transport have widened extensively the economic area accessible rom that base.

The worker-peasant community cannot persist because of the socio-ogical changes capitalist development produces in the community. In the 920s, Gosheim, like near-by Bubsheim today, was a worker-peasant ommunity. All the families owned land and the majority had members of he family working in someone else's factory or in the family concern. The ntrepreneurs may have been a wealthier group, whether or not they lisplayed it, but the door was still open to newcomers. Now it is not. Currently it is very difficult, if not totally impossible, to set oneself up in usiness; not one of the immigrants has succeeded. Cheap labour no longer xists; generally there is a shortage of labour, especially of the skilled ariety. Initial investment charges are high and it is doubtful if the per apita earnings of a one man or two man outfit would exceed the earning apacity of a skilled factory worker. Certainly the distinction between those who are dependent upon wages alone and those who are worker-peasants as almost disappeared. Within a very short period of time higher wage ates and shorter working hours will render the contribution of five o'clock arming to the family income of such marginal significance that its con-inuance will be explicable only on therapeutic grounds. The rise in the irth-rate amongst the native born Gosheimers means that the existing roperties will be subdivided further when the rising generation claims its nheritance. Many properties will be so small that their partial development s building sites will be the only sensible course. *Realteilung* and the binary conomy have pulverized the holdings to the extent that individually they will soon be useless for agriculture.

Sociologically the effect of industrialization has been to diversify, differentiate and stratify an originally homogeneous population, but at the same time it has produced a larger and increasingly homogeneous class of factory workers; and by so increasing the levels of living amongst the worker-peasant class it has removed its *raison d'être*. Industrialization has put an end to the peasant economy.

Thus our theory of the worker-peasant class rests ultimately upon certain assumptions concerning the evolution of the capitalist system, as well as upon the theory of the peasant economy. As an extension of the peasant chef's labour commitment, particularly under the conditions of high population densities, rapidly increasing populations and relatively poor yields, the ready adoption of factory work is easily explained, especially when prevailing inheritance practices encourage the decentralization of industry. *Anerbrecht*, the conveyance of the holding to one heir only results in the production of a rural proletariat which migrates to and provides the labour supply of the towns, to which industry is decentralized whilst *Realteilung*, the physical division of the property amongst all members of the family, helps to maintain a fairly dense small farm population in the genuinely rural areas which can be tapped as a labour supply as the needs of capitalist industry arise.[24] The fact that with *Realteilung* a large part of the rural population has not been de-rooted, that a peasant structure has been maintained, means that industry has been forced eventually to seek additions to its labour supply in the countryside, and the freedom of movement permitted by the electric motor and the internal combustion engine has facilitated the development. Our forecast for the future rests upon an appreciation of certain trends manifest within the capitalist sector. Greater productivity, higher incomes, social security benefits which the industrial system can provide, the levelling up effects associated with greater wealth, above all the elimination of massive industrial unemployment, seem destined to wipe out the necessity for a worker-peasant class. At the same time technology and industrial organization favour the large, joint stock concern against the small, independent establishment, particularly in the modern growth industries. This all seems to indicate that an industrial reorganization within the villages is highly probable in the future. Increases in the scale of operation are most likely and the owners of small plants are likely to be placed at a disadvantage. The decentralized pattern of the industrial population need not be affected though particular changes may be unavoidable. But the progressive industrialization of the rural communities will entail a greater homogenization of the rural population and their closer identification with the urban model of existence.

If the advanced level of industrialization in Gosheim makes the dis-

[24] Röhm (1959): 5, also Röhm (1957).

ppearance of the worker-peasant class seem all the more inevitable, that loes not mean it is generally imminent. In their daily lives people are usually not as impressed as academics with the inevitableness of things or y long-term trends. They work on assumptions based upon past and usually outmoded experience. In the past, three less sound arguments have een advanced in favour of part-time farming: it provides an insurance gainst unemployment, it increases the volume of income, it prevents de-rooting of the population in the process of industrialization. It is vorth recording, without pursuing the point, that as late as 1966 some very esponsible people in the Federal administration had not dismissed the nemployment issue as irrelevant to this age. In automation they foresaw general threat to employment and in the residual function of the part-ime farm they were prepared to seek a haven. There is no doubt that art-time farming in the past has increased the volume of income for many marginal farmers, and that in the early '50s the worker-peasant farms were etter off than many family farms in Baden-Württemberg. They were etter off than some working-class families too.* The income argument is a ood one with respect to the agricultural population, i.e. it is better to be a art-time farmer than a marginal full-time farmer; but it does not follow hat it is better to be a worker-peasant than an industrial worker. And he income argument has particular force at certain stages of economic evelopment. The high price of food has been one important reason why he contribution of the farm sector to the household economy has been vorthy of the chef's consideration in the past, and it is one of the rigidities n the economy that will influence the evolution of the agrarian structure n the future. What the chef's indifference curve looks like no one knows, ut the decision to abandon farming altogether depends upon more than he marginal contribution of the farm to the family income. It depends pon the ease with which the chef can dispose of his property and obtain he current or expected value of his equity. At current prices agricultural

* Kuhnen (1954): 135–48 gives some data for Baden-Württemberg parishes in 953/4.

Monthly income DM	*Per family*	*Per head*
Worker-peasant	513	103
Factory worker	480	125
Shop assistant and office worker	378	129
Railway worker	345	102
Full peasant holding with additional source of income	311	76
Full peasant holding	109	20

See also Wagener (1958): 76–7.

land is so costly that many individuals wishing to enlarge their holdings t
an economic level can afford the expenditure only by spreading it over
number of years, and the capricious and piecemeal manner in whic
individual properties and strips of land reach the market makes the proce
all the more costly and difficult. Some part-time farmers are undoubtedl
retaining their properties until a propitious time arrives when they ca
dispose of it on the more favourable urban market. There is little doul
that the function and attractiveness of the part-time holding is closel
related to the biological cycle of the worker-peasant family. It has a ro
to perform in the early years of marriage when the children are numerou
and growing and there are a lot of mouths to be fed; in the declining year
too when factory work can be rigorous and demanding. And when th
prevalence of moonlighting and overtime amongst industrial workers
acknowledged the part-time farm does not appear to be so out of place i
an industrial society.

Nevertheless, the long-term trend towards the dissolution of the worke
peasant class is unmistakable. In Hessen between 1949 and 1960 full-tim
farms of less than 2 ha declined by a quarter as did those between 2 an
5 ha. The part-time farms of less than 2 ha declined not so fast, by
fifth; but those between 2 and 5 ha increased by a quarter. Obviousl
small full-time farms and the smallest of part-time farms are on th
decline, and the ranks of the larger part-time farms are being swollen by th
conversion of some full-time farms to part-time farms. This movemer
disguises the general tendency. The conversion of some 7,000 2–5 h
full-time farms to part-time farms did not balance the net loss of part-tim
farms in the less than 5 ha category which amounted to 10,000 holding
13 per cent of all part-time farms in existence in 1949.[25]

The emergence of the worker-peasant community has produced one c
the most dynamic countrysides in Europe. A great degree of diversity sti
exists within the general context we have been describing. Table 2.1
illustrates the varied socio-economic conditions in a number of Baden
Württemberg settlements. Nevertheless a progressive and seemingl
irresistible incorporation of the rural population within the capitalis
system has been under way for over a century; and as Hesse's map
indicate, since the inter-war period the process has accelerated.[26] In th
Baden-Württemberg of 1939, a broad band of industrialized communitie
stretched from Mannheim southwards along the course of the Rhine plai
towards Baden-Baden, branching eastwards at Karlsruhe, throug
Stuttgart to Aalen, where it was joined by another band of industrial an
worker-peasant communities stretching from the borders of the Blac
Forest, near Villengen, north-east along the line of the Jura, throug

[25] Staat und Wirtschaft in Hessen (1963): May 109–15. [26] Hesse (1965).

TABLE 2.16 *The evolution of six typical parishes in Baden-Württemberg, 1939–61*

Village Kreis	*Schlossau (Buchen)*	*Hausen ob Rottweil (Rottweil)*	*Gosheim (Tuttlingen)*	*Brigach (Villingen)*	*Wildentierbach (Mergentheim)*	*Weil unter den Rinner (Balingen)*
Gemeindetypen* Community Type						
1939	D	D	C	E	E	D
1961	D	B	A	B	E	C
Population						
1939	757	368	1,097	442	503	251
1961	907	430	2,219	541	480	329
Over 65, % 1961	14	13	7	8	15	11
1961						
Labour force in agriculture %	64	49	7	43	87	37
Auspendler % of labour force	21	43	7	47	8	35
Households (Nos.)	232	114	653	157	111	103
% which are farms	50	49	25	36	79	70
Farm types %						
Part-time	66	68	99	52	19	100
Small peasant	23	23	1	11	20	—
Full peasant	10	9	—	37	60	—
Taxable capacity per head. DM. Realsteuerkraft	41	44	249	59	58	51

* Hesse's classification: A–Industrial communities and service centres
B–Dormitory communities
C–Worker-peasant communities
D–Small peasant communities
E–Middle and small peasant communities

Source: Hesse (1965) and *Gemeindestatistik Baden-Württemberg* 1960/1.

Reutlingen and Göppingen. Large peasant communities dominated in three regions, in the north and south-east of the State and in the central parts of the Black Forest. Elsewhere small peasant communities were prevalent; but by 1960 they had all but been eliminated. The only concentration of predominantly peasant communities persisted in the north and south-east regions, which, significantly returned the highest rates of increase in *Auspendlern*. Almost everywhere else the peasant element within the community had been reduced to the level of a minority.

For those who are not particularly well acquainted with the deceptions of the German countryside a statement like the preceding one is often a cause of misapprehension. As a view from any of the Autobahns will inform one, the German countryside, apparently, supports a predominantly

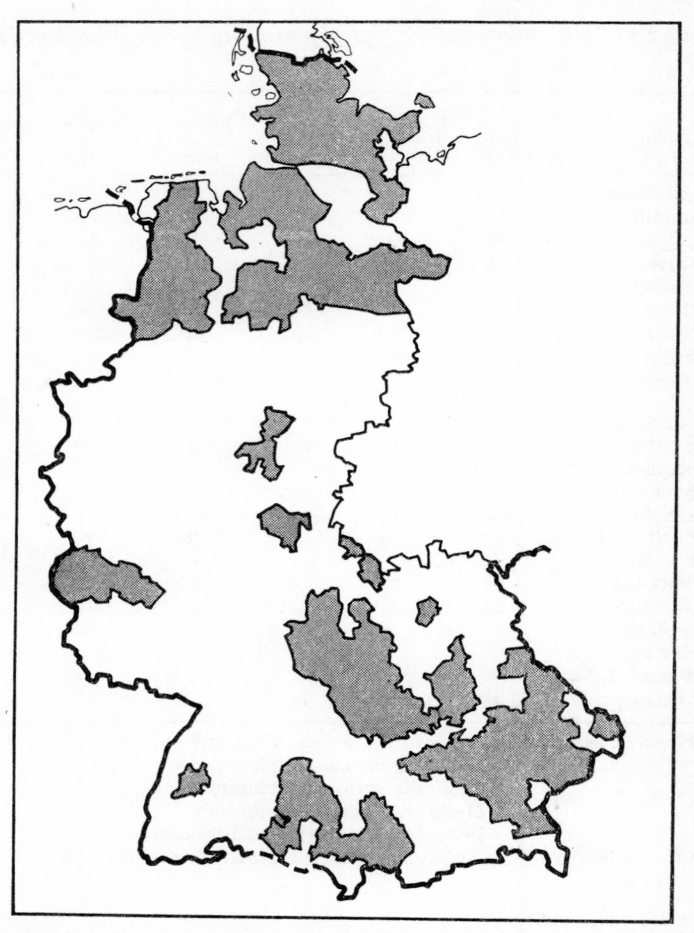

Fig. 2.3. The agrarian communities of Federal Germany; 40 per cent or more o active population engaged in agriculture

agricultural population. There is the variegated pattern of the strips. Th farmhouses and the villages are as quaint and as old-fashioned as an landscape artist could wish for; and if the season is right, one can see th families dotted about the fields, harvesting or mowing. What one does no see are the new commuter suburbs attached to the old village centre, or th factories concealed by their architecture and cleanliness. The visua dominance of the strip system hides the economic transformation of rural society. According to van Deenen's map of community types in 1961 only in three areas were agricultural communities dominant: in th northern parts of the Republic (Schleswig-Holstein and parts of Lower Saxony), in the Eifel, and Bavaria, including Schwaben. In these areas either 40 per cent of the working population were engaged in agriculture, and less than 25 per cent in secondary manufacturing, as in Middle Franconia and Lower Bavaria; or, and more frequently, 40 per cent of the active population was dependent upon agriculture, and something between one-quarter and one-half were dependent upon manufacturing. Throughout the remainder of the Republic, the greater part of Rhine-Westphalia, Rhine Pfalz, Hessen and Baden-Württemberg, the rural community with more than 40 per cent of its population engaged in agriculture had become a rarity.

Underdeveloped regions

In some parts of West Germany the small peasant problem acquires markedly regional characteristics and a diversification of the region's economic structure through the decentralization of industry to local centres, or even villages, becomes in the light of the experience in Baden-Württemberg and other *Länder* the obvious solution to seek. By the adoption of regional development programmes and the selection of development poles the Federal Government in conjunction with the administration of relevant *Länder* have gone some way to dealing with these problems.[27] In comparison with France a far greater reserve exists in Germany concerning the appropriateness of interventionist measures in a market economy, and it is only reasonable to stress that in the context of the whole German economy regional problems are small fry in contrast to the French and particularly the Italian situation, where about a third of the whole population is affected by regional underdevelopment. Nevertheless these regional problems acquire an exaggerated importance because an obvious solution is to close down parts of the regions – to abandon them, one could say, with skill, forethought and care. Deserted villages and wastes have been associated in European history with all that is worst in life: war, plague and famine. A retreat of the area cultivated has been too frequently the long-term manifestation of the despoliation or destruction of civilized life, and it is understandable why a deep and atavistic revulsion exists against the abandonment of an area, though, for the first time in history, the society is rich enough to afford the luxury of not having to make a living wherever it is practicable. One may draw some of the heat from the discussion by talking of Development Shut-Down Agencies, or as the Germans are doing by talking of the farm population of these regions as 'park-keepers'. In economic terms the maintenance of farming in some regions, they argue, cannot be justified. But so that the cultural landscape

[27] Langer (1964) and *Raumordnung Bericht* (1963).

can be preserved – for the benefit of future urban generations – it is advisable to keep the peasants in these regions as 'park-keepers'. The pros and cons, and ironies, of the argument are pretty obvious, and the English should be the last to smile at them. What the suggestion does underline once again is the fact that in the modern society the farmer is being reduced to the level of a dependent agent of a state subsidized sector. The price of wealth!

The accepted indices for recognizing the existence of backward zones, dramatic and disturbing though they are initially, lose their force because they are normative. One has only to look beyond the national borders of a given underdeveloped region to realize that the per capita income which makes that region backward in a national context, makes it relatively advanced in a European sense. In this light some problems of underdevelopment appear to be rather selfish issues; but in truth they are not and neither do they disappear because of this relativism. The condition of under-employment may reveal itself in terms of per capita income, or a high proportion engaged in argriculture, but the nature of underdevelopment lies in the inability of the regional economy to provide employment at current standards of remuneration for the present and projected labour force. This definition explains how underdevelopment can occur and is likely to occur in very advanced economies, such as the Federal Republic's. And since agriculture at its present stage of evolution in Germany can provide better jobs only by providing fewer jobs, in all regional development programmes the burden of achieving success falls principally upon the industrial and the associated tertiary sectors.

The underdeveloped regions of West Germany are all influenced by their frontier positions, with the exception of some of the markedly rural and un-industrialized areas of Bavaria. Along the eastern borders of the Republic from Schleswig-Holstein to the Danube in the south-east, a whole series of economies have been disrupted through the erection of the Iron Curtain. They form the most concentrated area in the region of the Bavarian Forest.* In the west, the economy of the Eifel-Hünsruck suffered a similar but earlier impairment after the severance of its economic contacts with Luxembourg, the Saar and Alsace-Lorraine following the First World War.[28] These political events have aggravated a condition that is fundamentally agrarian in origin and industrial in its solution. For the Eifel-Hünsruck a specific exercise has been carried out to assess the possibilities for structural reform in agriculture and the related need to provide non-agricultural employment.[29] The investigators discovered

* A lot of valuable material on this region is provided in Leffler and Schall (1964).

[28] Bergles (1961): I, pp. 165–82.

[29] Cramer (1964) and van Deenen (1963): 27–36 for a useful summary.

that out of a total of 199,200 employed persons, 57,700 were engaged in agriculture, 33,700 were *Pendlern*, the majority being worker-peasants, about 10,000 of them commuting over considerable distances. Only 4,100 persons were considered surplus to the agricultural labour force and capable because of their youth of changing their occupation. A larger under-employed group were considered to be immobile because of age and the structure of the family labour force. The long distance commuters and the 4,000 surplus agricultural workers were regarded as constituting a potential labour force that could with advantage be found industrial employment within the region; and the creation of an estimated 1,750 new jobs per annum was considered necessary to cope with the rising generations. To reorganize the agrarian structure it was proposed to prefer the part-time unit, and the family unit – enlarging the potentially valid holdings with land recouped from the marginal holdings of more than 2 ha. The criterion used for the family holdings has already been outdated by the rise in parity income, a risk which any exercise of this nature runs. And the calculations for the redistribution of land, without ever touching upon the critical issue of the institutional means by which it could be achieved, revealed again what an intractable problem re-structuration is. Without furnishing the figures, which is unfortunate, the investigators concluded that in certain districts the disintegration of the agrarian structure into a multitude of very small holdings had left no basis upon which a new structure could be erected. The immediate prospect was a phase during which the area under 'social fallow' could only increase – tantamount to a sort of unorganized shut-down. In other districts insufficient land was available to stock up all the potential family farms. Only by degrading some to part-time farms could the needs of a portion be satisfied.[30]

A number of regions have promising agrarian structures, not always for the same reasons. In Schleswig-Holstein and the northern parts of Lower Saxony, it is the prevalence of middle- and large-sized family holdings; in Upper Bavaria the combination of this with good soils that accounts for the promising structures. But since all three areas are not highly industrialized, they are all the more dependent upon maintaining and improving these favourable structures to ensure their economic future. The Lower Rhine plain is favoured with a middle peasant structure, good soils and the proximity of industrialized areas. In the band of country stretching from the Ruhr eastwards beyond Munster, Osnabruck and Paderborn towards Brunswick, Hannover and Göttingen lies a zone in which small family farming prevails, and there is little doubt that the high degree of industrialization and the demands of the associated urban markets offer the small

[30] Cramer (1964): 62.

family farm the best chances of survival through intensification, but onl because the soil conditions are among the best. The same is true for th valleys of the Rhine, Main and Neckar in the vicinities of Frankfurt Mannheim and Heilbronn. But in the Siegerland, the Westerwald, th Saar, throughout much of Hessen and Baden-Württemberg, intensificatio is severely restricted by the environment, and the combination of poo soils and small holdings gives these areas some of the worst agraria structures of any. But because these are well industrialized and thei economy as a whole little dependent upon agriculture, their economi future is not nearly so bleak as it is for the larger part of Bavaria, th eastern borders of Baden-Württemberg and the Eifel-Hunsruck, where high degree of dependence upon agriculture exists alongside a prevalenc of small holdings and poor soils.

By the adoption of part-time farming the West Germans have gon much further towards solving the problems of their farmers than thei agriculture. Incomes in most rural areas are now much higher than the would have been if the population had remained dependent upon agriculture alone.* Of the 6·1 million members of the labour force residing i parishes with populations of less than 2,000, i.e. living in distinctly rura circumstances, in 1961 only 2·5 million (41 per cent) were employed i agriculture, and four out of every ten of them were females. From a tota of 12·4 million people classed as residing in these small settlements onl 1·0 million people lived in dominantly agrarian parishes, 3·7 million live in agro-industrial parishes and the remainder lived in settlements wher manufacturing was the principal source of employment.[31] But industrialization having freed these people from a dependence upon agriculture ha not at the same time unlocked their land for consolidation into larger units This predial immobility of real estate constitutes the overwhelmingl important problem facing German agriculture in the future and the tota want of any institutional means for coping with it represents a grav lacuna in agrarian policy making. Family farming has been able to absor technology and capital without difficulty and a corresponding improvemen in output has been recorded on farms of less than, as well as on farms o more than, 10 ha. But the evolution of a valid form of family farming wi be seriously impaired unless these farms are able to meet economic pressures by raising their scale of operation. Despite all the real improvement of the post-war period very large areas of the German countryside are stil burdened with restrictive and inelastic agrarian structures; and in thos

* Kuhnen (1961): 439–53 estimated that farming families drew from non agricultural sources an income of between 4 to 6 milliard DM during the mid-'50s when the saleable output of agriculture amounted to 17 milliard DM.

[31] van Deenen (1965): 24–30.

areas with more promising structures – where more than 50 per cent of the land is in holdings capable of sustaining family farming at a little below currently accepted standards[32] – the need for some widespread means of transferring land from the marginal to the potentially economic holdings is just as pressing.

[32] van Deenen (1965): Karten.

3 PAYSANS: property, family and farm in France

The enigma which French farming presents to the outside observer arises from a combination of a paradox with an aversion. For the majority of people, Frenchmen as well as lesser mortals, French farming is thought of as predominantly peasant farming, which as a matter of counting heads is true; and agricultural issues are regarded mainly as peasant issues, which as a matter of economic reality is not so true. However, as a matter of practical politics, since last century it has been very convenient to confuse the demographic truth with the economic truth. Consequently, the attention of the public, and of the majority of writers upon rural matters, has been averted from the fact of the existence of a strong and economically significant capitalist farming sector, located in regions where the effects of depopulation have been far from detrimental to farming or society. In the areas of peasant farming, depopulation of the countryside, which theoretically is one of the conditions for its survival, seems on the contrary to have accelerated its decadence.[1] For electoral purposes this paradox has been used by the middle classes who regarded the maintenance of the peasantry as a guarantee of their own survival in the small towns and villages,[2] to confuse the issue of the economic survival of the family farm, which in part is a matter of occupational migration, with the issue of regional decadence and revival, which is a matter of geographical migration and industrial decentralization. By short-circuiting the argument they have been able to suggest that the maintenance, rather than the reduction, of the peasantry would have the double effect of preventing regional depopulation and regional decadence. Since, furthermore, it became a tenet of radical political thought in the late nineteenth century that social stability was dependent upon the conservation of a solid electoral base amongst the peasantry, it has been fairly easy for the interested parties to confuse the national demographic threat posed by the decline in the birth-rate with the question of rural depopulation and the decline of the peasantry. It has been easy in these circumstances actively to propagate a

[1] Mendras (1956).
[2] Mallet (1962): 15.

myth of the peasantry,* and at the same time to regard the system of small-scale, rather extensive, little modernized, low-productive polyculture, carrying the burden of too much labour, as portraying the eternal essence of agriculture;[3] to insist upon its protection, and to effect its subsidization. Only in the post-war period has the myth been seriously challenged within the peasantry itself, as well as within the administration, and then, for electoral reasons, with only limited success. Despite the real changes which have occurred since the war, and which reached a climax during the Pisani era, Edgar Faure, who replaced Pisani because of the withdrawal of political support from the Gaullist regime by the farmers in 1965, could announce the following year: 'L'exploitation à l'échelle humaine est une conception plus avancée que le type d'exploitation latifundiaire.' That he, himself, favoured a form of agriculture that was 'personalisée, à l'échelle humaine et non salariale'.[4]

Socio-economic structure of French farming

According to the one in ten farm survey conducted in 1963 a total of 6·8 million people belonged to farming families and lived on farms; 4·3 million of them participated in the labour force, 1·65 million as full-time workers, 2·65 as part-time workers.[5] Aged farmers and wives of the *chefs d'entreprise* composed most of the part-time group, so that the term itself does not have the same meaning or significance as in Federal Germany. It is not the French custom to apply a socio-economic classification to the data on agrarian structures but there is no reason to forgo this convenience so long as its limitations are recognized.† Because farming in France is much less intensive than in Germany the areal limits applied to the different categories are somewhat higher. Up to 50 ha, for instance, farms remain essentially family concerns, being dependent upon hired labour for

* One of the most fulsome and most recent (1958) contributions to the liturgy went:

> 'In agriculture the father is head of the household and *chef d'entreprise* at the same time, he commands with a double title. The mother is queen of the hearth and the hearth is the centre of attraction and the convergence of the farm and family. Under the direction of their parents the children work according to their capacity and contribute to the success of the farm, exercising their spirit of initiative, economy, sense of administration and responsibility. The peasant's simple life is less agitated, less noisy, less complicated than that of the town dwellers who are subject to the levelling process of the collectivity. In the countryside he finds time to replenish and renew himself, time to meditate and to search deeply into human and divine affairs both during his working and leisure hours, especially those of the long winter evenings.'

[3] Gervais (1965): 31.

[4] *Le Monde*, 21 June 1966.

[5] Premiers résultats de l'enquête au 1/10e pour les structures agricoles en 1963.

† See footnote (†) on next page.

less than 30 per cent of their requirements. Only as the 100 ha limit is approached does the employment of hired labour exceed the use of family labour and farming acquire an essentially capitalist form.

Of all the elements contained in Table 3.1, the capitalist group is the

TABLE 3.1 *The Socio-economic structure of French farming, 1963*

Type	*Size*	*Farms 'ooos*	*%*	*Area % S.A.U.*	*P.A.T. 'ooos*	*%*	*Family members incl. chefs. millions*	*%*
FAMILY FARMS								
Small peasant – part-time	1–10 ha	817·8	45	12	908·2	29	2·53	38
Medium peasant	10–20 ha	484·9	27	22	931·1	29	1·93	29
Large peasant	20–50 ha	393·7	22	37	945·7	30	1·73	26
FAMILY CAPITALIST	50–100 ha	84·9	4·7	17	267·9	8	0·37	5·5
CAPITALIST FARMS	100 ha +	23·4	1·3	12	119·6	4	0·10	1·5
Totals		1,804·7	100	100	3,173	100	6·66	100

Source: *One in Ten Survey* 1963.

S.A.U.= Total farm area less the amount in woodland and non-agricultural land, e.g. roads, lakes and ponds.

1 P.A.T.= 1 person (of whatever age, sex or status) who works on the farm, for at least 300 days of 9 hours each; cf. and ct. 1 U.T.H. (unite-travailleur – homme) = one adult worker working on a farm for at least 300 days of 9 hours with reduction coefficients to standardize child, female, and aged person's labour. One U.T.H. is in principle comparable with the German one V.A.K., Vollarbeitskraft. In this chapter the anglicization S.L.U. (standard labour unit) refers to P.A.T.

† J. Chombart de Lauwe has recently (*Le Monde* 15 Nov. 1966) provided some data which fills out the material in Table 3.1.

Per farm

Type of farm	*Nos. 'ooos*	*Area ha.*	*S.L.U.*	*Capital d'exploitation Fr.*	*Revenue Fr.*
Part-time	403	4·0	0·4	18,000	2,200
Small and medium peasant (<20 ha)	884	10·2	1·5	27,000	7,700
Large peasant (20–50 ha)	380	30·2	2·4	73,000	19,600
Family-capitalist (50–100 ha)	83	66·3	3·2	145,000	29,600
Capitalist (>100 ha)	23	161	5·2	322,000	48,000
Specialized farms	167	—	3·0	92,000	25,100

most distinct and homogeneous. It displays a remarkable degree of geographical concentration, 49 per cent of all farms exceeding 100 ha being located in the Paris Basin, principally in Picardie and Champagne. Large farms exist in the southern regions too but their size is a reflection of poor soils and a difficult climate and rarely do they display the high technical

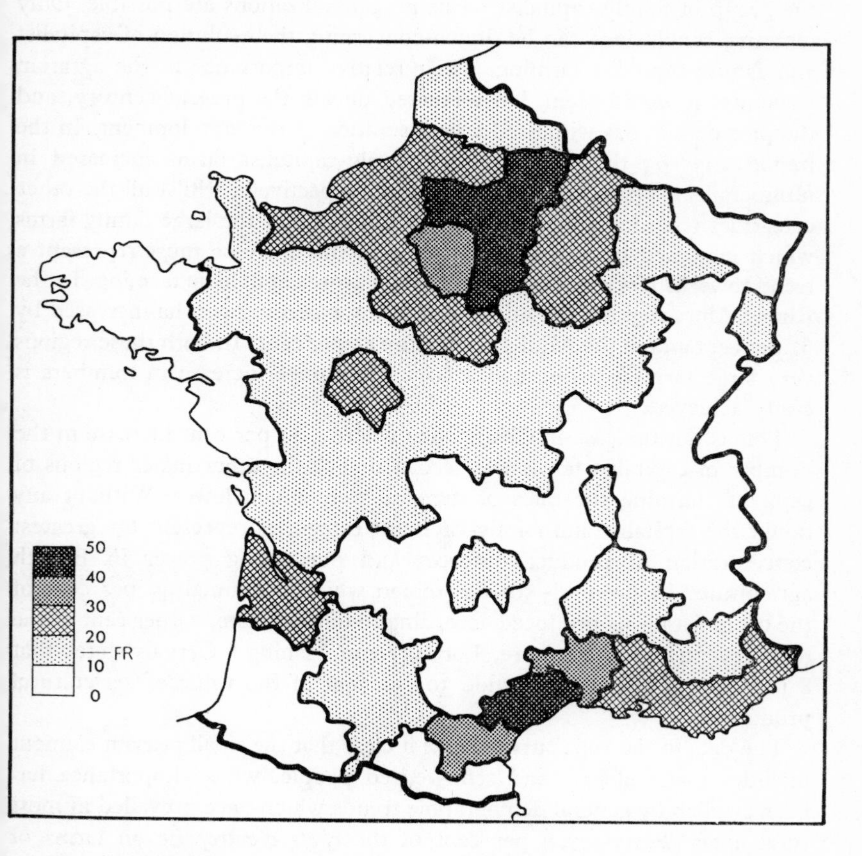

Fig. 3.1. Hired labour as a percentage of total labour force (S.L.U. 1963)

levels with which the 'grandes fermes' of the north are associated. Some farms of smaller acreages, intensively cultivated but using a lot of hired labour – the vineyards of the Gironde and Languedoc for instance – are capitalistic in organization. Until it is possible to classify enterprises according to their volume of output and labour character – and it will be some time before this is possible – one has to be content with an inflexible system of classification. Similar qualifications have to be made for the farms classed as Family-Capitalist enterprises. However, as a group they are, to a surprising degree, concentrated in the North, 35 per cent, alongside the capitalist farms, and they represent the other wing of the most progressive section of French farming. With regard to the remainder of the group of family-capitalist farms no generalizations are possible. Only tentative conclusions can be drawn concerning the evolution of capitalist and family-capitalist farming. Their relative importance in the agrarian structure, it would seem, has increased during the present century, and the past decade has witnessed an acceleration of this development. In the period 1955–63 the capitalist and family-capitalist farms increased in numbers by 16 per cent and 13 per cent respectively, whilst all the other categories recorded a decline with the exception of the large family farms which increased by 4½ per cent. Some of this increase must represent a trend towards more extensive rather than more capitalistic farming. In the Rhône-Alpes région* the number of farms exceeding 100 ha increased by 67 per cent and in the Midi-Pyrénées by 85 per cent. In both those regions very large farms are rare and a large percentage increase in numbers is easily achieved.

This is not the case in Champagne where a 44 per cent increase in the number of capitalist farms was recorded. For the other major regions of capitalist farming the rates of increase were much lower. Without any doubt the capitalist and family-capitalist categories represent the greatest concentration of productive forces and purchasing power in French agriculture. In the mid-'50s the region which contained 49 per cent of the capitalist farms produced according to one estimate, 24 per cent of the total revenue of Agriculture, Forestry and Fishing.[6] Gervais states that 8 per cent of all farms provide 30 per cent of the value of agricultural production.[7]

The data in the 1963 survey make it clear that the small peasant element includes many elderly and semi-retired people, whose importance has been swollen by general demographic trends which have prevailed in most rural areas. Forty-seven per cent of the *chefs d'entreprise* on farms of between 1 and 5 ha were over 60 years of age. On farms of 5–10 ha the proportion was 38 per cent; on farms of more than 20 ha it was below 20 per cent. Sixty-eight per cent of the 125,000 *chefs d'entreprise* who were women possessed small peasant holdings; 62 per cent were over 60 years of age and the overwhelming majority were more than 50 years of age. In

* Région, refers specifically to *régions de programme* which are called by their proper French names, e.g. Bretagne. The term region carries its usual English connotation and the regional name is Anglicized, e.g. Brittany.

[6] Études et Conjuncture (1959): 601. [7] Gervais (1965): 84.

ll 43 per cent of all chefs on farms of less than 10 ha were in their 60s.

Within the medium peasant category the elderly *chefs d'entreprise* form . substantial group. Out of a total of 485,000 chefs, 133,000 (27 per cent) vere over 60 years of age. In the large peasant class they accounted for ;5,000 out of a total of 394,000. They are not spread evenly throughout he agricultural districts of France and tend with the elderly elements ·f the small peasant class to be more than proportionately represented in he western and southern parts. When these districts have a record of lemographic stagnation, as many of them do, and when they remain ighly dependent upon the agricultural sector for their livelihood, then he problem of small farm structures acquires both demographic and 'ocational characteristics that render it particularly intractable; more so vhen, as is so often the case, many of the holdings are without successors. 'oung married chefs between 25 and 35 years of age are in the minority. Chey represent only 10 per cent of the medium peasant class and 12½ per ent of the large peasant class. The principal socio-economic group within hese two categories is made up of men between the ages of 35 and 60, vho intend to make their living from farming during the next twenty-five 'ears and who represent the principal recipients and critics of whatever olicies the government chooses to promote. Their ranks must include some ·f the earliest supporters of the C.N.J.A.* movement, a movement which elieves that family farming can find a place for itself in a modern society.

In total the chefs under 60 years of age in the medium and large peasant 'ategory represent a block of almost 650,000 active and interested voters. t would be going too far to call them a solid block of voters because of he differences within the group which in all probability will become more pparent as they engage in the struggle for survival in the coming years. Chose located in the Alps, the Massif Central, the Pyrénées, will be andicapped by the limitations of the environment. Those located in egions that are still over-populated, like Brittany and Alsace, even though he farming is intensive, will need to improve the man-land ratio in order o raise per capita earnings. They will need to overcome the legacies of agriculturalization' and the disadvantages of their remoteness from the oles of development. Those located in regions where the demographic ressure on farming has been reduced by decades of low birth-rates and . considerable volume of migration will still be faced with the enormous osts of structural costs reform and the capital charges attendant upon nvestment programmes. A fortunate but as yet indetermined proportion vill be able to grasp the opportunities provided by a favourable location, ;ood soils and climate; the possibilities of new outlets and markets.

Our knowledge of the disparities within the family farm sector is very

* C.N.J.A., Centre Nationale des Jeunes Agriculteurs.

TABLE 3.2 *The agricultural regions of France*

	Régions de Programme	
ZONE OF CAPITALIST FARMING A Good structures, high farming standards, high returns per hectare and per unit of labour. Capitalist farms control most of the agricultural land. Less than 30 per cent of the male labour force dependent upon agriculture.	PARIS PICARDIE	
B Capitalist farms control most of the agricultural land, but large peasant holdings farm 30–40 per cent of the total area. Average and above average returns per hectare and per unit of labour. Less than 30 per cent of the male labour force dependent upon agriculture.	HAUTE NORMANDIE CHAMPAGNE CENTRE BOURGOGNE	
ZONE OF PEASANT FARMING A Good structures, high returns per hectare and per unit of labour. Less than 15 per cent of the male labour force dependent upon agriculture.	NORD	
B Poor to weak structures, areas of above average returns per hectare and per unit of labour within the general context of below average returns. 30–45 per cent of the male labour force dependent upon agriculture. Demographic difficulties associated with overpopulation, depopulation and high average age of *chefs d'entreprise*. Small peasant properties contain a significant proportion of the agricultural area in regions marked*.	BASSE NORMANDIE BRETAGNE* PAYS DE LA LOIRE POITOU-CHARENTES AQUITAINE*	The West and
	LANGUEDOC PROVENCE	
	ALSACE*	
C Poor to weak structures, low returns per hectare and per unit of labour, in largely mountainous or isolated regions. Very high dependence of male labour force upon agriculture, often exceeding 45 per cent. Detrimental effects of depopulation evident, high average age of *chefs d'entreprise*.	LIMOUSIN AUVERGNE	Massif Central
	MIDI-PYRÉNÉES	
Less dependence of male labour force upon agriculture. Small peasant properties important.	RHÔNE-ALPES	
D Large peasant farms account for 36–48 per cent of the agricultural area and capitalistic farms are important in certain districts. Structures and returns per hectare and per unit of labour vary accordingly, from weak to poor in the case of structures, from below to above average in the case of returns. Less than 30 per cent of the male labour force dependent upon agriculture. Age of *chefs d'entreprise* below average.	LORRAINE FRANCHE-COMTÉ	

imited. We know, for example, that average farm incomes in Brittany vere some 70 per cent higher than in the department of Haut-Rhin and ;ome 30 per cent higher than in the Vendée, all of them being peasant 'arming areas. Within Brittany itself, the range in average farm incomes vas as much as 70 per cent.[8] We know that within the same commune or ırrondissement significant differences exist within the peasant community)ut the available information is quite insufficient to the task of evaluating hem. And the monographs and articles on various rural communities are ;enerally deficient in typologies and data on incomes and living standards.

It is impossible to obtain anything more than a generalized figure for he worker-peasant element in France from the one in ten survey. Of the otal family members living on farms 370,000 men and 60,000 women are :ngaged on non-agricultural activities. The areas where they are concen- rated are better known: the mining areas of the North, Lorraine, Alsace, he Lyon area and Savoy, around the ports, the Paris region, and in areas)f recent industrial decentralization, such as Rennes. But with rare :xceptions[9] very little has been written about them as a class, and little is :nown about their incomes and living standards.

During the past few years, 1955–63, though the number of large peasant 'arms has increased by 4½ per cent, the number of medium farms has leclined by almost 10 per cent, the number of small farms by about 25 per :ent. It is impossible to be precise about the long-term character of these rends or to set a date when the trend began to favour conspicuously the ;rowth of the family-capitalist and capitalist farms. But the trend is there ınd it has been conspicuous in the post-war era .However, it must not be 'orgotten, whatever implications for the future one may attach to this rend, at present the French agrarian structure is still dominated by 'amily-sized farms, small medium and large, which between them control 'o per cent of the agricultural area and employ 89 per cent of the agricul- ural labour force (S.L.U.).

Tour de France

'rench agrarian issues insist upon a regional treatment. The fundamental livision is, of course, between the areas of predominantly capitalist and redominantly peasant farming. On the basis of the concentration of ıgricultural land within the various size categories, the Paris and the 'icardie régions stand out as the node of the capitalist farming system. n the régions of Haute Normandie, Champagne, Centre and Bourgogne, arge peasant farms are of greater importance, but on the whole these égions are most suitably classified within the zone of capitalist farming. The remainder of France is dominated by family farming structures. In

[8] O.E.C.D. (1964): 190. [9] Le Balle (1958).

the west and south-west, in Bretagne, the Pays de la Loire, Poitou Charentes and Aquitaine a third of the family farms are located. Midi Pyrénées and Languedoc contain 14 per cent of all family farms as does the région of the Rhône-Alpes. Two smaller concentrations are to be found in Basse Normandie 7 per cent, and the Massif Central 7 per cent.

Of course it would be true to say that the regional problems of farming in France are only the particular expression of the general problems raised by the incorporation of peasant economies in increasingly dynamic capitalist systems: problems of scale, overmanning, outmoded structures, commercialization, and differential rates of growth in agricultural and industrial incomes. However it is too common a mistake to attribute the socio-economic difficulties of the various regions always to the same combination of causes, and to ignore the changes, which are discussed in some detail below, that have occurred during the past century. Changes which indicate how strenuously peasants will struggle to adapt and survive, and which explain some of the chagrin and violence that arises when their efforts lead only to apparent failure.

The West and South-west

For instance, co-operation was established quite early amongst the peasantry of Poitou-Charentes when they were forced to adopt dairying as a result of the destruction of their vines caused by the spread of phylloxera. The first co-operative dairy was established in 1887 at Chaille, near Surgeres. Today, however, the dairy factories are too numerous and too small, sometimes in competition with one another for supplies and often incapable of changing or diversifying their production.* Short on reserves and capital for improvement, integration is an obvious solution, but it will entail the disappearance of one in four co-operatives. The butter they produce is reported to be amongst the dearest in Western Europe and exported only through the assistance of heavy subsidies.[10] Despite the region's dependence upon livestock, only 2·8 per cent of the milk cows are included in milk recording schemes, compared with 7 per cent in the région du Nord. Although Poitou-Charentes has 40 per cent more milk cows than the Nord it spends only 20 per cent more on the control of tuberculoses, and the average yield per milk cow is only 1 per cent above the national average.[11]

Flatrès writes of a 'second agricultural revolution' in Finistère† during

* 'le secteur co-opératif, bastille de l'anti-productivité'—de Virieu (1967): 255.

[10] France de Demain 6: 28–30. [11] Statistique Agricole 1964.

† Despite the prevalence of tenant holdings and the low return on agricultural investment which has hindered the modernization of tenant farming, a practice which is widespread throughout the West: in Aquitaine 70 per cent of the agricultural land is owned and exploited by the *chefs d'entreprise*. North of Bordeaux,

the post-war period;[12] but the region remains one of the principal zones of peasant discontent.

Ley farming, the introduction of temporary pastures into the rotations, has been almost universally adopted in Finistère and this this has been accompanied by an increase in the yields of the arable crops associated with the simplified rotations. Only half of the pre-war acreage is now required to raise the equivalent of the pre-war cereal production. The increased volume of forage has stimulated the production of livestock, pigs and poultry, factory farming making its appearance. A preference is being displayed for the qualities of non-local breeds of cattle better suited, it is thought, to the greater feeding capacities of the farms. The mechanization of farming has been rapid and largely individual in organization, little account being taken of its profitability. Although the consumption of fertilizers has risen it remains behind the levels of the other more advanced areas such as the Nord. The application has not always been intelligent or economic. Though extension services have multiplied there remain many areas of farm management which need closer supervision and investigation. In its attack upon the structural problems the local office of S.A.F.E.R., one of the most active in France, has run into difficulties of a fundamental character, which will be discussed later,* whilst the problems associated with the commercialization of the farm produce, a principal cause of dissatisfaction and violence in this area, have not been overcome satisfactorily. Thus it is in the field of production, not of vulgarization, farm management or institutional reform, that the best and quickest results have been obtained. The economic returns on all this effort have consequently been less than satisfactory. According to a limited number of farm budgets which are available, the annual income per unit of family labour averaged out at between £360 and £450; and the range in earnings within one system of farming on medium peasant farms was enormous. Opposed to the advances in Finistère, which can be matched but not exceeded in other parts of Brittany, are some areas in the interior of Morbihan; archaic, socially, materially, and agriculturally, utilizing a large amount of labour for their root crops, still cultivating rye and buckwheat.[13]

and particularly north of La Rochelle, owner-occupiers become a minority, without changing the essentially peasant character of the farming, though the non-farm propertied classes introduce a significantly new element into the social structures, and constitute an influential factor determining the agrarian future of these areas. In the régions of Basse Normandie Pays de la Loire, most of Bretagne, in the departments of Vendée and Deux Sèvres, less than 40 per cent of the land is owned by the *chefs d'entreprise*. Only in the department of Finistère does the percentage exceed 50. Nowhere in this part of France does the number of owner occupied farms exceed 50 per cent of the total.

[12] Flatrès (1963): 5–55. * See pages 107–8. [13] France de Demain 7: 110.

The introduction and extension of hybrid maize has produced a majo evolution of the farming systems in Aquitaine. The increase in area ha been accompanied by a considerable rise in yields and a rapid increase i mechanization. The production of seeds has provided the small farmer with a larger and relatively assured source of income, as tobacco has don in Lot and Garonne. It has also helped towards a fuller utilization of th chefs' labour force. Much of the maize is fed locally to stock, thoug nothing like a North American corn belt has arisen; or it is exported a feeding stuff to the rest of France and other parts of the Common Market But the improvements it has brought to the peasantry, and the chanc it offers them for the future, have been accompanied by wholesale an apparently irreversible changes, which though ensuring a brighter futur for agriculture in the region, do nothing to preserve any traditional feature of peasant farming. The agrarian structure proved to be a serious obstacl to the mechanization of harvesting operations. Only 6,000 of the 32,00 holdings in the Basse Pyrénées exceeded the minimum size for the efficien utilization of a mechanical harvester – 20 ha – when the post-war expansio commenced.[14] The depopulation of the past hundred years severel restricted the supply of farm labour. The optimum fertilizer requirement usually surpassed the financial capabilities of the farmers. The greate degree of commercialization revealed the inadequacy of the storage facili ties both on the farms and in the warehouses of the merchants and th co-operatives, as well as the insufficiencies of the port facilities at Bayonne upon which there has been a great demand owing to a growing expor trade, itself now vital to the economic stability and welfare of the region These changes have not had time to run their full course, and the availabl statistics are not always a satisfactory guide to what is happening. In th Basse Pyrénées a 14 per cent rise in the number of 20–50 ha farms occurre between 1955 an 1963; an even larger rise, 40 per cent, occurred in the 50- 100 category though the absolute numbers involved are only in the hun dreds. But in Landes, the other considerable producer in the South-west all categories of farms registered a decline. If the mechanization of maiz cultivation is leading to either concentration or an increase in the averag size of holding, then in this case it is being obscured by the decline o farming on the more marginal areas. Significantly as the production o maize has increased in these predominantly peasant areas it has also bee adopted on a large scale in the capitalist areas to the north.

In the vine growing area of the Gironde it is the capitalistic element which have prevailed in what on first sight would appear to be a pre eminently peasant activity. The peasant producers outnumber the large concerns but supply little of the total amount marketed. They are in th

[14] Lerat (1961): 106.

majority in the less important producing zones but even there they supply only a quarter to a third of the sales. The large-scale producers prevail in the main production zones and supply two-thirds of the output. Consequently the mass trade and the quality trade is dominated by the bigger châteaux, increasingly supported by investment capital from outside the region. Commercial interests have sought the integration of marketing and production and to reduce their risks they have sought to include a range of vines within their production line. Competitively the prospects for the

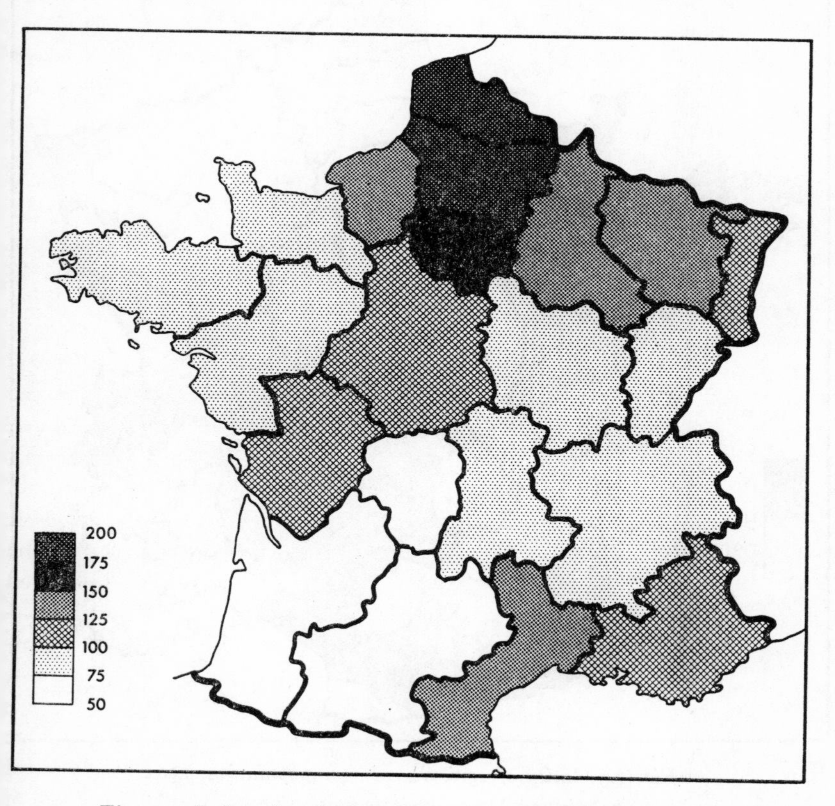

Fig. 3.2. Index of agricultural income per active person, 1962
France = 100

capitalist concerns are much better, and co-operation amongst the smaller producers is only a partial solution to their problems. The demand of the adjacent urban centres has, however, opened up the possibilities of vegetable and milk production for some of the peasant enterprises.[15]

[15] France de Demain 6: 35–41.

It is not the absence of change in the West and South-west which explains the region's difficulties; far from it. In the adoption of new ideas, new techniques, new institutions the area has on the whole a good record. The number of *Centres d'études techniques agricoles* and the membership of the *Centres de gestion agricole* are both above the national average. Almost without exception the departments of the West and South-west

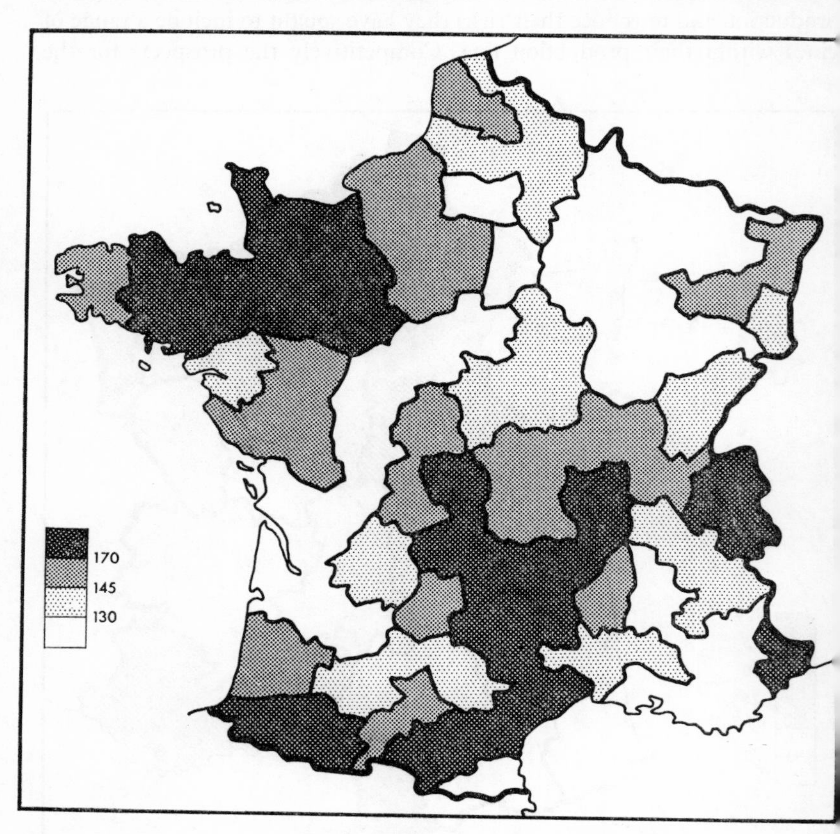

Fig. 3.3. Index of agricultural over-population, 1962

$$\left(\frac{\textit{population active agricole masculine}}{\textit{population techniquement nécessaire}} \times 100\right)$$

register a gross output per hectare equal to, and in some cases, Finistère, Côtes du Nord, Loire Atlantique, Manche, well above the national average. With few exceptions these same departments return a below average figure for gross output per worker. The estimates of the amount of surplus labour in agriculture help to explain this inversion. Out of an estimated surplus totalling 863,000 male agricultural workers, 350,000 – 40½ per cent – are located in these regions, which in 1962 contained only 36 per cent of the male labour force in agriculture.[16] Despite the long-term migration from the land, despite the 18–26 per cent decline in the male labour force throughout the region in the most recent period, 1954–62, too many people are still forced to make a living from land which only the investment of human capital has made so productive. Although the decline in the male labour force in agriculture has been a considerable one, only in rare instances has the rate attained the level of the national average. With the exception of the Massif Central, the declines have been greater in those regions less dependent upon agriculture for their livelihood.

The past achievements of peasant farming have rested on the system's ability to achieve high productivity through the intense application of human labour. Thus Brittany, at the time of Arthur Young an impoverished, backward area,[17] progressively intensified its agriculture during the 19th century until it was able to support some of the densest agricultural populations in France. Those achievements were never sufficient to match the rate of natural increase. Hence it became a notable area of emigration which was never adequate to the task of reducing the region's over-population. This condition was worsened through the process of 'agriculturalization'. Brittany, like many other areas of France, became relatively more dependent upon agriculture for its livelihood as the nineteenth century progressed. Though this trend has been reversed in the post-war period, the implantation of new industries and the continuing out-migration have been insufficient to overcome this original checking of its industrial development. Hence the intractability of the surplus labour problem is explained in part by the process of 'agriculturalization' and in part by the nature of the peasant economy.

The most persistent feature of rural life is the prevalence of the small farm divided, according to the particular district, into a few, and in most cases, a large number of parcels. The basic immobility of rural life in the West and South-west is a structural one, and as the following table portrays, whatever the productive changes in Brittany or Aquitaine, however rapidly the number of small farms may decline, even disappear from the records, the physical reorganization of the landscape, by remembrement (field consolidation) or through the agencies of institutions like S.A.F.E.R. is not keeping pace with the needs of a modern system of family farming.

It is clear that within the general context of this region of peasant farming quite diverse conditions and potentialities exist. The economic forces

[16] Bontron and Mathieu (1966): 28.
[17] Chombart de Lauwe (1946): 15–53.

which have instigated a process of socio-economic differentiation and competition amongst the peasantry must lead also to geographic differentiation and probably an intensification of geographic as well as socio-economic disparities amongst the peasantry. In Aquitaine the advantages of climate and the continuing possibilities of maize production indicate a

TABLE 3.3 *Remembrement in the West and South-west compared with the area controlled by small and medium peasant farms, 1964*

Région de Programme	*Area in farms of 1–20 ha 'ooos ha*	*Remembrement in course or completed 'ooos ha*
Basse Normandie	557	152
Bretagne	1,288	453
Pays de la Loire	981	246
Poitou et Charentes	558	346
Aquitaine	1,037	117

line of specialization which once pursued must have countless ramifications. At the same time the intensification offering in certain privileged areas opens up attractive prospects. But in a period when labour costs are rising, and in some cases labour is in short supply, this can only be achieved through managerial and organizational adaption. For Brittany Flatrès poses as alternatives the intensification or the extensification of farming.[18] The coastal areas of intensive cultivation require the managerial and organizational adaptation that is equally necessary in Aquitaine to make it more profitable. In addition, as Flatrès notes, they require an outlet for their produce in the urban populations associated with the decentralization of industry, or in the urban markets across the Channel. For those areas of Brittany dependent upon forage production Flatrès wonders whether their fate might be like that of Ireland, rapidly passing from a state of overpopulation to one of underpopulation, ultimately acquiring the character of a vast ranch. Already in terms of the objectives and standards of the 1970s the agriculture of the West and South-west is heavily overpopulated. Whether the outflow of labour will be sufficient to achieve an equilibrium in the next decade is unpredictable. A simplification of agricultural systems and an extensification of farming in many areas appears to be more certain. But the abandonment of agricultural land, the reduction of the area farmed, the chances of this happening in the environmentally less favoured regions of the Massif Central and the Alps seem greater than in the regions of the West and South-west.

[18] France de Demain 7: 112.

The Massif Central, the Midi-Pyrénées and the Alps

The effects of overpopulation, depopulation and wastage of population are all evident during a traverse of the Massif Central. In the earlier part of the last century pressure of population led to the terracing for arable purposes of slopes now quite unsuited to modern farming practice, which, nevertheless, are still cultivated according to the economies of the aged person's small holding. The pastures of the higher plateaus, above all the poor untreated character of the woodlands, bear the marks of insufficient manpower being available to ensure their proper care. The image of one old man supervising the grazing of his two milch cows, of an antiquated school-building in a minute isolated settlement, recall the wastage of population in two senses: labour lavished on unproductive agricultural activities, inadequate facilities for the vocational preparation of the young. 'The development of the cash economy led to the consumption of non-local products and broke the fragile and mediocre equilibrium of the past based upon autoconsumption at the family level. Confronted by the difference between the price at which they had to sell and the price at which they had to buy the rural population lost heart and deserted the countryside.'[19]

The crisis of the agricultural sector is not the only cause of depopulation. In the past it not only proved impossible for the young to find sufficient employment in agriculture; because of the effects of 'agriculturalization', neither could they find it in local industries. An unfortunate tendency currently exists which underrates both the importance of industry in rural areas during the pre-industrial epoch and the relationship between the peasant economy and manufacturing. By the time of Colbert the tapestry industry of Aubusson and Felletin, based on the wool production of the upland areas, the enamel, the textile, paper, armaments and porcelain industries of Limousin had all achieved a considerable reputation. But in the post-Revolution period the textile industry fell away before the competition of the factories in the North. The flax industry disappeared, as did the local coal and iron industry and many of the food processing industries, again because of competition from outside the area. As a consequence of a weak agrarian economy and a debilitating industrial history the whole economic structure of the région is in need of repair and renovation. Those industries which have persisted, porcelain, paper and leather, have all experienced considerable difficulties and are now in the process of re-adaptation to modern marketing, organizational and production techniques. Characteristically the population is heavily weighted towards

[19] France de Demain 8: 59.

the older age groups. The returns per hectare and per man are both at the lowest end of the scale. The recent indices for migration reflect these economic facts.

TABLE 3.4 *Net migration, 1954–62, by région de programme*

	The West and South-west			The Massif Central	
	Net loss '000s	% of total population 1954		Net loss '000s	% of total population 1954
Bretagne	−93·0	−4·0	Limousin	−20·3	−2·7
Pays de la Loire	−53·6	−2·3	Auvergne	−15·0	−1·2
Poitou-Charentes	−37·1	−2·7	Midi-Pyrénées	−31·9	−1·3
Aquitaine	− 9·4	−0·4			
Basse Normandie	−52·2	−4·5			

The departments of the region Midi-Pyrénées display characteristics and indices similar to those of the departments of the Massif Central, and there is little need for separating them except to emphasize certain original features – in particular the appearance of the North African *colons* with their large-scale, mechanized farming. The establishment of capitalist farming demonstrates what can be achieved in zones of peasant farming, not especially well endowed, when capital and know-how become available, at the price, of course, of destroying many family farms. Many metayers were not given the chance of retaining their tenancies once they expired, and the rise in land prices resulting from the constitution of these 100 to 200 ha farms, prohibited them from purchasing the holdings for themselves. The rural depopulation of the communes affected by the change was accelerated, but at the same time the chances for specialized agricultural labour were improved. Concentration on cereals did increase the risk of soil erosion and the financial exigencies of some of the operators may have rendered them careless in this respect, but on the whole the *colons* had coped successfully with the problem in the Maghreb. These developments were concentrated mostly to the north of Villefranche de Lauragais and between the rivers Ariege and Gers. It is too early to judge the results, but the changes are indicative of what can be effected through the introduction of mechanized capitalist farming in peasant farming areas, particularly how the structural problem can be overcome. In contrast to the trends in the Massif Central, farms of more than 100 ha are in full evolution in the region of Midi-Pyrénées. In the region of Limousin they declined by 22 per cent in the period 1955–63, and in Auvergne the numbers remained about the same. In Midi-Pyrénées they increased by 33 per cent. The biggest numerical increases were as follows: in the department of Haute Garonne farms of 100 ha or more rose from 108 to 280; in Gers they rose from 90 to 200, and in Lot from 66 to 120.

Despite their long-standing record of depopulation, the régions of Limousin, Auvergne and Midi-Pyrénées contain, it is estimated, 19 per cent of the surplus male agricultural population, even though they contain only 16½ per cent of the total male agricultural labour force. The proportion of the population surplus in the Midi-Pyrénées is comparable with the average for the whole of France, about one-third. In Limousin and Auvergne the surplus approaches 60 per cent of the total. Unselective migration will not help to solve the agrarian problems of these regions. Already the age structures are distorted by an extended period of depopulation and low rates of natural increase – to the extent of leading one to question the significance of assessments of surplus population without reference to age structures. These two areas in fact suffer at one and the same time from a surplus and a deficiency of people. There are too many old men, and a surfeit of under-employed young women in agriculture. There are a number of young men at present in agriculture who will never make a decent living from farming because their numbers exceed future requirements. But at the same time there is a deficiency of adequately trained young men who might carry out the necessary organizational changes, and unless efforts are made to obtain a better balance between the generations throughout the whole region, in the urban as well as the rural sectors, then when the opportunities arise, they will be available neither in sufficient numbers nor at an adequate standard of training. The young can be retained in these areas primarily only by providing attractive employment opportunities outside of agriculture; secondarily by improving the prospects for those who remain in farming.

One vital piece of information is lacking, the real size of the demographic fundament upon which the future farming population is to be built. On a double front these regions demand assistance: aid to overcome the retardation caused by the destruction or obsolescence of long-established industries and to stimulate the establishment of new industries; aid for agriculture. In the latter context the recommendations of the Commission for the '*Plan régional de développement et d'aménagement du Limousin*' make interesting reading, for that region displays most of the features which characterize the backward economy of the Massif Central at its worst.[20] The average return per person engaged in agriculture was calculated at 2,000 F in 1960, and in consequence the planners accepted the raising of agricultural incomes as a prime objective. This is to be achieved by increasing production. Their recommendations have a familiar ring. The adoption of modern farming practices, e.g. the use of temporary

[20] Journal Officiel, 96 Annee, No. 268, 16 & 17 November 1964.

pastures* and much more fertilizer; reafforestation, along organized lines linked with the needs of a prospective industry; the repair and renovation of the whole agrarian infrastructure; the re-tooling and establishment of agricultural processing industries and systems of marketing – these are the methods and means by which the ends will be attained. Correspondingly the evolving patterns of agricultural settlement and population will need co-ordination within a new framework of urban hierarchies. For more agricultural extension work (vulgarization), better agricultural educational facilities, model farms, centres for the establishment and analysis of farm accounts, the need is very pressing; and at the disposal of the government and administration there are a whole range of institutions, laws and accepted formulae. Since 1963 the department of Creuse has been classed as a *zone spéciale d'action rurale*, which entitles it to priorities in public investments, especially for small industries and education, and freight tariff relief.† The *Société pour la mise en valeur de l'Auvergne et du Limousin* (S.O.M.I.V.A.L.), a semi-public body with a capital of 1·6 million francs, has a particular interest in the development of agricultural and silvicultural resources, as well as irrigation and tourism; whilst S.O.D.E.C.C.O. ('Société pour le développement économique du Centre et Centre-Ouest) has wider geographical and economic interests. In Limousin their loans have been mainly to industrial concerns.

One piece of legislation of which the authorities have availed themselves is the section in the Code Rural designed to facilitate the establishment of agricultural families from overcrowded areas, like the West. In the past few years about 150 families have been established annually in Limousin. The Commission for regional development in Limousin appreciates that in some of the most disfavoured agricultural areas the resident population is incapable of providing the necessary demographic means for renovation, and it therefore supports the immigration of younger, more vital elements; a recommendation which serves like many of their other recommendations to bring the issue of agrarian structures to the forefront. On this issue the views of the Commission are at once daring, cautious and ultimately dispiriting. They recognize that 25–35 ha are necessary for a viable two-man livestock farm. Remembrement, they stress, improves the internal functioning of the farm, it does not lead to general structural change. The work of the local S.A.F.E.R., which is structural in purpose, has been

* Dumont, 1956: l'intensification fourragère, levier essentiel du progrès de l'agriculture du XXe siècle, comme la betterave sucrière fut le premier agent améliorateur de l'agriculture européene au XIXe siècle. Page 481.

† Lamour (1964): 99, wrote, with respect to the departments of Lozère and Morbihan, the first to be designated as special zones: practically, the decrees have had little effect, because they are primarily financial in concept, and for want of specialized agencies responsible for the programme and its results.

carried out on land that has been abandoned or gone out of cultivation. More is required, they insist: a policy of creating larger units which will place farms in the hands of competent men, with capital and acquainted with modern methods. Unfortunately, there is no substance to this revolutionary proposal. Only remembrement receives mention in their list of specific recommendations. And they recognize ultimately the prospects for change by 1975 are not really great. The average size of farm in 1960 was 15·7 hectares; by 1975 the figure will lie in their estimation somewhere between 18 and 19 hectares. The density of labour per hectare will have declined from 16·3 to 14 by 1975. About 25,000 men, they forecast, will have left the agricultural labour force – equivalent to two-thirds of the estimated surplus. But as the provisions for migration during the second part of this decade make clear, the ages of the bulk of the migrants will lie between 20 and 30 years. In the words of the I.N.S.E.E. report,[21] referring to both Aquitaine and the Massif Central, 'Le faible dynamisme démographique de ces régions pose probablement les problèmes les plus difficile à résoudre à long terme'. There are no grounds for doubting the general accuracy of this prognostication, and therefore the outlook for agriculture in the Massif Central is indeed bleak, for a healthy agriculture economy must be based upon a young working and managerial population.

Demographically the région d'Aquitaine has more in common with the regions of Midi-Pyrénées and the Massif Central than the regions of the West. Its departmental age structures display the same distortions, a relative deficiency of the young and under-40s, a marked relative excess of over-50s; whereas the regions of the West display the characteristic age structures of areas with high rates of natural increase and marked emigration – a relative excess of the under-fifteens and a relative deficiency in the working age groups. A weak flow of farmers and their families from the West to Aquitaine and the Massif Central has been one result of these pressures arising out of the rate of natural increase. As an outlet the flow pales into insignificance beside the high geographical movement towards Paris and the occupational flow to the non-agricultural sectors. It is of interest, however, for demonstrating what little importance inter-farm migration has had for the solution of the agrarian problems of both regions; and the experience is worth bearing in mind because of the possibilities of non-nationals migrating to these depopulated areas once the conditions within the Common Market permit. In fact the South-west already has a history of Spanish and Italian peasants establishing themselves as farm operators, and successfully too. The organization of the migration from Brittany and the Vendée has largely been the responsibility of what is now the *l'Association nationale de migration et d'établissement rural* (A.N.M.E.R.). Of the

[21] Études et Conjuncture (1966); 1: 77–131.

8,684 families, involving 44,885 persons, who have quit the western ar northern departments since 1949, the majority have gone to the régio of Poitou-Charentes, Aquitaine, Midi-Pyrénées, Limousin and Auvergne. The principal motives for migration have been the insufficient size the holding in the migration foyer – half the migrants are tenants and th

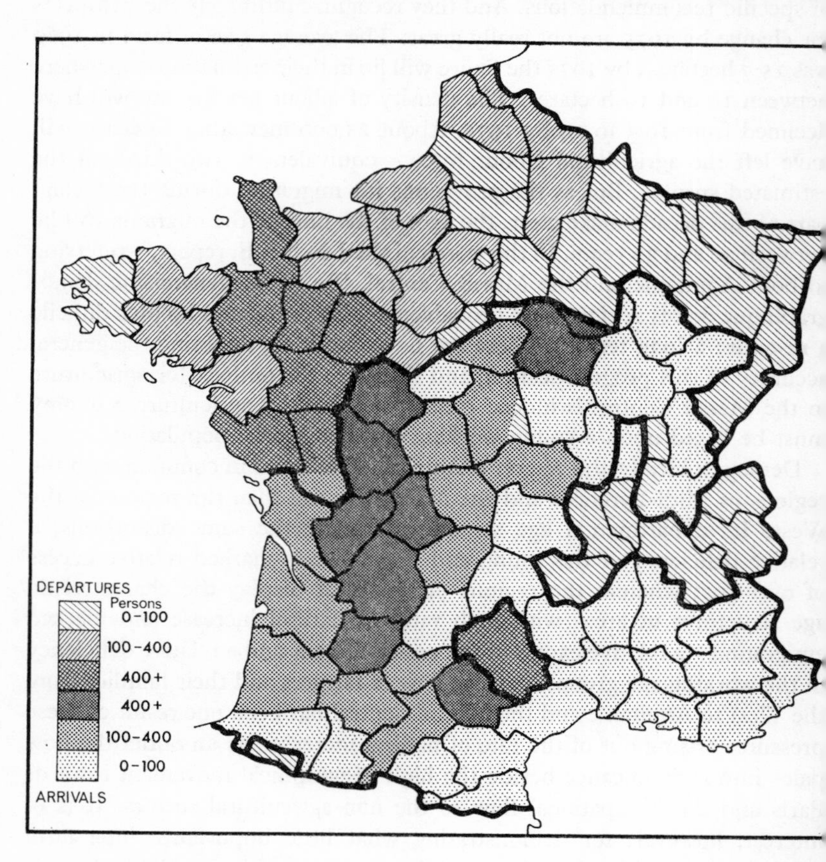

Fig. 3.4. Migration of farm population under A.N.M.E.R. auspices, 1949–6

remain so in the reception areas – and the difficulty of obtaining a farm usually the motive of farmers' sons and agricultural labourers. The socio economic promotion which accompanies the migration explains, in part why only 15 per cent of the migrants are proprietors in the migratio foyer, and 35–40 per cent are proprietors in the reception zone. Accordin

[22] Statistique Agricole (1964): XXXII–XXXIV.

Christiane Pinede's survey, the average size of holding increased by
·8 ha, from 11·8 to 22·6 ha as a result of migration.[23] But a 20–25 ha
lding is rather marginal in Aquitaine in present circumstances. A
fferent type of migrant family has appeared in recent years as a conse-
ience of the troubles in the Maghreb; 5,947 families (23,940 persons)
ve been involved. And as we have seen some have been of very different
ckground and outlook.

The agrarian problem in the Alps does not assume the same proportions
in the Massif Central, or the South-west and the Pyrénées on account of
e region as a whole being less dependent upon agriculture for its living
d containing in the Lyon district one of the major poles of growth in
ance. Only the departments of Hautes and Basse Alpes display age
uctures heavily weighted towards the older age groups, in contrast to
e youthful profiles of Haute Savoie and Savoie. With almost 8 per cent
the total male agricultural labour force the region contains a slightly in
cess proportion of the surplus manpower, so that while it is true to
gue that as a whole the region possesses a more favourable economic
ucture, the agricultural sector itself suffers from many of the debilitating
itures found in other mountainous regions: aged *chefs d'entreprise*, a
perabundance of small holdings, below average returns to labour; whilst
thin the agricultural sector itself great variations are displayed, Haute
ivoie being generally superior to the rest. Despite the carefully organized
stems that were evolved to maintain farming life in these regions,
riculture is in a process of decline, even disappearance, and geographical
ncentration. A reassessment of the environment's potentialities is under
iy and accompanying it the geography of the region is changing. Evidence
a period of over-population and of a more recent period of regression in
e limits of cultivation is available in many districts. The Col du Glandon
Savoie is instructive in this respect.

The ascent from the north-east gives one a view back across the valley
the Arc. In the immediate foreground are the small cultivated strips of
id, with vines, belonging to the few villages crowded between the narrow
ills of the valley. Beyond, lower down, amidst somewhat larger fields
d pastures along the river valley columns of smoke rise from the large
ectro-chemical works. Within this small circumscription the farmers
ve an urban market for their produce and employment opportunities.
a backdrop to this scene there are the extensive high pastures of the
ountains, and the rocky peaks. At the summit of the Col it is possible
take a closer look at these vast summer pastures, so extensive that the
own herds of milk cattle and the summer houses are difficult to discern,
pecially as they are camouflaged by the sour brown-green of the pasture.

[23] Pinede (1960): 5–43 and 399–423.

On every hand there is evidence of small patches of land, even at th height, 1,900 metres, having once been terraced and cropped. The desce to the valley of the Romanche provides one with a superb view of th Belledonne range. Along a glacial bench lie a string of villages amid a set of small cultivated strips of land arranged like a compact orga keyboard, the product of an era of much greater population densitie Presently the area under woodland is being rapidly extended, and not onl in the higher and remoter parts, for in addition to the plantings of the sta authorities and the farmers themselves, urban speculators are participatin

As a whole the Alpine region displayed some of the largest declines i the number of holdings during the period 1955–63. In Haute Savoie th number of small peasant holdings declined from 18,000 to 8,000, in Savoi from 20,000 to 11,000. Of the four Alpine departments only Haute Savoi had a population in 1962 that exceeded the population existent in 1861. I Savoie, the Hautes and Basse Alpes the 1962 population was only 97, 7 and 63 per cent respectively of the 1861 figure. Since 1936 the populatio of the rural communes in these departments has declined by 31,000 – fro 268,000 to 237,000 – an 11½ per cent decrease. What is still not evident the ultimate level at which an equilibrium in agriculture will be found.

The capitalist zones of the north

The landscapes of peasant farming districts retain human proportions a single glance can encompass the whole extent of one farm, or a numbe of farms. The proportions of capitalist farming in Northern France requir an aerial view. That way the extent of these enterprises with their hug blocks of land, their large nucleus of farm buildings, the distant silo railway tracks and market centres can be encompassed. At ground leve the individual is dwarfed by the extensiveness of the landscape, and hi conception of the regularities is dispersed by the more immediate variation of topography and land use. This diversity is reflected in the agricultur statistics. In the region of Picardie there are some 9,000 small peasan holdings occupying 41,000 ha and 18,000 medium and large peasan holdings occupying 382,000 ha. These holdings are beset by the familia problems of the peasant enterprise, though it is impossible to judge accur ately their relative standards and levels of living compared with those c the peasant families in the West and South-west. Their problems, further more, cannot be solved by imitating the evolution of the larger concern because their evolution has often occurred in quite different physica conditions. Hence the diversity is both geographic and socio-economic The district of Thierache in the north of Picardie towards the border wit Belgium, for instance, has a grassland livestock economy in need of diversi fication. It would benefit too from the addition of fruit production and th improvement of its processing industries. Opposed to the family enterprises are the capitalist concerns. In Picardie 5,000 farms of between 50 and 100 ha, and 2,500 farms of 100 or more hectares, control 350,000 and 496,000 hectares of land respectively; twice the area contained in the peasant properties. Geographically they display marked localizations and certain variations. In Picardie they are dominant in Soissonais, Valois and towards Laon and St Quentin. Further east, in the Champagne *pouilleuse*, the utilization of machinery and fertilizers has permitted large-scale cereal

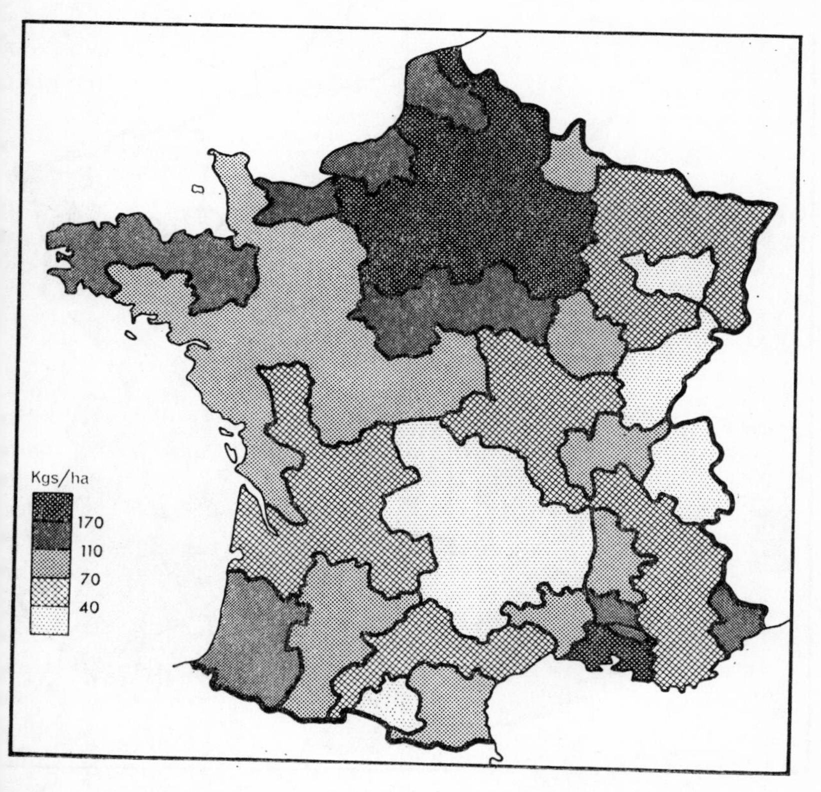

Fig. 3.5. Consumption of fertilizers per hectare, 1963–4

farming, with very little attention to livestock or root crops, on land considered a century ago to be fitted best to re-afforestation. Immediately to the east of Paris, in Brie, to the immediate south in Beauce, at a greater distance between the Loire and Indre in Berry, lie the other major regions of large-scale farming. In contrast to Picardie these regions have curtailed labour-demanding activities, livestock and sugar-beet, in favour of colz and maize. But on the general map of France these diversities are wiped o and as a block, with the region of Picardie as its node, the capitalist are distinguish themselves from the rest of the country on the basis of whatev indices are chosen: yields per hectare, return to labour, utilization fertilizer, the volume of cereal production, the degree of mechanizatior they lead in every case.

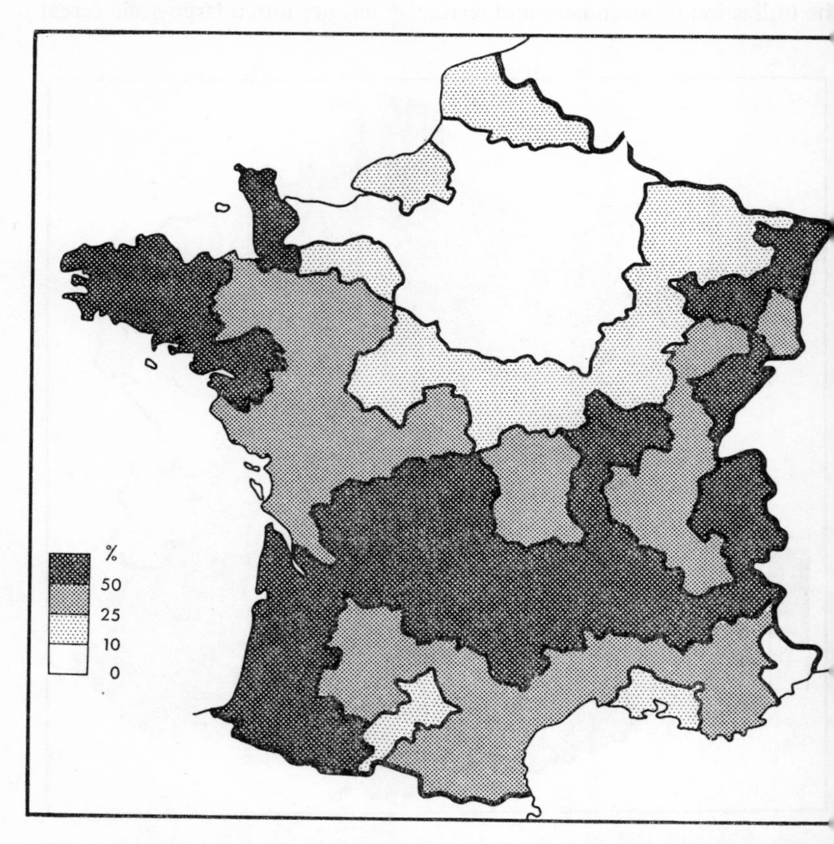

Fig. 3.6. Percentage of commercial wheat sales delivered by producers whos total consignment was less than 75 quintaux

Not surprisingly Picardie is one of the few areas of France for whic farm accounts are available for peasant as well as capitalist farms, and for lengthy period of time.[24] The analysis of the consolidated average return

[24] The documents were made available on condition that their confidential natur was respected.

is valuable, whatever its limitations, in demonstrating some of the important features of the capitalist farms' economy. In area they average out between 190 and 260 hectares, and they grade themselves from those that are overwhelmingly arable farms, with 97 per cent of their surface area under the plough and half their area under root crops, sugar-beet principally, to those which have something more than 10 per cent of their area under permanent pasture, less than 10 per cent under root crops, and two-thirds under cereals, with maize recently playing a much more important role. These contrasts are carried through to the livestock sector, the row crop farms carrying 11 livestock units to the 100 ha compared with the 20 livestock units carried by the cereal farms, which is equivalent to one-third of the livestock density of the large peasant farms in the same region. There is very little difference between the cereal and row crop farms in the degree of mechanization. The cost accounts reflect the differences in the cropping systems. Not only do the row crop farms bear about twice the labour costs per ha as the cereal farms but they expend more on fertilizers, seeds, petrol and pest control, and their expenditure on the upkeep of machinery and buildings is higher. Only for animal foodstuffs do the cereal farms bear higher charges. The investments of the row crop farmers pay off. The returns per hectare on potatoes are almost twice, and on sugar-beet almost two-thirds greater than on cereals, and on the row crop farms the returns on wheat are some 20 per cent higher than on those farms on which wheat is the principal source of income. The final result is an income minus expenditure difference of 392 NF to the hectare on the most intensive row crop farms ranging down to 159 NF per hectare on the cereal farms. Converted to sterling this represents on a 200 ha farm a net profit of approximately £5,600 in the first case and £2,200 in the second. Returns to management on a 200 hectare farm vary from £2,000 to £1,200.

The contrasts between the capitalist farms and the peasant farms are along lines that one might expect. It needs stressing that the sample is small and on average the farms are all above 35 ha in size. The very fact that they are participants of a farm budget scheme suggests that they are likely to be in the better class of peasant farms. The emphasis is on cereal and livestock production, between 50 and 70 per cent of the total output is derived from these two sources. Some are more intensive and obtain 25 per cent of their output from row crops. The global charges per hectare are comparable with those of the capitalist farms, not as high as the most intensive row crop farms, but neither as low as the cereal farms. Much less is expended upon fertilizers, motor fuels, seeds and pest control. Animal feeding stuffs are by far the greatest charge. Reflecting the lower technical level of farm management the output per hectare of cereals is well below the level of the predominantly cereal farms and almost a third below the level of the row crop farms. On the more intensively farmed peasant holdings the output of sugar beet is again well below the per hectare level of the highly intensive capitalist farms. Since arable crops supply anything from 40–60 per cent of the gross output of the peasant holdings these lower levels have a depressive effect on the total income which the contributions of the livestock sector cannot remedy. The final outcome is a very small difference between total income and total expenditure. On a 40 ha farm the net profit might average out between £56 and £166. On an intensive 40 ha peasant holding the return for management and labour is of the order of £640. Such are the disparities within the farming sector.

The Nord and Pas de Calais

Many of the indices which are used to separate the zone of capitalist farming from the rest of France appear also in the adjacent région du Nord, which by any measure must be classed as a zone of peasant not capitalist farming; though as a provider of employment the agricultural sector as a whole is relatively unimportant. Agriculture in the Nord is not without its problems or insufficiencies, but within the context of peasant France its achievements are remarkable. In terms of output per hectare, return to labour, consumption of fertilizers and degree of motorization the region stands in the first rank, and for the yield of some individual products heads the list of all departments. Compared with another highly productive area of peasant farming, Finistère, the weighting towards the medium and large peasant properties in the Nord becomes obvious and reflects a trend in evidence since the inter-war period. The farming districts are numerous and varied. They range from the coastal districts around Dunkirk where arable farming, with sugar-beet, barley, flax and chicory, and around St Omer, horticulture prevail, through the vegetable growing areas around Lille, to the region of Ternois, one of the most rural of all areas, to Hainault, where livestock farming is important. But they display much in common also. Few of the farming areas are isolated and overwhelmingly rural; their contacts with the industrial sector are maintained through industries processing their products, the ready markets afforded by the urban centres for their fresh produce, the investment of urban finance in rural properties – the majority of farms are tenant or partly rented – and finally through the frequent residence of a commuting population in the rural areas. The result, according to Nistri and Precheur, is a state of mind amongst the farmers more receptive to modernization, more attentive to the requirements of the market.[25] It is not without significance for the future that peasant farming in France displays some of its best aspects in what is a largely industrialized region and structure, even though that structure is

[25] France de Demain 2: 44.

itself in need of reconversion. Though the returns incorporate the farm budgets of only 100 farms, and 25 of these exceed 50 ha, the net profit is as follows: on farms of 20 hectares, £370 – return for management and labour £800; on farms of 40 hectares, £915 – return for management and labour £1,050.

The Centre and Eastern regions

On the perimeter of the Paris Basin there is a decline from the high standards associated with the principal areas of capitalist farming. The pattern is neither regular or concentric, the diversity of the physical geography ensures that quite contrasting situations are in relatively close proximity. To the south the more specialized agriculture of the Loire Valley based on vines, fruits and vegetables lies west of the cereal growing areas of Berry, with the desolate region of Sologne separating it from the large-scale farming region of Beauce. In the régions of Champagne, Bourgogne and Lorraine, a similar sort of degradation occurs. In Champagne large cereal growing holdings remain important. In the departments of Maine, Aube, and parts of the Yonne conditions correspond closely to those prevailing in the departments nearer Paris, but further eastwards peasant properties predominate, and where large holdings remain important the statistics indicate the presence of an extensive rather than capitalistic type of farming. The depopulation of the East – only the industrialized departments of Lorraine showed in 1962 a marked increase on the population of 1861 – has left its mark on the landscape in many areas, in the form of low quality pastures, unkempt hedges and acres of poorly tended land and forest. But the overall result is not as dismal as one might expect. The dependence upon agriculture as a livelihood is below the national average. Together the three régions contain 9 per cent of the males in agriculture but less than 6 per cent of the surplus labour force.

These figures must not be allowed to draw attention away from the variety of conditions they mask. In the industrial districts of Lorraine part-time farming has been the solution to the problems of many peasant households. Meurthe et Moselle and Meuse are amongst the rare cases of departments returning an increase in the number of 1–2 ha holdings for the period 1955–63. The departments of Bas-Rhin, Nord, Oise, Vaucluse and some in the région Centre, are the only other claimants to this distinction. Holdings of more than 50 ha are generally on the increase in the East, and in some cases the numbers involved are impressive, but in the coming decades the inadequacies of their present standards of farming are likely to be exposed through competition, and they must be amended in a more rigorous climate than that which prevails in the Paris Basin. The family farms, the small and medium ones especially, are in full decline. Many are located in harsh, repulsive environments, like the Morvan, the plateau of Langres and parts of Vosges. Others, more favourably placed near to growing industrial centres, stand a better chance as do the family farms in specialized regions like the vine areas of the Côte d'Or, Beaune, and

TABLE 3.5 *Decline of family farms and increase of capitalist farms in the East, 1955–63 ha.*

Région de programme	1–10	10–20	20–50	50–100	100 +
Champagne	– 3,123	– 1,490	– 1,762	+871	+84
Bourgogne	– 16,240	– 2,496	– 302	+478	+49
Lorraine	– 19,355	– 3,073	– 539	+ 1,015	+38
Franche Comte	– 7,068	– 3,883	+ 1,536	+306	+ 17

Beaujolais. The early achievements of an intensive dairying economy in the Jura, the high degree of co-operation which developed, has not ensured protection against the effects of changing economic fortunes, external competitors and rising technical requirements. In the words of Blanc,[26] the family holding is at the centre of the agrarian problems of the East. It would only be boringly repetitious to enlarge any further on this issue. The eastern provinces of France do not have a natural vocation for agriculture, and it is fortunate that they are less dependent than most upon farming. For the capitalist farms the lines of evolution they must follow are obvious, and it is with these farms and a technically high standard livestock economy that the future of the region lies.*

The emergence of a structural policy

The regional diversity of the present scene, the accelerating pace of change over the last fifteen years, make the preceding decades appear even more immobile than in fact they ever were. Mallet's contention – that only in the last few years has the traditional mode of life forged under the absolute monarchs and legalized by the Revolution collapsed – is, in general terms, probably sound.[27] However, during the reign of Napoleon III there was a period of agricultural development, and free trade, which certain writers on agrarian and economic affairs now regard with some nostalgia. Then the capitalist classes had an interest in keeping food prices low, and agriculture benefited from the trade with Britain in wine, eggs, butter and vegetables. Under the Third Republic the fears of the farming classes arising out of the fall in agricultural prices were associated with the indus-

[26] France de Demain 3: 51–91.

* Space prohibits one from dealing with Alsace and the regions of Languedoc and Côte d'Azur.

[27] Mallet (1962): 118.

trial elements who now wanted protection of their nascent industries. A whole structure, still maintained, of agricultural protection was erected which cut short the agricultural revolution so that the small peasant structure of French farming atrophied. After the First World War, in which the peasantry made an enormous contribution in personnel and suffered staggering losses,* the appearance of world-wide agricultural surpluses, the reality of demographic and economic stagnation created the right atmosphere for the introduction of a system of price support and financial aid from which no subsequent French Government has been able to extricate itself. The aim with all these programmes was to sustain and improve the condition of the peasantry, not to revolutionize it. Only as the enormous costs of these programmes under the newly created productive conditions of the post-war period became apparent did the search for an alternative programme of re-structuration commence.

In France, as in the Federal Republic of Germany, the post-war period has witnessed an enormous rise in the input of materials and capital, a considerable increase in agricultural output, a rise in incomes and per capita incomes, but in the opinion of the farming population, a quite unsatisfactory rise in comparative living standards. The post-Liberation shortages of food warranted official encouragement of increased agricultural output. Later, within the context of the First Plan for Modernization, the growth of agricultural output received further encouragement, as a means of raising national income, in order to save foreign exchange, in fact, to increase overseas earnings. At the same time the representatives of the agricultural community were seeking higher incomes, and as a means to this end, firstly in 1946, the cost of production was accepted as a basis for the price of sugar beet, and again in 1947, as a basis for the price of wheat. The following year wheat producers received an increased bonus for the area planted. Overproduction and falling prices were the immediate consequence in 1949.

From that time onwards French agrarian policy becomes a field of confusion and controversy; of charge and countercharge, of threat, manifestation, submission, retraction and resubmission, of indexation, non-indexation and partial indexation of agricultural prices; of arguments concerning the validity of common agricultural prices for wheat as opposed to maize, and so on and so on. Amidst all this one is liable to lose track of certain regularities, and certain lacunae in the controversy. Throughout the whole period and in spite of repeated surpluses, gluts and marketing difficulties, the successive governments encouraged investment in agriculture and its modernization, thereby raising the technical standards of its

* Marcel Faure reckons of the 3,700,000 peasants mobilized, 673,700 were killed and 500,000 were so gravely injured, they were unable to resume farming.

performance, and thus constantly increasing the likelihood of surpluses and gluts. Between 1951 and 1965 the sown area under wheat remained almost constant; but the yields doubled and so did the total output. In the same period the yield of maize doubled, the sown area increased nearly threefold, and production rose from 6 million quintaux in 1951 to 38 million quintaux in 1963. Meat production rose during 1951–65 from 1·9 million to 3·1 million tons; milk production almost doubled. Accompanying this growth in output, and reflecting both the improved living standards within France, and the strenuous efforts of the family farms to raise incomes was the shift from vegetable to livestock production. In 1950 livestock products supplied 54 per cent of the total agricultural output; by 1965 that percentage had risen to 61. Correspondingly the input of fertilizers, the expenditures upon machinery had expanded, as had the provision of credit to agriculture, and above all state aid, which increased sevenfold between 1954 and 1966.

A quite involved argument has arisen concerning the effect of all these changes upon the remuneration and living standards of the agricultural population, involved, and ultimately vitiated, because the contending parties are unwilling to admit or agree upon certain facts or principles. One base year, 1955 for instance, will show that agricultural producer prices have risen faster than costs and a little faster than retail prices. Another base year, 1948 – hardly a wise choice – presents a quite unfavourable picture for agriculture; but it does reveal that since 1955 the relative position of agriculture has only slightly worsened. Per capita income in agriculture has increased by 44 per cent since the commencement of this decade, and its standing relative to the national average has been maintained. But of course, any discussion of these matters has little meaning, as the previous sections ought to have made clear, unless placed with the context of the highly differentiated socio-economic and regional character of French agriculture; and until very recently none of the interested parties has shown any willingness to make this concession to reality.

It has been of enormous advantage to the capitalist farming interests which have dominated the agricultural federations for most of the post-war period, to have consistently maintained the fiction of a farming community, which if not totally homogeneous, nevertheless possessed identical interests and needs; which would benefit from the exclusive advocation and implementation of common policies. For the farms of the capitalist zone, which have overcome many of the structural, technical and marketing problems still facing most peasant holdings, which, whatever their deficiencies, are comparatively far better placed than most to withstand the rigours of competition, an agrarian policy based upon price supports and guarantees ensures a quasi-rent, or a surplus above costs, far superior to anything received by the majority of farmers. Furthermore a policy directed towards the amelioration of living conditions in rural areas conflicts in no way with the particular interests of the capitalist farmers. On the one hand, by supporting such policies they achieved an apparent common purpose with the large mass of the peasantry; on the other, any success such policies might register, by helping to maintain the peasantry rather than diminish

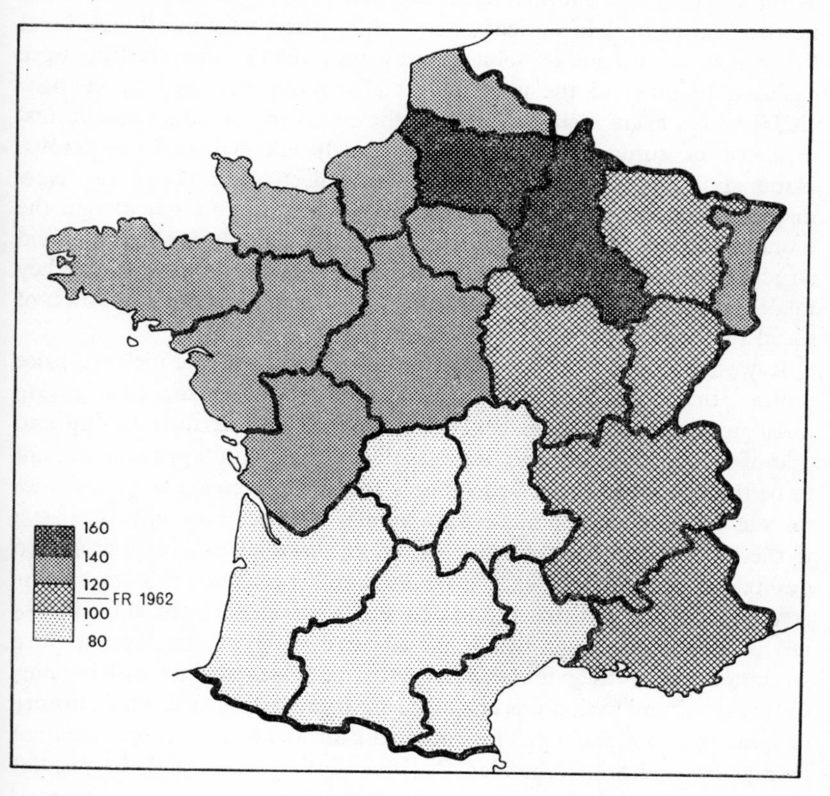

Fig. 3.7. Index of agricultural income, 1962
(Constant Francs, 1954 = 100)

them, would, at the same time, help to sustain the peasants electoral importance, and by extension increase the pressure which the capitalist led federations might bring to bear upon the various governments. This chosen practice of obscuring the marked differentiation within the farming community has itself contributed to the enigmatic character of French farming. But under the pressure of events this ascribed homogeneity has been subjected to criticism and re-evaluation by the once youthful leaders of the younger peasantry still desirous of making farming their vocation as well as by the more youthful section of the capitalist farmers who seem prepared to dispense with the political strength which alliance with the majority afforded them.

Rather late in the piece, in 1964, the spokesmen for C.E.N.A.G.* argued that it was a confusion to speak of agriculture in general terms.[28] Without being too specific regarding policy, they recognized that the needs of farms in defavourized zones, whose chefs were mostly aged and for which no economic solution was immediately conceivable, were different to those of the potentially viable farms managed by younger chefs; which again were different to the needs of the large-scale farms, capitalist or co-operative, that were already adapted and prosperous. National policy, they argued, ought to reflect these variations. New markets were more important than costly price support schemes to the economic future of the competitive producers, whilst price supports and structural reforms were needed to sustain the younger farmers whilst they made the necessary readjustments. For the old it was more a question of social than economic policies that were required.

It was the dissatisfaction with the unfair results of the inelastic price policies that stimulated the C.N.J.A. leaders during the late '50s to insist upon the distinction between the needs of their membership and that of the capitalist section; 'the question of agricultural prices ought not to be the sole pivot of the Federation's action. An increase of 50 centimes for a litre of milk, or 100 francs for a quintal of wheat represents very little if the holding produces only 10 or 15,000 litres of milk a year or 100 quintals of wheat. There exist other important problems.'[29] They elaborated a policy that was structural in emphasis as well as financial in character. In an administration which had come to recognize the necessity of a structural policy they found a receptive and sympathetic collaborator, so that the Pisani period was one of the most inventive in the whole history of agrarian policy making. This apparent coincidence of interests must not betray the reader into thinking that the administration and the peasant movement achieved a solidarity they in fact never possessed. On the rigour and implementation of policies there were considerable divergencies – the debate over the amendments to the *Loi d'orientation* is a case in point – and in the end dissatisfaction and disapproval prevailed.[30] What is more the C.N.J.A. were never able to detach themselves politically from the older, more conservative, more capitalist, members of the F.N.S.E.A.,† as at

* Le Centre des chefs d'entreprises agricole. [28] Le Monde, 17 June 1964.
[29] Debatisse (1963): 171. [30] Rimareix and Tavernier (1963).
† Fédération nationale des syndicats d'exploitants agricoles.

rst they thought they might. Though they have gained a larger say in the ffairs of that powerful body it has not been easy to clearly distinguish r divorce the interests of the big and the small. In face of the apparent heck to structural policies the former leaders of the C.N.J.A. now appear nore willing to emphasize the unity of the farming community for the olitical effectiveness it brings with it, whilst the government for its part as acceded to the political pressure exercised by the farming community uring the Presidential elections of 1965, so that the clarity with which grarian policy was enunciated a few years ago has now been replaced by ess disturbing obfuscation. One ought not to be surprised at this turn of vents. The fundamental problem for the leadership of the C.N.J.A. and '.N.S.E.A. is that in seeking a place in modern society for the family arm, the political nature of their power prevents them from expounding pon the nature of the problem except in the grossest of terms. They are nable to say to their membership that family farming can be preserved only t the cost of eliminating a large, but as yet undetermined (and given the ynamics of the current situation presently undeterminable), proportion f the farms in existence.* The only possible line of action open to them, iven the dilemma created by industrial society for the peasant holding, is o seek to preserve as many of the existing farms which the wealth of the ndustrial state and the electoral exigencies of the parties in power currently enders feasible. Nevertheless for all its ambiguities, as one of the most xciting and intellectually agile attempts to deal with this dilemma, the hilosophy of the C.N.J.A. deserves attention, for it has recognized and aced up to some of the fundamental weaknesses of the peasant economy vithin the modern state, and then within the context of the values and eliefs of a Christian and capitalist society it has sought institutional nnovations and has been instrumental in their propagation.

Sans entraîner la prolétarisation des travailleurs'†

'he C.N.J.A. philosophy was founded upon three rejections which have een the basis for decisions, policies and actions. First, it rejected the lienation of the individual in a modern capitalist society. It viewed the xercise of responsibility in a working life as a fundamental personal ecessity, which, it was pointed out, can be achieved in the modernized

* 'Il est ainsi difficile d'apprécier d'une façon exacte dans quelle conditions et uivant quel rythme évolueront les structures d'exploitations agricoles. Des dimenions d'exploitation, valables en 1970, risquent notamment d'être dépassées en 985.' J. de Vaissière, Inspecteur General de l'Agriculture (1966): 12.

† '. . . dans les principes qui animent le C.N.J.A. s'il fallait la résume en quelues mots, nous disons: efficacité économique et liberté des hommes. Nous voulons ue le progrès technique dans lequel nous croyons, et qui conditionne l'amélioraion du niveau de vie des hommes, puisse se développer sans entraîner la proléarisation des travailleurs.' Debatisse (1963): 264.

peasant holding. It justified the maintenance of the peasantry on moral and psychological grounds as well as for reasons of economic democracy. Secondly, it rejected the cultural and psychological impoverishment of the individual, the crushing burden of unmitigated and routine work, the deprived conditions of the rural female, which have so marred the image of the traditional family farm: *l'exploitation familiale se traduisait par l'exploitation des familles.* But to modernize the traditional family holding, it was recognized, required a change in outlook, a reorganization of the working methods and an enlargement of the scale of operation, a reconstruction of marketing systems; in short: at least a continuance of and, at best, an acceleration and improvement of the trends already in existence; trends which were reducing the number of peasant holdings and aggravating both regional and socio-economic differences in the farming sector. The leadership avoided dealing with the conflict of interests which is inherent in the numerical preservation of the peasants as opposed to the economic modernization of the family holding. Instead it advocated a series of measures, and sought to balance the unfortunate consequences of one set by the application of another. Thus for the old and inadept it sought the security that the farm has always offered in the provision of government assistance for old age and ill health and in retraining schemes available to those who must quit agriculture. For those that remained, however, it sought to destroy the very same association of security and property. As one of their leaders argued: 'To maintain in the peasant mind the idea that he should be the proprietor of his own land, that he should immobilize his capital in the possession of real estate, this is to sterilize his efforts rather than direct them towards progress; a progress achieved by the industrial worker who long since has left behind the artisanal stage. To maintain at all costs the traditional idea of property in the world of agriculture, this is to maintain agriculture on the margins of the modern world.'[31] Thirdly, the C.N.J.A. leadership rejected the tutelage of the agricultural syndicalist movement by the interest of the large northern farmers, and the domination of the young by the old. But they recognized they would be more effective in obtaining their ends through co-operation with the larger more powerful F.N.S.E.A. 'We understood this essential truth, for ideas to become realities they need to be supported and carried by a structure or organization.'[32] Furthermore, as Christians, or as heirs to a Christian movement motivated by the Jesuits (Jeunesse agricole catholique), they believed that 'in all civilized countries, the dialogue, not the dialectic, is the source of progress'.[33] With their adhesion to the F.N.S.E.A. they gained a notable victory by obtaining

[31] Debatisse (1963): 126–7.
[32] Debatisse (1963): 142.
[33] Debatisse (1963): 142.

membership for the sons and daughters of peasant households previously excluded by the fact that they were not *chefs d'entreprise*. But as we have seen, once in harness it proved impossible, and in part unnecessary, to pull in different directions.

With the membership of the F.N.S.E.A., in part at least, interested in structural reforms and not exclusively concerned with price policy, during the early '60s, particularly with Pisani at the Ministry of Agriculture, the administration pushed ahead, at times were driven ahead, with a series of reforms which are best dealt with systematically; for the chronology is rendered difficult by the delays in promulgation or revision of laws and ordinances. Reluctantly following the pattern long since established in Germany (1955) Article I of the 1960 *Loi d'orientation* recognized as an aim the establishment of parity with other economic activities. Unlike the German legislation it included nothing as specific as the *Vergleichslohn* – a parity wage against which the progress of the farmers' income might be matched. The French were content to expose the nuances of the concept rather than specify standards: parity implied comparable but not identical conditions with other socio-professional categories. In fact, the dirigists queried, was it possible to compare something as dissimilar as the life of a family farmer and factory worker? Would it be realistic for the Government to try to ensure that one category of workers never had anything to envy about another category? In the government's opinion parity meant it should have regard to the well-being of the farming population, to its income, its chances of social promotion and its protection against insecurity and inclemency. It should also have regard to the changes which the play of economic laws were likely to produce, to see that these changes operated in humanly acceptable conditions. In sum, parity was meaningfully approached, in the opinion of the administration, if agriculture shared in the economic expansion of the national and Common Market economies as the causes of economic disparities were eliminated. If in terms of the provision of social security, the rural dwellers were not at a disadvantage with respect to the urbanites. If the family farm was compensated for the natural and economic disadvantages it suffers with respect to the other sectors of the economy. Whatever the peasant leaders may have thought of the proposals, they at least could not complain at the dialectic skill with which they were put forward.[34]

Having established a principle, the peasant leaders had to seek elsewhere for the reality. The singly most important structural reform, ultimately the responsibility of Pisani, was the establishment of the S.A.F.E.R. ('Sociétés d'Aménagement Foncier et d'Établissement Rural') – in short, Land Banks. When rural land comes up for sale, these societies have the

[34] Politique agricole française (Revue Française de l'Agriculture) – no date: 8–9.

right of pre-emption.* They can 'stock' the land for up to a period of fi years, and either sell it to existing farms, in order to increase their size ar viability, or they can consolidate pieces of properties to create brand ne holdings. In either case the farmer has to commit a fair proportion of h capital resources to the acquisition of the freehold of the property, th curtailing the sums available for investment in reproducible capital. I the end of 1966 about 170,000 ha had been acquired and about 80,000 had been retroceded. The respective totals for 1964 had been 60 and 20,0 ha. Languedoc-Roussillon is the largest of the regional S.A.F.E.R., wi Brittany and the regions of the South-west following in importanc Finance has been a difficult problem. There has been a tendency to use t the budgets in purchasing land, and because the rate of retrocession h been slower than anticipated the revolving funds have not accrued and t functioning of the S.A.F.E.R.s has been slowed down. The pieceme fashion in which properties have come on to the market has made plann and concerted efforts difficult. The attitude of some S.A.F.E.R.s has be to stock land against the time when a more rational reallocation of prope ties would be possible. Their initial experience has enforced the idea th the reorganization of agricultural properties needs to be seen in a wid economic and social and regional context. In a sense they have tended inflate their functions, perhaps displaying ambitions to plan, justifyi thereby the apprehension of some conservative critics, who recognized the original formulations an inevitable tendency towards state control the land market. A final difficulty has been associated with the very diver conditions and structure of the French countryside, so that the geograpl and demography of the region has influenced the location of their activiti and the ease with which they have been able to instigate them. Not alwa has this coincided with the location of the most problematical and mo populous parts of their territories.

The mobility of the agriculture properties has been assisted by t expenditure of monies derived from the *Fonds d'action sociale po l'aménagement des structures agricoles* – F.A.S.A.S.A. – established l the Pisani Law. Principally, old farmers receive an indemnity (Indemni Viagère de Départ) if they quit their holdings so that the regroupment properties may take place at a somewhat earlier date. One hundred ar seventy thousand beneficiaries were reported at the beginning of 196 located mostly in the West of France and the Massif Central. Somethi like half a million hectares have been recouped by these means, ar

* This hard-fought right was granted by the Loi Complémentaire à la L Agricole (the Pisani Law, 1962); as opposed to the establishment of the S.A.F.E. which was authorized by the Debre Law, 1960 – the original Loi d'Orientati Agricole.

stributed amongst 50,000 small holdings they have increased the area by average of 10 hectares. As de Virieu points out, since most of the aged rmers possess very small farms, this process will take a very long time fore the structure of a region is seriously modified.[35] These funds also sist the migration and settlement of farmers from densely populated eas like Brittany, to the less densely settled parts of the South-west. hey provide the major part of the finances of A.N.M.E.R. (see pages 91–93) tablished in 1949; and under the aegis of A.M.P.R.A.* they finance the training of those who quit agriculture for good. During its first two years operation 37,000 persons, principally from Brittany, availed themselves the facilities and only 17,000 in fact completed the project. In comrison with the actual outmigration from agriculture the numbers affected e very small indeed. From the beginning of 1967 the disposing of A.S.A.S.A. funds was made the responsibility of the *Centre nationale ur l'aménagement des structures agricoles.*

The second major step in dealing with structural reform has never been mpleted, partly through the innate opposition of 'grave doubts', and cause of certain real difficulties. The Pisani law envisaged the establishent of *Sociétés agricoles d'investissement foncier* (S.A.I.F.), joint stock ganizations which would direct non-peasant capital to the rural market, that the farmer, particularly the tenant, would be freed from the burn of providing the capital for the purchase of the freehold, and could ilize what capital he possessed for productive purposes.[36] He would be ven, subject to certain good farming clauses, security of tenure, and the ght to benefit from the improvements he had made. The shares of the lding would be marketed as other industrial shares are. The immediate servation with this scheme is that at present, and in the foreseeable ture, industrial investment and investments in urban land will be much ore attractive. Secondly no one in his right mind would expect much of a turn with farming in its present state, and the prospects for capital gains such shares appear to be remote. In fact the scheme appears to suit a rming system which has attained a much higher level of productivity an most French peasant farms are likely to achieve in the near future. seems to be designed for a structural reform which has been complished rather than one which is in progress. Other advocate shower have indicated their belief in state monies being made available to sist the programme, which to conservative eyes looks like an underhand ay of nationalizing some of the land. Nevertheless the proposals do highht a real problem associated with the inheritance laws of France – and

[35] de Virieu (1967): 93.
* l'Association pour les mutations professionnelles en agriculture.
[36] *Le Monde*, 17 and 18 May 1964.

other countries, of course. The equal division of property imposes enormou burdens upon the heir who takes control of the farm, or on the tenant wh is forced to acquire the freehold because on the death of the owner th heirs decide to sell. Some sort of a joint stock arrangement would consider ably ease these difficulties. Equally, under present arrangements, a larg proportion of the agricultural credit which is made available is in fact use

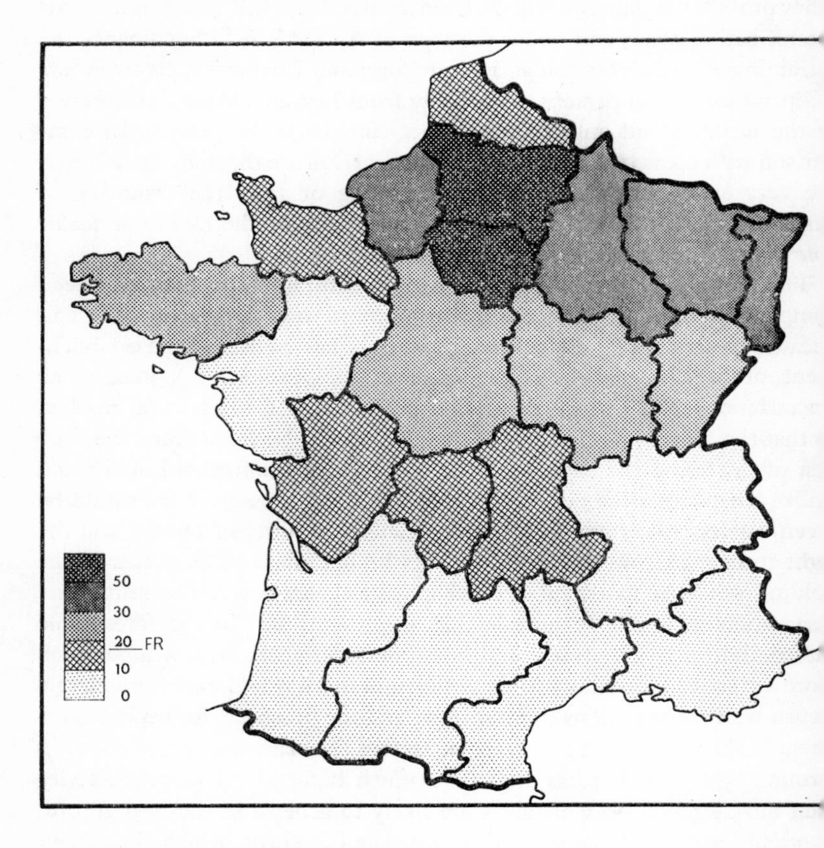

Fig. 3.8. Remembrement 1964 (Per cent of agricultural area (S.A.U.) consolidated)

to meet these genealogical exigencies, and eventually it supports an finances the training of the family members who migrate to the towns.

Remembrement has a much longer and costlier history than either c these two structural innovations. Between 1945 and 1950, half a millio hectares of land were consolidated; during the next fifteen years an addi onal four million hectares were treated. Progressively the cost to the state as risen from 14 million francs (1954) to 270 million francs in 1964. eographically the effort has been concentrated, in a remarkable manner, ı the regions where capitalist farming prevails.

All these reforms have been concerned with the predial difficulties of ıe family farm. Other innovations have sought to gain some of the dvantages of large-scale operation without destroying the family based ature of the enterprise. With the authorization of G.A.E.C.* by the isani law of 1962, it was hoped that the distinction between the family s a social and as an economic group would be emphasized and made more eal; that the disadvantages, social as well as economic, arising from the o close interconnection between family and farm might be diminished, ithout the family labour, the chef especially, being reduced to the status f hired hands. Membership of these groups is restricted to active chefs – articipation in the working of the farm is imperative – who combine their parate holdings to run them as a single joint enterprise. It is possible r a labourer without capital to be a member; and there is a ceiling pon the number of participants and the total area, and upon the proporon of hired labour that can be employed. The constituent farms are not ecessarily contiguous, but worked as a single enterprise a degree of pecialization in labour organization is achieved which is impossible within ıe confines of a single family. Some of the burdens that fall upon the wife re reduced, especially when investments result in mechanization of her rmer duties. The family is offered the real prospect of leisure on certain eekends; even annual holidays become practicable. By their attempt to lve socio-economic problems the G.A.E.C. have raised considerable ıridical difficulties. They are, at one and the same time, associations of eople, working together regularly but not living in common, joint ıvestment concerns, in which it is necessary to take account of each ıdividual's contribution; and finally they are going concerns in which ıccess demands a degree of permanence independent of the personal tuation of their membership. The G.A.E.C. have been granted legal xistence for the purposes of acquiring credits, tax relief and the signing of ontracts. A change in membership does not automatically result in their emise. Such a sophisticated vehicle, which represents a much higher age of co-operation than the long-established organizations for the int purchase and use of machinery and fertilizers, cannot readily become popular institution;† and despite the strong support it has received from

* Groupements agricoles d'exploitation en commun.

† Co-operatives for the joint ownership and use of machinery (C.U.M.A.) and r extension work (C.E.T.A.), have a longer history and are more popular. Unlike ıe G.A.E.C. they do not attempt to influence the same critical relationships, though

the most progressive elements of the farming organizations, the numbe established are few, and the impact restricted; though one must recogni that only a limited amount of time has elapsed since their inauguration.

By January 1967, 368 G.A.E.C. covering 46,000 ha had been create averaging in area anything from 14 to 85 ha, with the node in the 30–4 ha class. About one-quarter of the co-operatives had been formed b fathers and sons, an unexpected development which had required th authorities to accept the idea of only one holding constituting a co-opera tive. Another quarter had been formed by brothers and close relations; th remaining half were constituted by not closely related families. The popularity was greatest in the regions of capitalist and family capitali farming – 16,000 ha in the Paris Basin and peripheral regions; in th South-west 9,500 ha and in the Pays de la Loire and Poitou-Charente 7,400 ha. But in truth the vigour and strength of the movement is derive not from the area of land affected or the significance of its contribution to th structural improvement of French farming: rather it originates in a belief i the necessity of an alternative form of economic existence, a belief which ha received the moral approval of spiritual leaders, in an age when economic lif is increasingly centralized, cartellized and collectivized. In spirit and motiva tion the G.A.E.C. movement is frankly anti-capitalist and anti-collectivis By imitating and adopting some of the more superficial features of thes systems it seeks to preserve what it considers to be essential to its own.

one must agree with the official view of the Ministry of Agriculture that a familiarit with co-operative action obtained through an association with either of the two helpful in inducing a more favourable attitude of mind toward the more comple forms of co-operation; that their emphasis upon the technical and commerci functions of the *chef d'entreprise* is of use in eliminating the confusion of rol function and values, which exists in his mind. *The Centres d'études techniqu agricoles* service between 25,000 and 30,000 members. They are irregularl distributed throughout the country, with a tendency to concentrate in the depar ments of Brittany. The *Centres de gestion agricole* perform similar functions fo about 18,000 adherents but they tend to concentrate in either the Paris Basin o Normandy and Brittany. The *Co-opératives d'utilisation de matériel agricole* we highly popular after the war when they received preferential treatment from th government for the acquisition of machinery. An increased availability of equip ment, together with a certain degree of disillusionment associated with organiza tional inadequacies and mistakes in purchases, saw the number of C.U.M.A reduced from 10,000 to 4,500 by the mid '50s. Subsequently the number of thes co-operatives rose to 8,800.

* 'Les résonnances politiques de l'agriculture groupe sont claires: elle se propo pour l'agriculture comme *une voie* entre le capitalisme libéral et la collectivisatio (Lafon, 1967: 27).

Lafon classifies the participants in G.A.E.C. as: men and women strong influenced by the Catholic Action Movement for which co-operative farming is question of principle as well as means of economic transformation. They are in th majority. People who have used it as a convenient device to solve successor problems. Those who have adopted it as an astute means of benefiting fro prospective subventions.

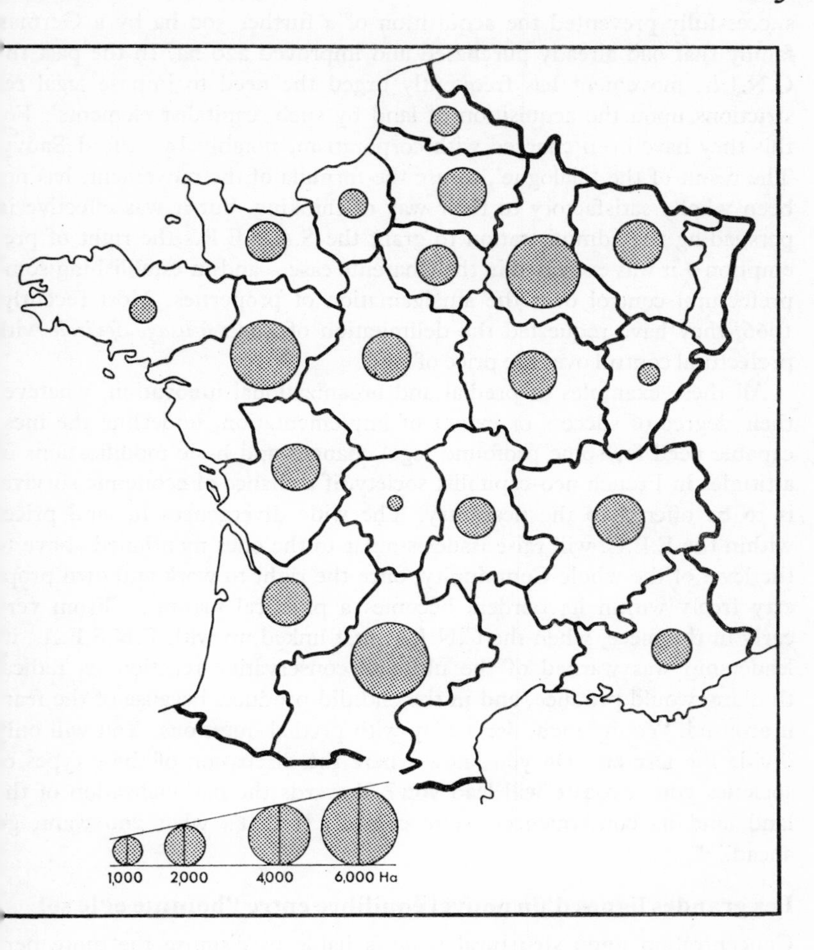

Fig. 3.9. Area worked by G.A.E.C. January 1967 in '000 hectares

The Jean Gabin affaire, 1962, brought to the attention of the general ublic the competition for farmland that had arisen in some areas between 1ose who hoped to make a full-time living from agriculture, and for whom, ıerefore, the enlargement of family holdings was an indispensable con- ition, and the non-agricultural classes who were using the wealth derived om their urban occupations to force up the price of land and limit the ccess of the younger farmers to what used to be called in England the gricultural ladder'.[37] More recently in Charente, local farmers have

[37] Debatisse (1963): 211–26.

successfully prevented the acquisition of a further 500 ha by a German family that had already purchased and improved 220 ha. In the past the C.N.J.A. movement has frequently urged the need to impose legal restrictions upon the acquisition of land by such 'capitalist elements'. For this they have been charged with corporatism, notably by Alfred Sauvy. The result of the 'dialogue', to use the formula of the movement, has not been wholly satisfactory to their way of thinking, but it was effective in persuading the administration to grant the S.A.F.E.R.s the right of preemption – it was exercised in the Charente case – and in establishing some prefectural control over the amalgamation of properties. Most recently 1966, they have requested the delimitation of *Zones à usage agricole* with prefectural control over the price of land.

All these examples of predial and organizational innovation, whatever their degree of success or extent of implementation, underline the inescapable need for some profound legal changes and basic modifications of attitudes in French neo-capitalist society, if a chance of economic survival is to be offered to the peasantry. The wide divergences in land prices within the E.E.C. will raise issues similar to the ones mentioned above to the level of the whole Community, once the right to work and own property freely within its borders becomes a practical prospect. From very early in the piece, when the C.N.J.A. first linked up with F.N.S.E.A., its leadership was warned of the ultimate conservative reaction its radical thinking would produce, and in the end did produce, because of the fears it aroused. 'Young men, don't play with predial questions. You will only divide the farmers. Do you know where the discussion of these types of societies you advocate will lead you? Towards the nationalization of the land, and its consequences, state control. If that's what you want, go ahead.'[38]

Les grandes lignes d'un nouvel équilibre entre l'homme et le sol

Concentration upon structural issue is liable to disguise the more permanent and continuous character of state aid to agriculture, and perhaps over-emphasize the importance of the Pisani period. In the last ten years though expenditure upon agricultural research and vulgarization has expanded most rapidly of all, in terms of the rate of expansion as well as the volume of expansion, first and second place is taken by the provision of social security to the rural population, absorbing 44 per cent of the total aid in 1964, and expenditure on the stabilization and modernization of marketing (Table 3.6). There is no need to expand on the question of welfare. Regulation of the markets commenced in the 1930s for wheat and sugar-beet, and the post-war period has seen the extension of the

[38] Debatisse (1963): 163.

TABLE 3.6 *State aid to agriculture, 1954–64*

	Millions of francs			
	1954	%	*1964*	%
Agricultural research, education, extension work, and popularization	39	3	386	5
Improvement of structures and productive equipment	361	24	2,090	25
Aids, subsidies and indemnities	289	19	527	6
Stabilization and improvement of marketing	234	16	1,617	20
Social security for agricultural population	561	38	3,650	44
Totals	1,484	100	8,270	100

system to meat, milk, potatoes, fats and flax,* Since 1961 all schemes have functioned under the financial aegis of F.O.R.M.A. (Fonds d'Orientation et de Régularisation des Marchés Agricoles.)

In an attempt to combat the anarchic condition of agricultural marketing, which originates in the widely dispersed and petty nature of comercial production amongst the peasantry, the Gaullist regime has facilitated marketing by improving the telephonic information system between the main centres, and by investing in the building and rebuilding of market centres throughout France. Above all, in line with the trend towards vertical integration in farming it has sought to strengthen the hand of the individual producer in both fields of integration; through the promotion of discipline and solidarity of the producer co-operative and by preferring common or collective types of contract when individual producers make agreements with large commercial or industrial organizations. Greater organizational flexibility has been afforded the co-operative movement by the adoption of the legislation governing S.I.C.A.s,† so that agricultural and non-agricultural interests may be permitted to combine in co-operative ventures. Other recent legislation has been designed to encourage the grouping of producers of the same commodities on local, regional and eventually national lines for the purpose of disciplining themselves with regard to the quantity, quality, and packaging of their produce, and also to

* The various regulative bodies are: for cereals: O.N.I.C.; for sugar-beet: G.N.I.B.C.; for meat: S.I.B.E.V.; for milk: Interlait; for potatoes: S.N.I.POT; fats: S.I.O.F.A; and flax: S.I.LIN. Bodies concerned with the promotion of agricultural sales and markets are CE.N.E.C.A., SO.P.EX.A. and CO.F.R.E.D.A.

† Sociétés d'Intérêt Collectif Agricole.

encourage the adoption of long- and short-term contracts between producers and processors or marketing organizations. A more orderly, organized, informed and competitive – in short, planned – system of marketing is sought through the efforts of the agricultural community itself, rather than through the enforcement of state edicts and direction, or solely at the instigation of, and under the conditions of, the larger, more concentrated, industrial and commercial interests.[39] The failings of the co-operatives at the ordinary level of organization are accepted as grounds for seeking more supple and more advanced forms of joint action. The indiscipline and selfish practices of individual members, the competition between co-operatives with fundamentally the same interests, the excessively decentralized and autonomous nature of many units, the varied degree of comprehensiveness in the different fields of production have activated the dirigists' interest in the promotion of more comprehensive producer groups, which will be required to meet a number of criteria before receiving recognition from their respective national commissions. Regional committees, *Comités économiques agricoles*, will co-ordinate policy at the local level. Once the structure is in place it is open to the regional committee to request the obligatory adherence of all producers within the region. The members of these groups, and the various local associations, will be governed as to the volume, condition and quality of produce and they are required to support the costs of market promotion and research. On the basis of voluntary self-discipline and local, regional and national solidarity the government hopes to achieve a highly structured system of production, processing and promotion for the major agricultural products. By strengthening the collective hand of the peasantry it is hoped to improve their bargaining powers with respect to the large wholesale and retailing organizations, but prices will ultimately reflect the conditions of the market and the relative bargaining powers of the interested parties, not the state's prescriptions. By mid-1966, 411 producer groupings had been recognized by the administration, about half of them dealing with fruits and vegetables. Nineteen C.E.A.s were in existence, with the horticultural ones again in the lead. Production under contract has rapidly expanded in the frozen fruit, eggs and poultry lines. But indicative of the progress still to be made was the experience of the Federal German organization that was unable to find any producer, co-operative or private, which could guarantee an annual supply of 50,000 tons of fruit and vegetables according to the standards it specified.[40]

All these reforms are planned to take place within the context of a

[39] Politique agricole de groupe (Revue française de l'agriculture) 1965: 127–50.

[40] Cuisenier (1966) provides a comprehensive account of all the major forms of organization in the agricultural sector.

diminishing agricultural labour force and a buoyant industrial economy which will contribute its share to the revival of the rural areas through the programme of industrial decentralization. The Vth Plan forecasts a 25 per cent decline in the active population employed in agriculture between

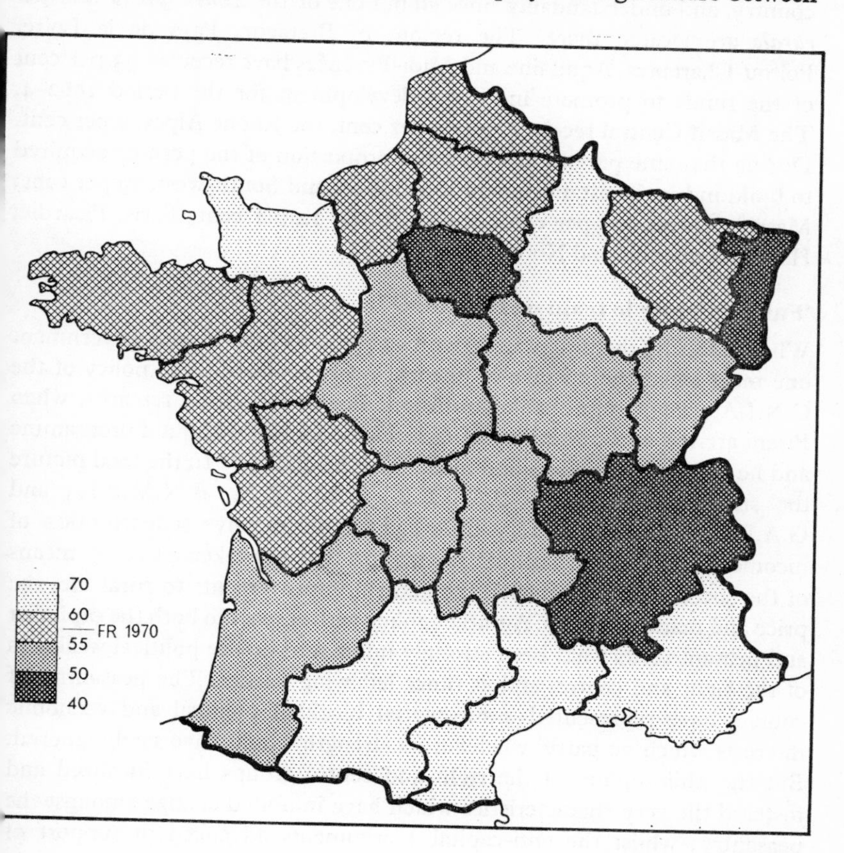

Fig. 3.10. Forecast of active population in agriculture, 1970 (1954=100)

1962 and 1970. Since 1954 the total has fallen from 5·0 million to 3·7 million, 1962, and it is projected to fall to 2·8 million by 1970. But it is clear from the regional projects that below average declines will occur in some of the régions with the largest agricultural populations and above average levels of overpopulation: for instance Bretagne, Basse Normandie and the Pays de la Loire. Thus the need to modify the economic structures of the primarily agricultural regions will be even more pressing. It is difficult to assess the immediate consequence and present achievement of the regional development programmes. The bulk of the money provided by the *Fonds d'intervention pour l'aménagement du territoire* (F.I.A.T.) have been used to finance schemes in the west, south-west and south of the country, and understandably since all but one of the *Zones special d'action rurale* are located there. The régions of Bretagne, Pays de la Loire Poitou-Charentes, Aquitaine and Midi-Pyrénées have received 43 per cent of the funds to promote industrial development for the period 1962–4 The Massif Central received only 5 per cent, the Rhône Alpes, 9 per cent During the same period, however, the proportion of the permits acquired to build industrial establishment were: West and South-west, 19 per cent Massif Central, 3·5 per cent; Rhône Alpes, 12 per cent; Paris, Picardie Haute Normandie and Nord, 28 per cent.

'Faire ralentir le train de l'histoire*'

When assessing the post-war agricultural policy of the French government one must avoid the mistake of unconsciously evaluating the policy of the C.N.J.A.; a not improbable confusion. For as de Virieu remarks, when Pisani arrived at the Ministry of Agriculture he was without a programme and he adopted their ideas and made them his policy.[41] In the total picture the structural reforms – S.A.F.E.R., A.M.P.R.A., A.N.M.E.R., and G.A.E.C. – amount to very little against the massive redistribution of income to the French farming population that has taken place by means of the social security benefits, the general improvements to rural life, the price and market policies. Agrarian policy with respect to both the capitalist and peasant sectors has been strongly influenced by the political weakness of the right and centre, and at times left wing parties. The peasantry, of course, have represented a substantial block of political and economic interests which no party, whatever its strength, could have safely ignored But the philosophies of the right and centre groups have idealized and fostered the very characteristics which have inhibited change amongst the peasantry; whilst the anti-capitalist arguments advanced in support of the peasantry have hindered the acceptance of concepts that are strictly technical or economic and have little inherent relationship with capitalism There seems to have been a convenient confusion, rather than collusion, of interests between the political parties and capitalist and peasant farmers The prompt response of the Gaullist regime after the withdrawal of agrarian support in the '65 Presidential elections is only the latest illustra-

* 'Michel Debatisse aime à dire que son objectif ces dernières années était de faire ralentir suffisamment le train de l'histoire pour permettre à ceux qui n'avaient rien compris de monter en marche.' de Virieu (1967): 256.

[41] de Virieu (1967): 193.

tion of the point. Now at least in Edgar Faure the peasants have a minister with views that are clearly appreciated by their older and more conservative ranks – 'Assurer la sauvegarde des exploitations familiales sans bouleversements juridiques.' Whether his policy constitutes a veritable reversal of his predecessors' remains in doubt. F-H de Virieu offered three hypotheses:[42] that for the next few years the government has decided to slow down the rural exodus by preferential treatment of the smaller proprietors. That Faure's* policy is no more than a manoeuvre to flatter part of the electorate in the meanwhile; that in fact there has been a genuine rejection of the Pisani policy and that a decision has been taken to dispense great sums in social assistance to the agricultural population at large. When one takes into account that it was the enormity of the financial burdens involved in modernization – a point now recognized by the C.N.J.A. – which prevented the realization of the Pisani reforms, burdens which also required a rejection of a policy based on prices alone; then in terms of these exigencies, a policy which temporizes and takes advantage of the residual function of the peasant family farm without loss of political support appears to be the most likely choice. Temporizing does not abolish the need to formulate some conception of the future structure of French farming, but it does have the advantage of avoiding any controversial implementation until the economic forces at work – the outmigration, the strengthening of the capitalist farming sector, the internal differentiation of the peasant, a process which incorporation within the E.E.C. will accelerate – have so weakened the strength of the conservative forces that their resistance has been undermined, whilst at the same time the increased wealth of the industrial economy allows the financial burdens of modernization to be more easily borne.

Two premises have underlain thinking about peasant agriculture in France since the last century – the redistributive and the enclave premises – and they are likely to retain some, if a diminishing, influence upon French thought almost to the beginning of the next. Two new premises have been introduced since the war – the industrial and the alienation premises – and they are likely to bear more heavily upon affairs as time progresses. The situation is not unlike the one frequently portrayed on the meteorological charts of western Europe. Within one system there are two distinct air masses. The beneficial warm air mass, which represents the older theses and which has so favoured peasant existence, still persists across the French landmass. Behind it lies a more disturbed, violent,

[42] *Le Monde*, 21 June 1966.

* M. Faure's transference to the Ministry of Education in the 1968 Couve de Murville cabinet and his replacement by M. Robert Boulin presages no great change in agrarian policy. Boulin is a young (b. 1920) Gaullist deputy from the Gironde, with a record in the Resistance.

colder air mass, representing the new theses, which, when it comes to prevail, will bring with it less congenial conditions for the peasantry.

The enclave premise assumed that peasant agriculture would continue as an historical remnant within industrial-capitalist society, governed by an autonomous set of economic laws, its relations with the rest of the economy being intermittent, with results that were largely unbeneficial to agriculture. In the inter-war period the premise was not a bad one, it seemingly corresponded closely to the prevailing situation. The economic laws of an industrial society did not seem to apply; there was for instance, no discernible movement towards concentration, much to the satisfaction of the supporters of the family farm. The detrimental effects of agriculture's relationship with industrial society – the depopulation of the countryside, the destruction of rural industries, the crisis of agricultural prices under the threat of sustained foreign competition – could not be denied, though they could be, and were, exaggerated. Conditions within this uncompetitive enclave, it was recognized, would deteriorate without further assistance. Hence the need for redistributive policies to sustain the income of this uncompetitive sector, by price supports, with schemes to improve the infrastructure of the rural communities and ameliorate the conditions of rural life, often with the justification that they would assist in staunching the demographic haemorrhage.

Neither premise, as we have seen, has been finally rejected. Even within the context of the Common Market, the enclave theory is still adhered to; the Germans have advanced the idea of a 'park keeper peasantry' and the French seem willing to adopt it. The massive funds available to the Community through F.E.O.G.A.* make the continuance of the redistributive and structural policies financially quite supportable. But under the influence of bodies such as C.E.N.A.G. and the C.N.J.A., and because of the market opportunities created by the C.A.P., capitalist elements in France are now beginning to recognize the need to differentiate agrarian policy according to the different categories within the farming community. They are beginning to appreciate the super-industrial capital intensity of modern agriculture.[43] The classic family farm based on polyculture requires as much capital per worker, 20–30,000 francs, as the textile and consumer goods industries. The large capitalist farm or one based on specialized activities or irrigation requires 200–300,000 francs per worker, comparable with the 500,000 francs per worker in the petro-chemical industries. Unlike the peasant family farm which is concerned with the full employment of labour, the modern farm must ensure the full utilization of its capital investment to remain competitive. Under these circumstances

* Fonds Européen d'Orientation et de Garantie Agricole.

[43] de Vaissière (1966): 21.

n increase in scale is unavoidable, vertical integration and a re-evaluation
·f function and nature of the holding become inevitable.

The advocates of the N.E.A. (Nouvelle enterprise agricole) hold to the ndustrial premise without however rejecting the alienation thesis. They 'isualize the farm as a workshop within the processing chain of the food ndustry, directed by the commercial and industrial norms of the larger nterprise. Farm organization, in one part of the process, is influenced by he advances made by the animal feed industry, in another part by the vol- ıme and scale requirements of the processing plant. All this implies a ıired agricultural labour force better paid than in any previous period and proletarianization of the bulk of the labour force that remains in agri- ulture. But at this point of the argument the advocates of N.E.A. join ıands with the C.N.J.A. in opposing the loss of exercise of individual esponsibility which is entailed in the process. Alienation is opposed at he same time as the institutions which produce it are advocated. Revolu- ionary ends are sought by non-revolutionary means.[44] The C.N.J.A. novement is fortunate in being able to utilise the sense of general dis- llusionment produced by the feeling of alienation in capitalist society to olster its arguments in support of a type of livelihood which is supposed to void it. Gervais and his collaborators estimate, without a nod to Marx, hat long before solutions to the general moral questions raised by the :.N.J.A. are discovered, capitalist farming will have become common.

It would appear that a profound misunderstanding about the nature of apitalism in the countryside exists in the West as well as in the East. There the misunderstanding revolves around the issue of labour relations n agriculture in the context of an expanding industrial economy. In the West the misunderstanding is of a socio-psychological order. The C.N.J.A. tself has pointed out that in a capitalist society the problem of security or the agricultural population is solved in a manner different to the way t is within the context of a peasant economy, when the proprietorship of he land is seen as an absolute necessity. Is it not therefore likely that the roblem of alienation in the capitalist society may be solved in an equally riginal manner, by re-ordering the daily significance of work and leisure, ather than by the preservation of outmoded economic forms?*

* The burden of state aid to agriculture is now so great that the Treasury has ittle scope for budgetry manœuvring – hence the talk of a 'new' agricultural policy for 969. The regime is indebted to the farmers for their support during the May '68 roubles and the subsequent elections. A complete rupture with past policies is herefore unlikely. A modified rather than a 'new' policy is more probable. Limita- ions upon the production of wheat, milk, sugar beet and fruits: an 'economic' ather than a 'social' prices policy; a programme adjusted to the needs of the various ocio-economic categories – all appear certain. There are hints too of a more adical predial policy. In June '68 M. Pompidou said the goverment had adopted he principle of a minimum income for *les petits agriculteurs*.

[44] Gervais (1965): 123.

4 CONTADINI: peasant and capitalist farming in the Mezzogiorno

Three, at first sight rather inconsistent, trends have appeared in the agricultural evolution of the Mezzogiorno in the past two decades. First, there has been an extension of owner-occupancy. More proprietors, both big and small, have assumed the direction of their farms, rather than leaving them in the hands of tenants and managers who commonly sublet. A large number of peasant families have acquired the freehold of their property; the most striking and publicized aspect of this trend being the land reform programme. Secondly, peasant farming has been generally promoted by the State as part of a social and economic policy which has also promoted the expansion and intensification of capitalist farming, primarily in association with large-scale irrigation projects. This aspect of the programme has received a greater share of the finance and a smaller share of the publicity, and only as the clamour concerning the land reform died down did the long-term preference granted to this sphere of agrarian development become readily apparent. In the context of a Common Market a highly organized, intensive capitalist farming sector has acquired an importance unforeseen in the immediate post-war years, when the social injustices and under-employment associated with both the peasant and capitalist sector of farming dominated most of the discussion in Italy and absorbed a fair amount of the emotional interest of sympathetic outside observers. Thirdly, the agrarian programme which has promoted both types of farming has been part of a general development programme designed to reduce the disparities between the northern and southern parts of the country and to establish the conditions for self-sustained economic growth in the South. Because this programme has been executed within the context of a dynamic national, and especially northern, economy it has allowed an enormous movement of labour to take place from the Mezzogiorno, and from its agricultural sector.

This change of circumstances has called for a re-evaluation of the role played by agriculture in the programme for social and economic advancement. Given the social and political circumstances of the late '40s, the function of agriculture was regarded at that time to be the provision of employment – hence the land reform and the promotion of the peasant sector with all its labour intensive characteristics. Given the socio-economic and political circumstances of the '60s, the need to render agriculture competitive on a European level has become the pre-eminent concern. Now it is necessary to provide the structural, credit, technological and marketing conditions which a modernized peasantry closely integrated in a market economy requires, and at the same time it is necessary to ensure the continuing outflow of low productivity labour from this sector, as a fundamental condition for rising living standards in the rural areas. Equally important is the need to ensure that the capitalist sector attains the levels of production and profitability which have already been established for it, and which in so many cases it has singularly failed to reach. As Rossi-Doria recognized in 1961, in these new circumstances, '. . . No longer are we forced to inquire as we may have done unconsciously, how much a certain area of land will produce with the application of technology, labour and capital. Rather our accounting may now be: what will a unit of capital and labour obtain when applied with the most suitable techniques to a given area of land?'[1]

The programmes of the Cassa per il Mezzogiorno, the budgetary and planning organization principally responsible for the development of the South, reflect this change of attitude towards the region's agricultural potential. Land reform and the promotion of peasant proprietorship were the prominent but not exclusive features of the agrarian section of the first fifteen year programme, 1950–65.* Irrigation, capitalist farming and the formation of a modernized peasantry are the prominent features of the second fifteen year programme, 1965–80. Later it will be convenient to treat these two prime aspects within the rather artificial framework of these historical periods, despite the degree of continuity within the Cassa's programme, especially with regard to the capitalist sector. It is in the regional context of programmes where the most abrupt changes have occurred. Out-migration, the changes in the structure of employment which have taken place and which are provided for, have been instrumental in altering the relationship between man and the land in the South. In its second plan the Cassa found it necessary therefore to cast its proposals for the economic and social improvement of the farming community within a quite different regional perspective to the one which had influenced thinking during the previous fifteen years.

[1] Caizzi (1962): 267.

* There was never in fact a first fifteen year programme. The time limit of the original programme was extended eventually to fifteen years by subsequent legislation, and the content was modified and the scope enlarged. It is now convenient to treat the amended programme as a single entity.

Agrarian and socio-economic structures

The agrarian structure of the Mezzogiorno remains highly polarized. The concentration of wealth, even in this decade, is still considerable. Whatever gains the landowning peasantry have made, the historic features of Southern rural society are still discernible. The small farm was the most common type; according to the 1961 Census of Agriculture, 92 per cent of the holdings were of less than 10 ha and they utilized 36 per cent of the agricultural area. One per cent of the holdings, units of more than 50 ha, farmed 40 per cent of the land; even when Sardinia, with its very extensive mode of land use, was excluded, 35 per cent of the land was occupied by large enterprises. Since the inter-war period the percentage of the agricultural land farmed by the large farms had declined from 48 to 40 and the percentage of the land worked by small farms had risen from 32 to the present figure. Farms of less than 10 ha are predominantly family farms and they constitute the class of small peasant holdings. They work both freehold and leasehold land, and it is not uncommon for one unit to incorporate both types of tenure. Together with inheritance practices, these tenurial arrangements create the morcellement of properties and the parcellation of holdings, thereby making fragmentation of farm units one of the most pressing structural problems of Southern farming.* Since the end of the war the area of owner-occupied land has increased by one million hectares, and the area of leased land has declined by the same amount. Approximately one-third of the area worked by peasant holdings, however, was still rented in 1961. Consequently the laws governing tenancies remain a sensitive issue in the South; and until most recently their reform has been largely ignored, in part because of the manner in which legislation of this nature jeopardized the interests of the land-owning middle classes.†

The other pole of the agrarian structure belongs to the capitalist farm, the *latifundia*, as most English-speaking people like to call it, without realizing quite the variety of labour and management contracts found within the category. In its simplest form the southern capitalist farm is large in area, managed by the proprietor and run with the aid of a small body of hired hands under annual contract and a larger body of less permanent, and less skilled day labourers – the *braccianti*. For purposes of management, however, the property may be broken up into a number of share-cropping farms, which in terms of labour organization are essentially

* On this subject see, Medici, Sorbi and Castrataro, 'Polverizzazione e frammentazione della proprieta fondiaria.'

† For example the law of 15 September 1964, No. 756: Norme in materia di contratti agrari.

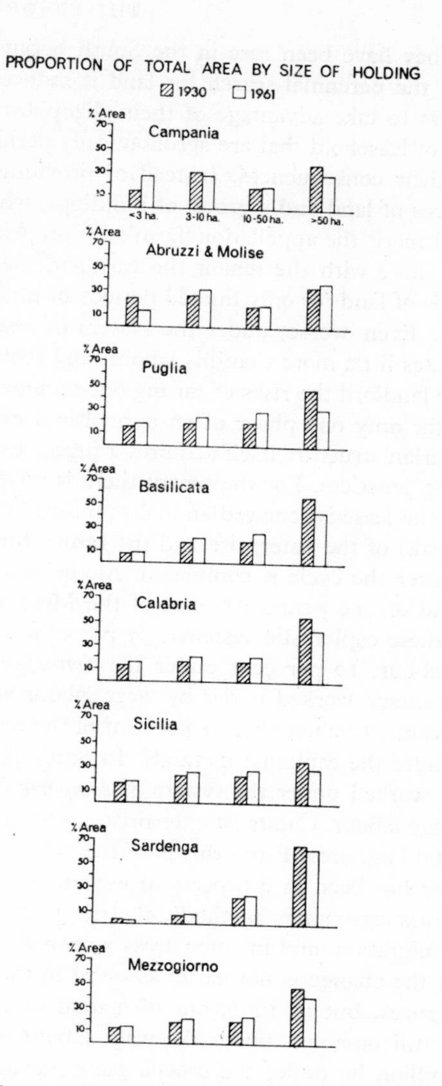

Fig. 4.1. The agrarian structure of the Mezzogiorno, 1930–61

familial in character, though because of the amount of capital and labour they are able to contribute, and hire, are larger in size than the average peasant holding. In these circumstances the term 'large-scale' is applicable only to the unit of ownership, not to the unit of operation. Contracts like these approximate closely to the highly regarded *mezzadria* system common to Tuscany, the system of *colonia parziaria appoderato*, but unfortunately they have been rare in the South because the pressure of population and the perennial search for land it induces has enabled the large landowners to take advantage of their oligopolistic position and to establish types of leasehold that are agronomically pernicious and socially deplorable in their consequences. Instead of providing the tenant with contiguous pieces of land and a group of buildings, which in the English language would merit the appellation 'farm', the proprietors have made it the custom to share with the tenant the care and management of non-contiguous areas of land for only limited periods of time, *colonia parziaria non-appoderato*. Even worse, under the system of *compartecipazione* the tenant contributes little more than his labour, and that of his family, and shares with the landlord the risks of raising one crop only, or worse again, responsibility for only one phase of an agricultural cycle. Under such a system the agrarian structure itself acquires a fugacious character inimical to good farming practices. For the tenant there is no security of employment, because the lease is renewed annually; but unlike the *braccianti*, he shares in the risks of the enterprise and the return for his labour is only determinable after the cycle is completed. At the end of the war 43 per cent of the land on the peninsular part of the Mezzogiorno was worked under one of these capitalistic systems; 27 per cent of the area with the use of wage labour, 10 per cent under the *non-appoderato* system.[2] In Sicily the percentage worked under by wage labour was 14, by the *non-appoderata* system, 26; altogether 51 per cent of the total agricultural area was worked under the capitalist methods. In Sardinia 13 per cent of the total area was worked under the system of *compartecipazione*, another 1[illegible] per cent by wage labour. Capitalist enterprises as a whole occupied 35 per cent of the total land area. From this base the system of contracts in the capitalist sector has been in a process of evolution, influenced by rising labour costs, new agronomic methods, the prospects for mechanization the effects of migration, and in some areas a growing shortage of labour The extent of the change is not easily assessed in the absence of strictl comparable figures, but in 1961, out of a total of 11·2 million ha, 3·[illegible] million were still operated under the wage labour or *compartecipazione* system, 0·3 million ha under the *colonia parziaria appoderato* contracts and 0·98 million ha under other types of contract, principally *non-appoderato* contracts. Since the war there has been something of a trend away from the *colonia parziaria* type of contract. In the South the area under the *appoderato* contracts has declined by 205,000 ha since 1946; the area under other types of contract declined by 515,000 ha; but the area worked by wage labour and *compartecipazione* contracts has increased by 771,000 ha.

[2] Medici (1952): 227–8.
[3] Campus (1965): 279–333.

'able 4.1 provides the 1961 data for the methods of operation prevalent ı the various regions of the South.

ABLE 4.1 *Systems of management, 1961*

	'000s ha			
'rovince	*Family farming*	*Wage labour and compartecipazione*	*Colonia parziara appoderato*	*Other*
;ampania	731	391	39	59
.bruzzi-Molise	655	519	171	22
.pulia	1,070	463	29	221
asilicata	541	303	33	25
;alabria	635	652	19	101
icily	1,126	696	38	483
ardinia	1,344	804	5	69
Aezzogiorno	6,104	3,830	336	981

Source: *Informazioni SVIMEZ:* XVI nn. 51–2, 1963.

The agrarian structure of the South, the classes and strata associated ⁄ith it, have created the principal components of the region's social tructure. The fundamental social distinction has been between those eople who work with their hands, the *contadini* and the *braccianti*, and iose who do not, the landowners – the *baroni* and the *borghesi*, their ıanagers and intendants. There is a polarity to the social structure of the outh as there is to its agrarian structure but this polarity is not exclusive. t does not prohibit a whole series of social and economic liaisons between he higher and lower orders, and it does not eliminate the existence of im-ortant but not absolute distinctions within the body of either the manual r non-manual classes. For instance the wage labour force, the *braccianti*, as always been swollen by additions from the under-employed family ıbour on peasant farms. By definition the *braccianti* are people with ısufficient land, even by local standaı.ds, to support a family enterprise. ;ffectively they are rural proletariat; but life in any agrarian region would e impossible without some access to a pocket of land, however infertile, owever unstable the contract. Within the life cycle of one individual, e might climb from the ranks of the *braccianti* through those of the small ɜnant class, to the status of a dwarf peasant proprietor; only to fall back gain, through bad management, ill health, or fate. The categories are real ut the fluidity of life does not always respect them. Before the land reform ome of the *latifundia* in the upland zone, near Potenza for instance, were ociologically closer to the conditions of small nucleated settlements of family farms than to the large agro-towns which house the *braccianti*, though under the terms of the *compartecipazione* contracts there was little in their life of the economic stability and security that goes with family farming. The landowning class is far from undifferentiated; it has included titled proprietors of under-utilized *latifundia*, now expropriated, the possessors of the modernized large cereal estates, the class of middle and small proprietors who may own poor cereal land, or intensively cultivated orange groves or horticultural land, and who may at one period of their family's history have belonged to the peasant classes. It is a characteristic of Southern life that the landowning class tends to confront the tenant and peasant proprietors not only as property owners and hirers of labour but in some professional capacity as well; as lawyer, doctor, chemist or bureaucrat. The relationship may not be at the face to face level, but it is sufficiently overt for the peasantry to be aware always of the influence exerted upon their daily life by the configuration of predial, political, economic, bureaucratic, and religious interests.

In a society from which an industrial and entrepreneurial group was largely absent, social structure and social life has centred round the propertied classes and their satellitic clientele in the artisanal and peasant classes. An economically undifferentiated society has nevertheless produced a considerable range of statuses and categories derived from the specialization of agricultural activities arising from the ecosystem, from the eternal competition for land and from the involution which job-finding produces in any underdeveloped society. Though the result has been a highly differentiated and hierarchical type of society, with enormous political, economic and cultural distinctions, that society derived some form of integration from the daily exercise of power over the lives of the majority by the rural oligarchies. But the very structure of power always prevented that integration from assuming co-operative and democratic forms which might lead to reform and advancement. The long-term deterioration of the rural propertied classes in the national socio-economic context reduced them to a category in tow to the rest of society – the words are Dorso's – able to defend themselves against the assaults of men and events, thanks to the astuteness of the politicians of the day, but finally condemned, for they were no longer *una classe dirigente*. They lived, until the last two decades, 'confirmed in the fatalistic idea that the one reality is the land, and that the lease is an invention of God's to assure the proprietor a mean but unassailable existence, an independence attained through the suppression or semi-suppression of civil life.'[4] Thus has rural society in the South been condemned to an immobility which all too easily might be mistaken for stability, were it not for the evidence supplied by

[4] Caizzi (1962): 423.

the frantic struggle to improve one's chance of security through upward mobility, and when this seemed quite unattainable, through migration, or riot and banditry. During the period 1881–1931, 3·1 million people quit the South; in one decade the outflow amounted to the equivalent of 89 per cent of the natural increase. In their hundreds of thousands the peasantry and their offspring left the provinces. Between 1871 and 1951 it is calculated that 723,000 left the Abruzzi-Molise, 847,000 left the Campania, 461,000 departed from Apulia, 326,000 from the Basilicata, 782,000 from Calabria, and 131,000 from Sardinia. Sicily lost 1·2 million of its inhabitants; but at the end of the period the Mezzogiorno supported approximately seven million more inhabitants than at the beginning, 83 per cent more than at the time of Unification, with an economy in which all structural change had been checked. In 1861 each square kilometre of land carried 77 persons, by 1951 the density had reached 142; even in the Basilicata, the poorest of all agricultural regions, the density had increased by 27 per cent. Since 1951, both the total population and the density per square kilometre have risen again, despite the migration of over two million persons; but the context is now different. The active labour force in agriculture declined by nearly 863,000 during the decade, the active labour force in the non-agricultural sector increased by 694,000, the structure of the economy began to change, and the pressure came off the land.

The flesh and bones of the South*

Unless placed within a regional cadre any discussion of the Mezzogiorno soon falls prey to over-generalization. Rossi-Doria first provided the four basic socio-economic regions of the South,[5] to which a further two have been added by the Cassa Mezzogiorno[6] in order to contain the emerging agricultural geography of the peninsula and the islands (Table 4.2). Basic to any understanding of these regions is the manner in which the elements of the Mediterranean ecosystem have been variously combined to achieve a maximum, and where possible, a well distributed input of labour; and the economic and social structures that have arisen when both environmental and institutional factors have prevented the attainment of these objectives. Family farming in the Mediterranean cannot exist without some combination of cereals, vine and olive, and some livestock; only capitalist farming can sustain a monocultural system.

Around Naples exceedingly intensive cropping systems have been elaborated, though this aboricultural abundance has been associated

* The expression, 'the flesh and the bones' is Rossi-Doria's: La polpa el'osso dell'agricoltura meridionale.

[5] Rossi-Doria (1956): 53–72.

[6] Cassa Mezzogiorno (1965) and Informazioni SVIMEZ: XVIII, n. 9, 1965.

with some of the vilest social conditions in Europe. To the basic trinity of cereals, vines and olives a considerable range of vegetables and tree crops have been added so that with the good volcanic soils, irrigation and urban capital, the region is able to support one of the densest rural populations in the Continent. Land accordingly is very highly priced, and the amount of capital per worker, and productivity per unit of land are amongst

TABLE 4.2 *The agrarian zones of the south*

Rossi-Doria's nomenclature	*The Cassa's*	*The English Version*
(1) Zone di agricoltura intensiva	(1A) Zone di vecchia agricoltura intensiva (1B) Zone di arboricultura specializatta	(1) The old zone of intensive agriculture (2) The tree crop zone (Jointly 1 and 2 as the intensive zone)
(2) Zone di agricoltura promiscua	(2) Zone di agricoltura promiscua contadina	(3) The zone of peasant mixed farming, or polyculture
(3) Zone di latifondo contadino (4) Zone di agricoltura capitalistica extensive	(3 and 4) Zone montane and Zone cerealicole estensive	(4) The zone of extensive peasant farming (5) The zone of extensive capitalist farming
	(5) Zone di nuova bonifica e irrigazione	(6) The new irrigation zone

the highest in the whole of Italy. In 1963 the minimum price for a hectare of citrus grove on the Sorrento peninsula was four million lire, the maximum price was around six million. Sown irrigated land between Acerra and Lola fetched 1·7 million lire per ha at a minimum. To obtain land at lower prices it was necessary to go out in the direction of Caserta.[7] Similar nuclei of intensive agriculture extend along the whole length of the Tyrrhenian coast, to reappear in Sicily, on the slopes of Etna – orange groves cost eight million lire a hectare around Caltagirone – and in the Conca d'Oro of Palmero. This *zone di vecchia agricoltura intensiva* represents one of the jewels of Southern agriculture, one of its great productive resources; to a surprising degree neglected by the post-war programmes. Speaking in London in 1962, Rossi-Doria said of the zone,

[7] Annuario dell' agricoltura italiana (1963): 66*–68*.

TABLE 4.3 *Economic characteristics of principal farming types, 1962*

Type of farming	Mode of operation	Province	Area ha	S.L.U./ha	Capital	Gross saleable output	Net product	Return per S.L.U. (manual)
					'ooos lire/ha			
Horticulture	Peasant proprietor	Campania	0·75	1·97	1,053	2,220	1,199	321
Horticulture	Peasant tenant	Campania	0·80	1·77	573	1,623	1,160	477
Olives	Peasant proprietor	Calabria	1·6	1·26	117	606	451	227
Olives	Wage labour	Calabria	35	0·22	216	381	248	423
Oranges	Peasant proprietor	Sicily	0·7	0·69	192	1,555	1,198	990
Oranges	Wage labour	Sicily	1·4	0·33	237	1,975	1,674	462
Vine	Peasant proprietor	Apulia	1·5	0·53	206	598	400	550
Vine	Wage labour	Apulia	5·0	0·35	259	441	298	551
Olives	Wage labour	Apulia	9·3	0·44	121	408	347	612
Olives	Peasant proprietor	Apulia	0·97	0·11	29	15	−4	−133
Cereals-vine livestock	Peasant proprietor	Campania	5·2	0·51	758	634	455	679
Cereals-livestock	Col. parz. appoderato	Abruzzi	12·5	0·29	275	235	167	354
Cereals	Peasant proprietor	Apulia	17	0·17	150	95	16	−38
Cereals	Wage labour	Apulia	161	0·05	91	69	41	400
Cereals-livestock	Compartecipazioni	Sicily	39	0·09	136	136	76	413
Cereals-livestock	Non-appoderato	Sicily	59	0·05	33	40	32	325

Source: *I.N.E.A.* 1964.

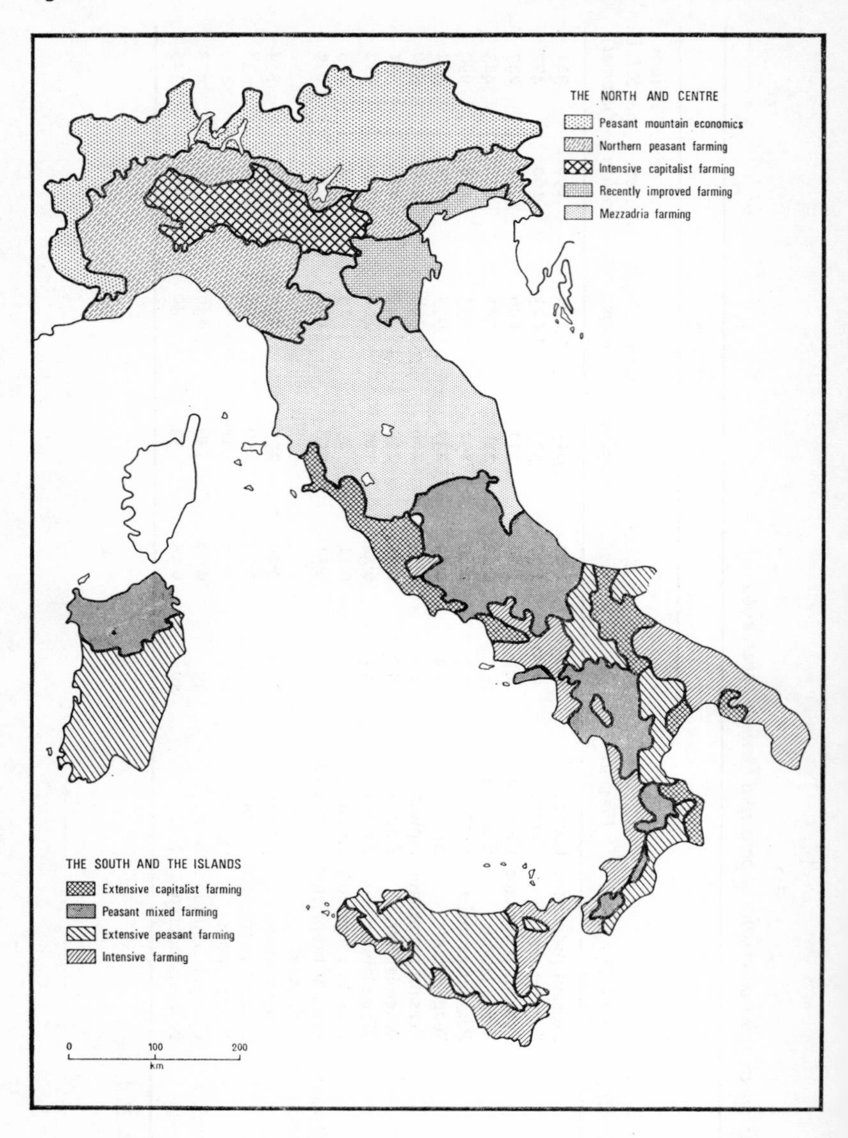
THE NORTH AND CENTRE
Peasant mountain economics
Northern peasant farming
Intensive capitalist farming
Recently improved farming
Mezzadria farming
THE SOUTH AND THE ISLANDS
Extensive capitalist farming
Peasant mixed farming
Extensive peasant farming
Intensive farming
0
100
200
km

Fig. 4.2. Types of farming

'Until now these areas have lived by their own resources. The Government has given them relatively few and modest public works – roads and aqueducts – no land reclamation, no irrigation programme, no land reform – only some modest contributions to private land investment . . . their situation has deteriorated. . . . As the country as a whole is moving from a modest semi-rural to an industrial economic system, the weaknesses – and there are many – of the productive and social structure of these areas becomes even more apparent.'[8] With only 3·6 per cent of the agricultural area this zone produced in 1961, 18·8 per cent of the South's net agricultural output. A slight, insignificant decline in its relative productive importance is forecast by the Cassa for 1980, but in terms of employment opportunities in agriculture its importance should increase.

The *zone di agricoltura promiscua*, the zone of polyculture, or peasant mixed farming as it is so inadequately translated, displays a falling off from all the high levels associated with the old intensive zone. In this zone the farms seek to maintain, and ultimately fail to maintain, the complex and involved cropping patterns of the more favoured areas in increasingly hilly and mountainous conditions, where the possibilities for irrigation are almost non-existent, except in certain valleys which have required a considerable investment of labour and capital to eliminate their marshy and sometimes malarial state. Around Avellino and towards Ariano Irpino the careful cultivation of crops and fruit trees on exceedingly steep slopes represents an inordinate investment of human labour, but the levels of productivity cannot match those of the lower areas, so that the investment per hectare of land falls off, as does the price. Irrigated land, or vine and olive land, in the favoured valleys will fetch at a minimum between 1·2 and 1·8 million lire per hectare; but sown land with trees brings less; and without trees the price falls to 420,000 lire around Benuvento, and 180,000 lire per hectare near Alta Irpina. Away from the Campania, westwards or southwards, there is a general falling off in productivity and an increase in the levels of misery, which are very difficult to compare because of the disparities that occur within regions as well as between regions. Certainly when given the opportunity to migrate the inhabitants of this zone have not been reluctant to leave. The Abruzzi-Molise has displayed the highest rate of migration in the post-war period. As a result labour shortages are appearing in a region where mechanization is difficult under most circumstances. Of all the *zone* this one is the least homogeneous, and some of the valley areas are destined for a more favoured future according to the Cassa's plans. In general, however, the zone of polyculture will produce a slightly smaller share of the total net agricultural production and employ a lower proportion of the agricultural labour force by 1980, than it does at present.

[8] Rossi-Doria (1962): 50.

Pre-eminently located in Apulia, the tree crop zone, the *zone di aboricoltura specializzata*, is the third densely populated, highly productive and relatively stable region of the Mezzogiorno, far richer and more productive than the zone of polyculture, without being quite as spectacularly productive as the old intensive zone. The three together are the flesh on the body of the South. Unlike the old intensive zone, the development and expansion of the tree crop region is of more recent origin, and concentrated in the last century. Since the 1870s the area under vine has increased from 96,000 to about 275,000 hectares; that under olives from 202,000 to 519,000 hectares, that under tobacco from 4,000 hectares in 1919 to 19,000 in 1965.[9] The practice over most of the zone is to specialize in the cultivation of olives and vines, often undersown with cereals. Only along the littoral, especially around the larger towns of Bari and Brindisi and the smaller fishing ports, are more intensive and diversified horticultural activities common. Hence there is a uniformity and regularity to the landscape quite absent from the landscapes of the older zone; olive and vine succeed one another mile after mile, to create a sea of deep green leaves that stretches from the high Murge down to the shores of the Adriatic. The harvests require an enormous assemblage of temporary help, often provided by women, so that the *braccianti* and the dwarf peasant element has been an important feature of the social structure of the numerous agro-towns spaced regularly throughout the area. Population densities are high in these communes but they never reach the levels common in the Campania. Specialized olive land near Brindisi costs, at a minimum 650,000 lires per hectare, at a maximum 2·5 million lire. Vine and olive land near Ostuni ranges in price from 800,000 to 1·25 million lire a hectare; near Lecce olive groves will fetch from 800,000 to 2·6 million lire, whilst some of the horticultural land near the sea in the Salentine peninsula is worth 3·5 million lire per hectare.

These three regions display the greatest concentration of small holdings and peasant enterprises throughout the South. In the Campania, 61 per cent of the holdings are crowded in the less than 10 ha category, and owner-occupied or leasehold peasant farms controlled 65 per cent of the productive area in the immediate post-war period. The regions of Brindisi and Lecce in Apulia, and the provinces of Palermo, Messina and Catania in Sicily have similar features. Between 40 and 45 per cent of the agricultural area is controlled by small holdings and the concentration of peasant farms in these areas is very marked.

In 1961 the tree crop, the old intensive and the polyculture zone, were jointly responsible for 53 per cent of the Mezzogiorno's net agricultural production; they provided employment for 47 per cent of the agricultural

[9] Colamonico (1960): 113–86.

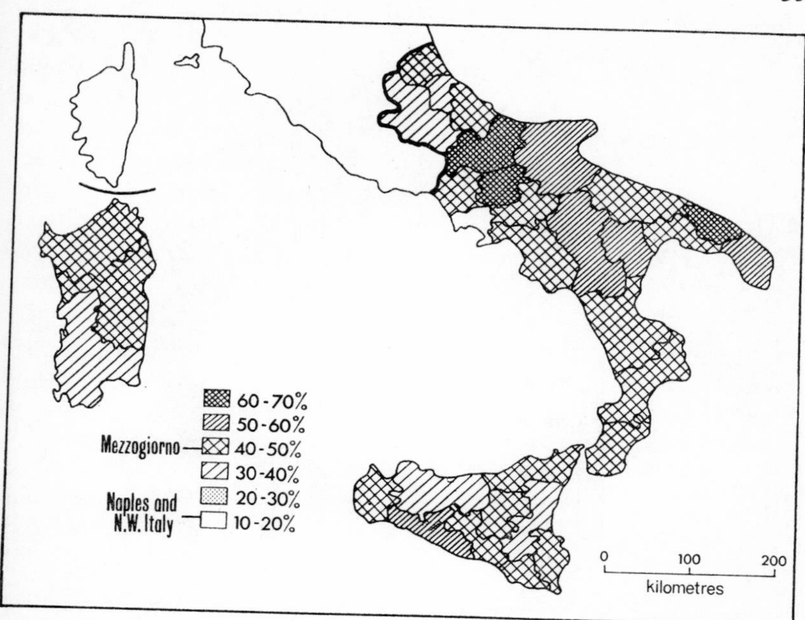

Fig. 4.3. Percentage of population active in agriculture, 1961
Based on Census of Population, 1961

labour force and incorporated only 27 per cent of the total area. Since the war their productive achievements, given the already highly productive bases from which further growth had to take place, outrank those of most other southern regions. According to the Cassa forecast, by 1980 they will still be responsible for 47½ per cent of the South's net agricultural production; they will still employ 47 per cent of the reduced labour force in agriculture. It would be quite misleading to regard these regions as undynamic areas. Each one, in its own way, has already experienced change in a variety of spheres, and a number of further changes are essential to maintain economic growth in the agrarian sector. At the same time their present and future strategic role within the productive and employment structures means that they constitute the pediment of any future agrarian planning in the South, and essentially they represent the stable farming zones of the Mezzogiorno.

The task of development in two of these zones is to preserve and improve upon the already highly productive levels which have been attained, and it will require a very careful and sophisticated tinkering with the whole delicate mechanism of the Southern intensive farming systems to achieve

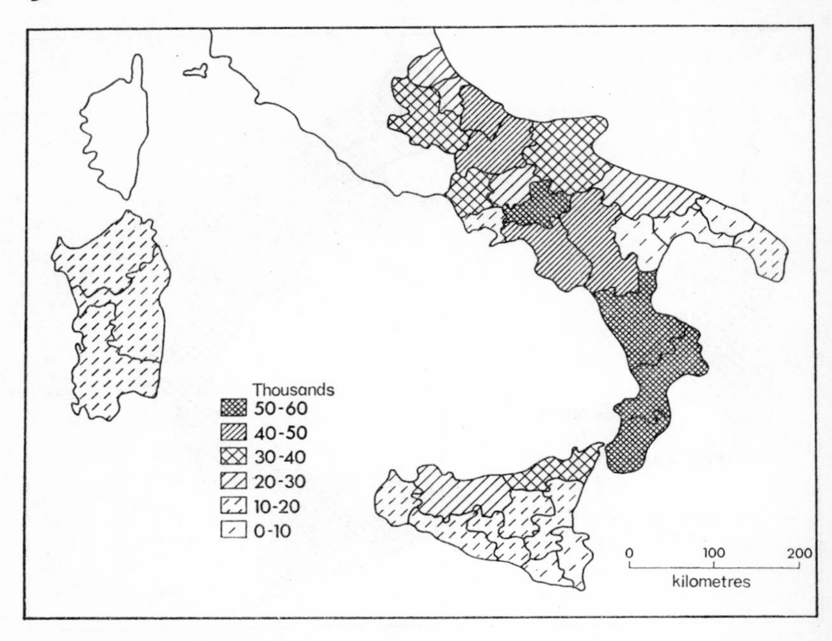

Fig. 4.4. Decline of population active in agriculture, 1951–61

these ends. Unlike all the other zones, capital and entrepreneurial ability are conspicuously present in the old zone of intensive farming, particularly around the centres of Naples, Salerno, Bari, Catania and Palermo. Large public works are not required in this environment, though local roading and services merit investment. More delicate and still largely unconfronted difficulties press for treatment: the amelioration of leaseholds, thorough-going innovations in marketing and the promotion of vertical integration, in addition to the ever present problems of mechanizing the small holdings pulverized into innumerable plots, their remembrement, and the achievement of a structure that can begin to support viable family farming. In this favourable habitat net production is forecast to increase by 22 per cent per unit of land, by 33 per cent per unit of labour. In absolute terms net output is expected to rise from 192 to 234 milliard lire by 1980, and the total public and private investment involved amounts to 250 milliard lire, about 8 per cent of the planned total.

Marketing and the mechanization of parasite control and of the harvest – technically a demanding project – are the dominant issues in the tree crop zone, where the expansion and renewal of labour intensive crops is a conspicuous and surprising feature during a period of rising wages. Over third of the zone – in those areas of most recent planting – the economic onditions of the vine and olive producing farms are regarded as satis- ctory by the Cassa. These holdings it is believed are suitable for mech- nization; they will be able to take advantage of the new processing plants nd the marketing innovations. They constitute the most competitive ector of the zone. Throughout the remaining parts of the zone a recon- ruction of the holdings, a renewal of the trees and bushes, a revision of ontracts, a rationalization of the productive and processing methods are ll necessary to remove the backward and low productive conditions which ne Cassa designates as pathological. In the next fifteen years, however, nat office estimates only half of the afflicted area can be treated. A reduction f the labour force to 67 per cent of its 1951 level, the eradication of the ine and the olive from marginal areas and those unsuited to mechaniza- on, ought to be accompanied by a 24 per cent increase in yields per ectare and a 77 per cent increase in yield per unit of labour. Again, about per cent of the total investment is destined for expenditure in this zone.

Without a wholesale re-ordering of the predial structure – the regroup- ng of strips and the recomposition of holdings; without a greater special- zation in crops and livestock, without – in the words of the Cassa – detailed apillary action not only of a technical nature but including a whole range f well selected and varied intervention, the renovation of the polyculture one cannot be accomplished. The zone has a total area of 1·3 million ectares; and of this 800,000 ha are occupied by undersized, self-sufficient arms. About a quarter of this land ought to be permanently retired to asture and woodland. Predial restructuring is an indispensable prelimin- ry to any rational investment programme for the remainder. Over about 90,000 ha prevailing conditions favour a more immediate intervention. bout 9 per cent of the planned investment has been set aside for this one. By 1980, with a labour force reduced to half the 1951 level, net roduction per ha ought to have risen by 16 per cent, per unit of labour y 83 per cent. In absolute terms net production is forecast to increase by 2 milliard lire, compared with 52 milliard lire increase forecast for the ree crop zone, and the 34 milliard lire increase forecast for the old intensive one.

Beyond Eboli

The *zone di latifondo contadino* and the *zone di agricoltura capitalistica stensive* appear in the Cassa's programme under the title of the moun- ainous and extensive cereal zones; they are the bones of the South. Together they occupied, in 1961, 65 per cent of the agricultural area. They roduced 35½ per cent of the net agricultural production and employed, n some fashion, 45 per cent of the agricultural labour force. The disproportion between the percentage employed and the amount produce is some indication of the level of misery to be found in the area. By 198 it is estimated only 30 per cent of a smaller labour force will be employe in these two zones, producing 26 per cent of the net output, thereb notably reducing the disproportion between labour and production. Mo of the change will be felt in the mountainous zone. Its share of the labou force will decrease from 28 to 15 per cent of the total, its contribution t output from 19½ to 11 per cent. Both a concentration of effort and closing down and withdrawal is planned; for in the midst of, or on th peripheries of, these regions the new zone of irrigation and intensiv agriculture is already emerging, combining both capitalist farms an peasant holdings drawn from the favoured areas of the land refor districts. In 1961 the new zone was estimated to produce 11½ per cent c the net agricultural output and to employ 8 per cent of the labour forc By 1980 it should be employing over one-fifth of the Mezzogiorno' agricultural labour force and producing a quarter of its output. Geograph ically the Cassa's programme is aimed to invert the pattern of land use tha reached its apogee during the last century. As the population increase and the demand for land attained excruciating levels, farming in th Mezzogiorno was pushed to higher and higher altimetric levels. Deforest ation and soil erosion were the physical consequences, isolation, povert and cultural impoverishment the social consequences, and declinin livestock numbers the agronomic consequences. Only in the last decad has the flow been reversed, and the Cassa hopes to accelerate the process raising, as a result of out-migration, the area per unit of labour in th mountains from seven to 18 ha; and lowering the ratio from four to tw ha per man in the irrigated zones as the land use intensifies. If the pla is successful then the Mezzogiorno will revert to a pattern of land use no in evidence since classical times.

Of all the regions of the South, the most notorious for the Englis language public is undoubtedly the zone of *latifondo contadino*, for it wa there that Carlo Levi spent his exile, on the borders of Calabria and th Basilicata. The zone extends from the Basilicata, through Calabria o the Ionic side and dominates the interior of Sicily; again some of Dolci' material is drawn from settlements within the zone. Peasant farming, a always, is based upon the vine, the olive and cereals, but topography altitude, drought, poor soils restrict the areas of intensive cultivation t the immediate vicinity of the settlements, and render the yields deplorabl low. Pressure of population and the shortage of fodder limited the livestoc carrying capacity so that low yielding cereals become the principal sourc of food and income. For this reason Rossi-Doria gave the zone its name Like the owners of the large *latifundia*, the peasant chef was practicall

monoculturalist, but without any of the advantages of scale, and be-
oured with all the burdens of iniquitous contracts, capital shortages,
uctural problems, often malaria and always ignorance.

From the hills on the edge of the Tavoliere, or from the ridges over-
oking the valleys which lead down to the Metaponto it is possible to look
t across the zone of extensive capitalist farming. Though the zone
ntains some of the principal sites of Grecia Magna, notably Metapontum
d Sybaris, in the last century it was a repulsive area, much of it still a
sert, like the Maremma north of Rome, a wintering ground for the trans-
mant flocks, malaria debilitating the sparse population. When the
sease was eradicated the environment, particularly the shortage of water,
ted as a bar to anything but extensive large-scale capitalistic cereal
ltivation, based on a biennial fallow system, or at best on cereals and
ans, the profitability of which depended upon state protection and an
tarkic economic policy. But wherever conditions permitted it, near
n Severo and Cerignola for instance, the relentless pursuit of more
tensive forms of farming by the land hungry could not be stemmed. This
netration of the tree crop zone into the extensive cereal zone, which has
en under way for more than a century was made possible, according to
ilone,[10] solely because the tenacious and indefatigable peasantry never
unted the hours of work, even though at one time their remuneration
as below that received by the *braccianti*.

By Rossi-Doria's original estimates the zone of extensive capitalist
riculture occupied only 5 per cent of the total area of the South. In
mparison with the 89 inhabitants per km. supported by the zone of
tensive peasant farming, it carried only 35 persons to the square kilo-
etre, but, and this explains the economic strength of the zone and the
litical influence of its landowners, the value of gross output per hectare
as twice that of the more densely populated districts. Current land
ices reflect these differences. Cereal land in the Tavoliere will fetch 500 –
0,000 lire per hectare; on the hills above the Basento it will bring no
ore than 200,000 lire. Near Corleone, in the extensive peasant area of
icily it costs between 100,000 and 350,000 lire per hectare – a range of
pproximately £20–80 an acre.

At the time of Mussolini's dictatorship 53 per cent of the area in the
gion of Foggia was concentrated in holdings of 100 ha and more; 64 per
nt in holdings exceeding 50 ha. Holdings of more than 50 ha held 56 per
nt of the area in the Basilicata; for Calabria, Sicily and Sardinia the
roportions were, respectively 52, 36 and 66 per cent. In the immediate
ost-war period many of the large estates in the Basilicata and Calabria
ere worked as capitalist enterprises, in the strict sense of depending

[10] Milone (1955): 793.

upon hired labour. In Sicily and Sardinia more than half the area wa worked under some form of leasehold contract. All the excesses of Southern rural life were concentrated in the extensive peasant and capitalistic zone almost every card in the pack called 'underdevelopment' had been deal in those areas. Inevitably, for political as well as ecological reasons, fo social as well as hydrological reasons, for economic as well as agronomi reasons, when the reform and regeneration of Southern life were undertaken, it was in these two zones that the most spectacular aspects of th agrarian programme were concentrated, the land reform and the programme for bonification and irrigation; thus separating the zone of new irrigation from the rest.

Over the next fifteen years the Cassa plans to spend 260 milliard lire on the mountainous zone. Having sustained some of the worst effects o over-population much of this tormented land is to be put out of commission, rested. In the folklore of geography wealth, it was always assumed, woul allow mankind to negate the environment, expand the oecumene to th maximum, grow tomatoes at the north pole if he wished. It appears now, to the contrary, that wealth permits contraction, the concentration o activity on the preferred areas, a withdrawal from the marginal zones. The Cassa's programme foreshadows the work of a 'developmental shutdown agency'; a 61 per cent drop in the labour force, a 76 per cent decline in net agricultural production, a 23 per cent fall in net production per hectare are planned, to achieve a 98 per cent increase in production per worker. Expressed in terms paradoxically suited to the situation, £340 will be spent for every job lost to the area. Already the effects of emigration, involving the equivalent of two-thirds of the population present in 1951, have been so disruptive, that Rossi-Doria has spoken of 'a falling apart of an economy and a traditional society'.[11] The task of the Cassa is to continue the work of soil protection and re-afforestation and to provide new economic foundations for this profoundly disorganized society. The Cassa itself speaks of action not confined to technical, agricultural or silvicultural matters, but incorporating an organic programme of assistance organized on a communal basis. The mountainous zone covers 5·1 million hectares and involves a population of two million persons. From a grand total of 1·7 million ha of arable land, a valid type of agriculture can be established on only 400,000 ha owing to the existence of minor advantages: small-scale irrigation, possibilities for mechanization, favourably sized holdings. These areas will receive intensive treatment. Another 400,000 ha will continue to be farmed by residual family holdings; 900,000 ha of arable land will be converted to pasture or woodland and large, 300–50 ha, forestry-pastoral holdings will be established. Tourism and whereve

[11] Rossi-Doria (1962): 49.

ossible, industry, are to be encouraged with the intention of maintaining labour force sufficient for the part-time requirements of the soil erosion nd re-afforestation works, which in themselves ought to provide a basis r some industrial activity. An additional sum of 231 milliard lire has been pproved to finance these ecological schemes.

Three hundred and seventy milliard lire are destined to be invested in at sea of hills, the zone of extensive cereal cultivation which composes ree-quarters of Lucania and the whole interior of Sicily whose character as summed up by the fleeting remark of the French governess to the alina family: '. . . c'est pire qu'en Afrique'. Large-scale, mechanized heat farming, as in Algeria, is the practical proposition for the area, but s introduction is inhibited and the returns to investment put at hazard y the slow decomposition of traditional structures in this semi-arid nvironment. Despite considerable migration, the price of land, as indicated, remains high, retarding the formation of adequately sized farms. hese can be obtained if family farming is to persist only by placing the ereal lands under collective management, whilst the individual family tains responsibility for the more concentrated and intensive type of ultivation – a far from promising scheme, given the political and social hos of Sicily. From a gross area of 2·5 million ha, 1·4 million are susceptible to development; 150,000 ha with restricted possibilities for irrigation representing the most attractive field for investment. Over 400,000 a where farm size and environment favour profitable farming the Cassa ill intervene to assist the development already under way; but on the 00,000 ha of residual farming, pre-eminently the zone of *latifondo ntadino*, the remembrement of land and a further reduction in the level population to half the 1951 level are prerequisites for investment. therwise the area will remain stagnant in a pitiful state of existence. A uccessful outcome is estimated to provide a net production per ha of land 3 per cent above current yields, which are equivalent to the present level the Basilicata, and a 94 per cent rise in output per unit of labour. The equired investment per unit of land considering its low productivity is ery high.

Amidst all the details of regional development generalities must not be nored (Table 4.4). By 1980, if the Cassa's proposals work out, 27 per ent of the Mezzogiorno's net agricultural product ought to be created in e newly irrigated zones; but 62 per cent of the total output will originate om the old intensive, polyculture, tree crop and extensive cereal production zones, which include some areas that have received very little sistance during the initial fifteen year programme, and which do not ntain within them mechanisms that will automatically ensure their evelopment. Yet the overall success of the Cassa's second fifteen year

TABLE 4.4 *The Cassa's agrarian programme, 1965–80*

Zone	Investment Milliard lire	Area %	Net product			Labour force '000s			
			Milliard Lire 1960	c. 1980	% Increase /ha	1960	c. 1980	% decrease	% increase product/man
di vecchia agricoltura intensiva	250	3·6	192	234	22	320	293	−8·4	33
di arboriculture specializzata	250	12·8	218	270	24	550	386	−29·8	77
di agricoltura promiscua contadina	270	10·9	132	154	16	345	220	−36·2	83
di cerealicole estensiva	370	21·5	162	202	13	450	289	−35·8	94
di montane	260	43·4	200	153	−23	720	279	−61·3	98
di nuova bonifica e irrigation	1,145	7·8	118	368	213	210	433	+106·2	51
Sub-total	2,545	100	1,022	1,381	34	2,595	1,900	−26·8	85
General works	435								
Total	2,980								

ogramme is dependent as much upon what happens there as what
entuates in the newly irrigated zone. All the zones desperately need
etter marketing facilities and improved processing plants, especially in
e context of the Common Agricultural Policy. The improvement of
ricultural contracts has commenced with the new laws related to
ezzadria and *colonia parziaria*, but enforcement and supervision are a
fferent matter to legislation, though the general reduction of pressure
pon the land works in favour of the tenant class. The least publicized
d the most crucial – theoretically speaking, the most exciting – aspect
the Cassa's programme is the institutional question. Structural change
as not automatically followed upon the rural exodus; the situation calls
r intervention and the mechanism of the market is incapable of the task.
his the Cassa admits; but what form the intervention shall take, what
stitutions it will be associated with, is not settled. In the zone of tree
ops and intensive agriculture spontaneous forces are reckoned to be
sufficient for what is needed. Successful intervention in the zone of
ixed peasant farming calls for 'the presence of a suitable development
ency capable of facilitating the gradual modification of the productive
ructure, especially where such modifications depend upon predial
form'.[12] The situation of the small peasantry in the zone of extensive
real cultivation calls for some collective organization of the sown and
asture lands, whilst an *Ente* with wide juridical and financial powers
pears essential to the successful improvement of the whole zone. In not
e of the cases is the co-operative immediately suited to the tasks im-
osed by the situation. Its democratic formulation and procedures do not
low the necessary degree of direction and authoritarianism required in
is case. To assume that the co-operative will be self-policing in the
outhern situation is to assume away some of the fundamental educational
sks facing the region. In a reorganized community the co-operative will,
course, have a major role to play; but in the process of reorganization
self there is limited scope for it. Only for the newly irrigated zones does
e Cassa display any real decisiveness, for there the *comprensori di*
nifica is a well tried, if not well proven, instrument ready at hand,
pecially now that the Cassa is prepared to strengthen the institution at
weakest point; by having the state participate in the transformation of
e individual holding itself. Fundamental to the implementation of this
oposal will be the farm study and the programme derived from it, which
ill become the basis for a contractual agreement between the land-owner
d the state agencies who as executive bodies will be represented in the
itary organization established, it seems, at the level of the *comprensori*.
what is the least historically burdened, the most accessible and the most

[12] Cassa Mezzogiorno (1965): 24.

capitalistic part of the agrarian sector, it is not surprising in an age of sta intervention to discover the most advanced development of state capita ism. Considering the huge financial burden already assumed by the sta for some of its capitalistic supporters, this trend seems destined to accentuated.

In terms of outlay per unit of labour maintained the planned investme varies considerably between the different zones; per unit of gross area th expenditure will be enormous. To illustrate from the zone of intensi agriculture: for every unit of labour in existence in 1980, over the previo fifteen years an investment of 850,000 lire (£500) will have been mad Per hectare of land it will have been £350, a very large sum in view of th already existing investment. Investment per additional unit of labour and this is relevant to the newly irrigated zone alone – will work out 5·1 million lire (*c* £3,000). The most meaningful assessment of the cos is to express them in terms of the ratio of investment to the increase in n production. In all cases the ratio is high; in some exceedingly high; but i these terms the investment in the newly irrigated zone is the most attractiv

TABLE 4.5 *Ratio of investment to increase in net production*

Zone	
Newly irrigated	4·58:1
Tree crop	4·80:1
Old intensive	5·95:1
Extensive cereal	10·80:1
Mixed family farming	12·25:1

Source: Cassa Mezzogiorno (1965).

All of this lies in the future. Now it is necessary to go back a little i history to see what has already been attained in the agricultural develop ment of the South. To see what was and what was not achieved by the lan reform, to see what progress the Cassa has made already with its develop ment of the newly irrigated zones.

The land reform

The Italian land reform, like most land reforms, was a response to particular socio-economic situation, made at a particular time within th confines of a given political structure. The execution of a general lan reform – Italy was one of the few remaining European countries which ha not made the attempt – was rendered impossible by the loss of the revolu tionary fervour characteristic of the partisan period; more important, b the technical difficulties arising from that delicate relationship of croppin system, labour organization, and land ownership which constitutes one of the major achievements of Italian farming, particularly in the central and northern regions. It was impracticable also because of the support the Christian Democrat Party derived from the middle classes of the rural areas. In order to restrain growing violence in the country areas, to lessen the persuasive powers of the Communists, to demonstrate in concrete terms the power and will of the new state to provide some hope for the future – the extraordinary laws promulgated to deal with the land confiscations in Calabria and elsewhere were extended to other areas of the South. To produce a land reform whose character was determined by the political decisions that were its basis: it should at once be popular without being revolutionary or punitive.

Land from only the very largest and most extensively farmed properties was expropriated. Approximately 673,000 hectares of poorly farmed, almost undeveloped land, was acquired, mostly from properties of more than 300 ha. The burden fell upon a very small class of rich and unpopular landowners whose shoulders were broad enough to bear the weight of an opprobrium that was more generally deserved. The geographical impact of the reform was therefore capricious. Brutal contrasts were created between neighbouring communes that were indistinguishable in terms of the clammering need for relief and improvement. As a further consequence the land acquired by the *Enti di Riformo* was totally unsuited to the immediate requirements of family farms. It was located, with rare exceptions, in the most isolated parts of the extensive peasant and extensive capitalist zones, where even the minimum of social services was absent. There were few roads, no water or power, no hamlets or villages, no schools, halls, churches or dispensaries. The *Enti* had to prepare not only the soil for farming, they had to create the social environment too. Hence the very high costs of development. To be popular the effect of the reform had to be felt amongst the largest possible number of recipients and the most deserving of cases. Generally therefore, the land was assigned to the *braccianti*, a class least prepared to meet the high standards required for successful family farming of a sort for which no precedent existed in the South. The social character of the assignees, the speed of execution required of the *Enti*, encouraged the marked paternalistic tendencies in evidence from the very beginning. For as Rossi-Doria pointed out, the reform was launched without any reference to the peasant movement, which in 1951 was in a phase of substantial depression.[13]

Despite the initial handicaps. Despite the fact that the social reform services were used progressively as political instruments to augment the electoral strength of the Christian Democrats. Despite the chicanery and

[13] Rossi-Doria (1958): 89.

the positive ill-will that marred the execution of the reform in Sicily. Despite the local imperatives of population density that made the reform in some areas, Calabria for instance, no more than an act of social solidarity, the economic results have been commendable; but this constitutes a fulfilment rather than an achievement considering the enormous expenditure incurred per family. Bandini reckoned on a figure of £2,000 per family when the cost of land development, farm buildings and stock were included. When the cost of social projects and public utility schemes was added the total lay close to £3,000.[14] And these figures have never been refuted, though it is questionable whether, in fact, they take account of all the costs that were borne.

To the criticisms of paternalism and the high costs involved a third was added which gathered weight with the passage of time and the changing economic circumstances of the South. Whilst the major proportion of the expropriated land was assigned as family sized units (*poderi*), half at least of the assignees received (*quote*) sufficient only to supplement their family's income. The majority of holdings established were therefore uneconomic from the beginning, a procedure for which good and bad reasons could be found. In the early '50s most Southern Italian holdings were uneconomic ones, and socially it would have been insupportable to have preferred in the midst of such universal misery a very small class of farmers selected from amongst their contemporaries. A widespread dispersal of the benefits made good political sense to many interested parties. Consequently 46,000 families received *quote* and 45,000 families received *poderi*. In Sicily the distinction between *quote* and *poderi* was not made, but the average size of holding assigned to the 76,700 proprietors was 4·35 ha (Table 4.6).

These average figures are unsatisfactory. They hide the dispersal of holdings amongst various size categories, and give no indication of the intensity of land use. The variety of conditions prevailing within the reform zones can never be ignored. In the Maremma, for instance, there were, in 1959, *quote* sown down with oats and nothing else, being too far from the communes of the assignees to permit more intensive cropping. Others, taking advantage of the proximity of the Rome markets, had developed into small market gardens, and attractive cottages had been erected through the enterprise of the assignee without the aid of the *Ente*. In the hill country of Lucania by contrast, quite large *poderi* were clearly marginal units. The environment restricted the assignees to a mixed livestock economy, and for this the farms were hardly of an adequate size. Because of limitations contained within the expropriation laws, the assignees had not received wood lots as part of their holdings. In not dissimilar environmental conditions, in Swabia or the Central Massif of

[14] Bandini (1957): 17–37.

France, such supplementary resources are considered to be indispensable to successful family farming but these peasants had to do without. *Poderi* in the Sila region laboured under the burden of similar difficulties.

TABLE 4.6 *Land reform: poderi and quote, 1960*

Enti di Riforma	*Expenditure milliard lire 1962*	*Total*		*Poderi*		*Quote*	
		Area assigned ha	*Families no.*	*Area ha*	*Families no.*	*Area ha*	*Families no.*
Delta Padano	41	35,300	5,626	35,026	5,305	274	321
Maremma	52	168,451	19,444	126,847	7,996	41,040	11,448
Fucino	11	13,495	9,026	—	—	13,495	9,026
Campania (O.N.C.)	10	14,936	3,632	11,685	1,684	3,025	1,948
Apulia-Lucania Molise	99	174,886	31,609	137,806	16,229	36,729	15,380
Calabria	44	77,373	18,902	61,276	11,411	14,735	7,491
Sicily*	29	76,723	17,602	—	—	—	—
Sardinia	31	57,756	3,584	54,068	2,794	3,404	790
	317	618,920	109,425	426,708	45,419	112,702	46,404

* The poderi–quote distinction was not drawn for Sicily.
Source: Cassa Messogiorno (1962).

It is not known what proportion of the assignees received holdings that would meet the standards of viability currently accepted as desirable. Certainly on the assumptions of the early '50s to have established these modern criteria as guides to action would have appeared totally unrealistic. With hindsight one appreciates the problems that have been created for the future. In comparison with the colonization of the Mussolini period, in the Pontine and Tavoliere areas, the *poderi* of the land reform were small; but as early as 1959 abandoned homesteads in the Pontine area were to be seen, whilst some of the Tavoliere farms were close to the limits of viability and many have been abandoned. Undoubtedly, some thousands of adequate family farms will emerge as a result of the land reform, especially following the planned increase of expenditure in irrigation zones. Hundreds of the *quote* appear to have been abandoned already. Around the nuclei of industrial development, near Bari, Brindisi, Taranto, and Ferradina and near some of the smaller settlements, Potenza and Cerignola, the *quote* and *poderi* are providing the basis for the emergence of a class of part-time farmers; though the process is not restricted to the farms belonging to the land reform schemes alone. In the majority of cases the living standards and income of the family farmers have risen. The recipients of so much investment, it could hardly be otherwise. Now as members of the small peasantry they are faced with the universal task of establishing a valid form of family farming in an increasingly industrial economy. To make them viable will necessitate considerably more investment. As an attempt, therefore, at solving a socio-economic problem the land reform must be regarded as being more successful in dealing with the social than with the economic aspects. A proletarian rural group has been raised to the status of a small family farming class, initially with very little effort on its own behalf. The markedly sociological consequences of the change, the considerable net import of capital goods and services with which the whole development of the South is associated; also the absence of effective participation at all points by the recipients themseves, reveal the land reform for what it is: a massive piece of social engineering, welfaristic in outlook, paternalistic in execution, and redistributive in intention.

Generalizations, however valid, ought not to detract from a recognition of the nuances in any situation. The land reform extended over a considerable area. Though that territory displays many common environmental features, peculiar geographic circumstances have given an original twist here and there to the programme, to the manner in which the reform was implemented and to its degree of success. The determination with which the reform has been executed has varied from *Ente* to *Ente*. The impact and concentration of other projects of the Cassa have varied between one region and the next. The result is a veritable geography of the Land Reform. It is not uniformly easy to obtain sufficient data for some *Ente* as others, however, and it is difficult to obtain firsthand knowledge over such a vast area. It is probably more instructive, therefore, to concentrate upon one region and its diversities – Apulia–Lucania – for which reasonably good data exist; where it has been possible for the author to visit the same settlements twice, in 1959 and 1966, and witness both the successes and disappointments.

The reform in Apulia-Lucania

In Apulia-Lucania the assignees participated in some of the major irrigation schemes for the South. In these settlements the most intensive types of farming were introduced and consequently most of the successes have been registered in these localities. In the Brindisi area they were dependent on subterranean water solely. The holdings created were rather small ones; 5,680 ha were distributed as *quote* amongst 2,741 families, 2·08 ha apiece; and 7,831 ha were assigned as *poderi* to 3,112 families; 2·53 ha each. In some of the adjacent communes the average area of both *quote* and *poderi* fell below 1·5 ha. But these properties were very close to the city of Brindisi and to the century-old areas of intensive tree cropping. The density of population in the surrounding districts is 209 km, accessibility is good, so that additional part-time employment was available in some measure, especially following the expansion of industry and building activity around the city. Certainly some of the larger irrigated holdings are now very productive, but the size of the family can be a factor reducing per capita income unless non-agrarian sources are tapped. One holding of 8 ha visited was worked jointly by a family numbering thirteen persons, including married sons, their wives and offspring, some of whom worked in the towns. The chef, a *braccianti* originally, had been able to organize an enormous input of effort, resulting in additions to the farm buildings and the establishment of a small herd of cattle, at the time of the visit suffering from brucellosis. The family was privately marketing its vegetables and milk. They had already added to the original size of the holding, but considered the acquisition of more land to be their greatest need in the coming decade. The chef of another 8 ha holding, supporting a conjugal family of only five, was busily investing in steel piping to extend the area under irrigation. His comments on the co-operative movement instigated by the *Ente* and then left to its own human resources were pretty scathing. Both chefs were able to indicate adjacent *poderi* which had been abandoned, underlining the influence of the individual upon progress. Many of the unirrigated *quote* had either been abandoned, or their farming had undergone no intensification. The sample *podere* for this area (Table 4.7) returned one of the highest gross and net returns per hectare for the whole reform district; also one of the highest net returns per unit of labour. This figure, however, is always partially influenced by the size of the labour force, and it is of more significance as an indicator of family income level, rather than the productivity of the cropping system which the other two returns reflect; as well as management, of course.

Over the rest of the Salentine Peninsula artesian water supplies were not always available, and therefore the *Ente* had to introduce a less intensive tree crop system, similar to the dominant one, but in localities where the rule had been extensive cereal growing and rough grazing. The pressure of population, and the impossibility of sustaining a family sized holding with such a system of cultivation meant that the proportion of *quote* was high, and the size of the *poderi* themselves was small. In all of the major areas of expropriation, Nardo (8,540 ha), Leece (4,870 ha), Otranto (2,600 ha), Melendungo (1,240 ha) and Aventrana (1,340 ha), the proportion receiving *quote* exceeded 40 per cent, whilst the *poderi* ranged from two to four hectares in size. Some of the poorest returns in the whole sample zone were derived from this area, where the only abandoned farm caught in the survey was also located.

In the Tavoliere and the Basilicata the settlements associated with

TABLE 4.7 *Economic returns for 10 of the 61 sample reform poderi, 1964–5*

Farm no.	Locality	Region	Cropping system	Farm size	Family size	S.L.U. /ha	S.L.U. /farm	Gross return /ha ('000s lire)	Net return /S.L.U. ('000s lire)
3	Brindisi	Salentine Peninsula	Intensive cash-crops, trees, wheat and livestock	5·08	5	0·68	3·5	546	658
6	Scanzano	Metaponto	Intensive cash-crops, trees, wheat and livestock	5·20	2	0·23	1·2	131	265
7	Scanzano	Metaponto	Intensive cash-crops, trees, wheat and livestock	4·90	5	0·51	2·5	325	506
61	Ginosa Marina	Metaponto	Olives and livestock	4·20	4	0·38	1·6	684	1,057
32	Lecce	Salentine Peninsula	Cereals, livestock with trees	8·97	7	0·26	2·4	81	164
16	Borgo Liberta	Tavoliere	Cereals, livestock with trees	8·70	5	0·40	3·5	123	160
27	Lucera	Tavoliere	Cereals, livestock with trees	6·8	3	0·38	2·6	329	666
37	Tacione	Fossa Premurgia	Cereals, livestock with trees	10·2	8	0·44	4·5	59	67
43	Gaudiano	Fossa Premurgia	Cereals, livestock with trees	7·1	5	0·28	2·0	137	297
57	Andria	Murge	Cereals and grazing	16·8	3	0·11	1·9	35	203

Note: This table displays the widely differing circumstances to be found between individual farms in terms of their productivity, labour force and family size. Table 4.8 deals with averages alone.

Source: Ente di Sviluppo, Bari.

barrage irrigation, unlike those near Brindisi, were established in what were, by Italian standards, sparsely populated zones; where there was little prospect of extra agricultural activity, except temporarily in the construction works associated with the programme or in the agricultural processing industries development by the *Ente di Riforma*. Consequently holdings had to be self-sufficient. In the commune of Montalbano Ionico around the new town of Policoro, 10,342 ha were distributed to 1,685 families (on average 6·1 ha each), and 251 families received *quote* of 4·1 ha. The basic foodstuffs of the family were provided by cereals, vines, olive trees, and livestock; cash earnings were to come from fruit trees, vegetables, sugar beet and tobacco, with some degree of specialization according to the immediate soil conditions. There is little doubt that in this locality the scheme has been, relatively speaking, quite successful. The proportion of departing assignees is probably the lowest of all. The cropping is developing along the prescribed lines, lucerne is being used as fodder and a renovating crop, the assignees can afford to utilize fertilizer, and the specialized crops and milk are being produced and marketed. Living standards are rising perhaps at a rather quicker rate than the re-investment in productive means.* Of the 63 *poderi* noted in the Scanzano district while thirty-one possessed television sets, only eleven had made additions to the farm buildings. Three *poderi* had acquired old cars, six had motorbikes, and bicycles were common. One family had established a local shop, and another man was working as a blacksmith, both ventures in their own small way indicative of an increase in the circulation of money, and of the initiative to find additional employment. Nevertheless the overall impression of the land reform in the Metaponto was that the productive resources of the farms were still not fully developed, an impression supported by the returns in the farm sample. In their original publications the *Ente* had forecast a gross return per hectare of 350,000 lire, as representative of the level of productivity which was sought.[17] In 1964–5 three of the farms in this area included in the sample had exceeded the figure, and another had approached it; but seven others were still well below the target. The range within the group was quite considerable, but this is a common characteristic of peasant farms, and it is influenced by a variety of factors. In this case, however, it is important to remember that although some

* Moschini made a similar observation, supported by figures, in his survey of the Maremma.[15] Official figures show that by 1960, one-third of the total investment made by the assignees on their own behalf consisted of durable and semi-durable household goods. In Apulia-Lucania, the percentage was higher, 52; in the Maremma it was only 24.[16]

[15] Moschini (1958): 294–388.

[16] Ministero dell' Agricoltura e della Foreste (no date): Tables 11–16.

[17] Ente Puglia-Lucania (1959): 34.

seventeen years have elapsed since the promulgation of the reform law, the irrigation schemes in the Metaponto have functioned only in the '60s. Some of the assignees will have reached retirement age before the settlements reach a period of maturity.

The reform settlements associated with the irrigation schemes of the Ofanto and Fonterosa in the Tavoliere had, like the ones in the Metaponto, an air of permanency about them, though the occasional abandoned homestead was observable. The development of the Ofanto cropping patterns was particularly impressive, for it should not be forgotten that the majority of assignees were accustomed only to monocultural practices, being by origin largely unskilled manual labourers. It is quite an achievement both there and in the Metaponto for the chefs to handle successfully the complex combination of livestock with vines and olives and cereals, together with the production of cabbage, lettuce, tomatoes, onions and fruit. The total area affected by irrigation in Apulia-Lucania far exceeds that incorporated in the land reform schemes; and within the context of the land reform scheme itself the importance of the irrigated areas is only secondary. Less than a fifth of the expropriated area has benefited from the irrigation schemes. Most of the land reform settlements have had to survive under far less favourable environmental circumstances. Over the major part of the Tavoliere, from Lake Lesina to the Ofanto; south from the Ofanto through the Fossa Premurgia to the far margins of the Metaponto cereals remain the basic crop of the reform farms, with wine and table grapes, forage crops and livestock on a modest scale, and a small recourse to vegetables to eke out a living. Given the environmental circumstances there was no alternative: a shortage of ground water, minimal rainfall in the spring and summer, spring temperatures as high as anywhere else in Italy, and summer temperatures surpassed nowhere else. Nevertheless the size of the *poderi* was no greater than those in the irrigated areas. The cropping programme was an inadequate insurance against the risks of crop failure and low yields, which only the economies of scale could combat. In the commune of Torremaggiore the *poderi* averaged 6·5 ha, in Orto Nova 4·5 ha, in Stornara 4·0 ha, and a fifth to a third of the assignees received *quote* only. In the communes of Stornarella (711 ha) and Ascoli Satriano (5,877 ha) – the numbers in brackets are the areas expropriated – the *poderi* averaged 7·0 ha; and as in Candela (1,335 ha), Bicarri (343 ha), Castelluccio (985 ha) and Lucera (2,900 ha), the proportion of assignees receiving *quote* was either small or negligible. But in Borino (225 ha) and Rochetta San Antonio (453) the proportion of *quote* reached 25 per cent and 30 per cent though the environmental circumstances were characteristically severe.

In the Basilicata the *poderi* averaged 8·0 ha; in the commune of Irsina here over 3,000 ha were expropriated, 7·0 ha; in Matera, and in Stigliano, ·0 ha. But spring drought hits this area eight years out of ten, Bernalda, Iontalbano Ionico, Cirigliano, and Matera being the worst hit comunes; Salandra and Grotto are a little less affected. Miglionico suffers o, but is worst hit by fog and spring frost. And the 'Stretta' – a damaggly early ripening of the wheat, caused by the hot winds blowing in om Africa – regularly destroys a third to one-quarter of the harvest ound the districts of Matera, Tricarico, Bernaldo and Policoro.[18] In the ommunes mentioned, approximately 10,000 ha were expropriated and nlike the 13,000 ha of Montalbano Ionico they will never receive the enefits of irrigation.

As one travels through these unirrigated districts it becomes apparent at the reform has been far less successful than in the irrigated areas. much higher percentage of the homesteads have been abandoned, and the atches of intensive cultivation associated with them are left unattended. he plough land, however, is still cultivated, by the original assignee ho has gone back to his original residence, or by a neighbour. The first ase constitutes a failure, because the assignee has reverted to his old onocultural practices. The second case is not much better, except with holding twice the original size, the economics of peasant monocultural rming are somewhat sounder. On the majority of farms the assignees ave remained, but their farming is largely unmechanized, their cropping ill leans heavily upon cereal production. Additions to farm buildings e rare. The population is composed of chefs, mostly over 40 years of age, ith a large proportion of young and old family dependants, the young ble-bodied men having departed in large numbers. The prime function f the farms appears to be the historic residual function of the small easant holding. The assignees now have a greater degree of personal nd economic security than when they were *braccianti*. It is difficult to ssess by how much their standard of living has improved since the period f colonization. Furnishings are still sparse, and clothes rarely new, but ere and there cars and television have made an appearance. Generally andards are low, but low in comparison with the steadily improving andards of the '60s, not those of the early '50s. The community centres how no sign of improvement, and in some cases they have deteriorated. onditions do vary from one settlement to another, and within settlements ere is little doubt that the age old process of differentiation is taking place ithin the small peasant class, as the data from the sample survey bears ut.

The community centre at Borgo Liberta had fallen into a remarkable tate of disrepair (1966,) grass was protruding through the macadam which

[18] Milone (1955): 869–72.

had been quite new seven years previously. Almost a quarter of the home steads noted had been abandoned and their plots of vines and fruit tree were no longer cultivated, but on the *poderi* still occupied they wer in production and well tended. Located in the middle of the Tavoliere thi settlement can do little more than grow cereals. Some of the lowest gros yields per hectare were returned from this district, but the size of th labour force, and family, exerted a big influence upon the returns per uni of labour and per capita (Table 4.7). Conditions at Centrogallo, where th environment is the same as Borgo Liberta seemed better. Admittedly fou of the twelve houses were abandoned but the standard of cultivation c the intensive crop was very good, and five of the occupied houses possesse television. One chef at least was able to afford toys for his children. Wher the *poderi* had been able to imitate the intensive vine growing practice around San Severo the productivity of the land was double that wher cereals prevailed. One of the most remarkable failures was at Ferradina adjacent to the new methane plant, where the land of fourteen *poder* irrigated by artesian supplies had gone out of production; where, on th majority of farms which had remained in production, the fruit trees ha been allowed to wither and the patches of intensive crops had bee neglected. Some of the farms had become part-time holdings; one or tw were offering lodgings for workers on the industrial site. The genera effect of industrialization had been pernicious in what had been a ver promising venture. Whereas isolation appeared to be helping the main tenance of settlements near Grassano, isolation and the shortage of wate had defeated many assignees in the bare semi-arid country of the Foss Premurgia, near Spinazzola and Poggiorsini, where 22 of the 47 *poder* observed had been abandoned; and in parts of the Murge, cereals an extensive livestock farming have not proved to be a very successfu solution to the needs of peasant farming. *The Ente di Riforma* official estimate that the proportion of abandoned homes varies from 5 to 29 pe cent within Apulia-Lucania. It is said to be lowest in the irrigate areas, but in the non-irrigated areas 35 per cent of the 351 homestead observed had been abandoned. In building expenditure alone this repre sents a loss of approximately two million lire per house.* Nothing ca disguise the wastage of resources and the partial failure of the reform i this area.

A quite considerable area of land, over 4,000 ha, was acquired by th reform office in the mountainous zone between Potenza and the Mont Vulture, most of it lying at an altitude of between 600 and 900 metre

* Cost for all types of houses were provided by the *Ente* publication *Case Colon iche*, 1958; the cheapest type cost 1·47 million lire, the dearest 2·84. The ones observed were in the slightly more than 2 million class.

ove sea level. Significantly the hunting castle of Frederick the Second Castel Lagopesole was central to the area. The clearing of the forest and e establishment of low yielding cereal cultivation had continued into the er part of the last century, leading to the erection by share-croppers of serable stone hovels (*casali*) as the limits of cultivation put them too far yond the pale of their native villages to permit the diurnal movement tween field and residence. The *Ente* officials recognized that the only onomically and agronomically sound form of land utilization for the vironment was one based on fairly large holdings with livestock farming edominating. The practicality of the system had been demonstrated the president of the local *consorzio* for land transformation on the tskirts of Potenza, who in 1937 had commenced the renovation of his tate (280 ha) worked by tenants and *mezzadri*. By deep ploughing, the e of fertilizers, the introduction of forage plants to the rotation; by proving the agricultural contracts of his tenants, making them all *zzadri*, he had raised the grain yields 25 per cent above the local aver-es, and had more than trebled the livestock carrying capacity. Even then e improved yield was only 11·58 quintals per hectare – though, indicating e potentialities awaiting release, yields of 20 quintals per hectare had en obtained. But fundamental to the economic success of the whole terprise was the fact that the average size of holding had been increased reducing the number of families farming the land, something which e reform agencies could never do.[19]

The density of population per square kilometre in that part of the ovince of Potenza falling within the jurisdiction of the reform agencies eraged 80. The variations around the mean were very great, and alone e sufficient to make one suspect that the whole human geography of the gion is far less simple than one might suppose. In the centre of the Vul-re vine growing district the density reached 270 km^2, something over 1 erson to the acre. In other communes containing poor cereal land, rough sture, and forest, the densities were only half the average: Atella 43 km^2, orenza and Pietragella, 50 km^2. But other equally impoverished moun-in communes returned densities twice as great: Ruoti 91 km^2, Avigliano 3 km^2, Oppido Lucania 99 km^2 (virtually 1 person per hectare), and San ele – incredibly – 170 km^2. Faced with such densities the reform agencies ere impotent.

In some communes expropriation has been negligible or non-existent. he vine-growing areas were excluded from the operation of the law ecause of their intensive land use. Others were small property communes. he main expropriations were limited to the communes of Avigliano ,103 ha), Bella (2,014 ha) and Melfi (3,106 ha), much of the land in this

[19] Cassa Mezzogiorno (1955): 149–51.

case lying at a somewhat lower altitude near the course of the Ofant
Under such conditions of population pressure the *quote* were numero
and the size of *poderi* small: five, seven, and in Melfi three hectare
impossibly small for any satisfactory mixed livestock economy to
practised. The assignees, nevertheless, appear to have held on to the lan
though not always for the same reasons; and in general the colonizatio
schemes of the *Ente* have retarded the decline of population in tho
communes affected by the reform. Drought is not such a problem in the
elevated parts, though it is not absent. The shorter growing season, t
steepness of the land, and the scarcity of level ploughable country, redu
yields and make farming a back-breaking business. It is still the practi
to break the clods of earth with a hoe after ploughing, usually women
work. Security of tenure has been a counter weight to these disadvan
ages and has encouraged the assignees to intensify their cropping pattern
whilst the lack of alternative employment opportunities combined wit
isolation has forced the assignees to concentrate on farming. In mo
accessible districts part-time farming has evolved producing a marke
feminization of the agricultural labour force.

For a composite picture of the reform farms in Apulia-Lucania an anal
sis of the 1964/5 returns for the sixty sample farms is useful, provided it
remembered that the sample includes *poderi* only; the *quote* are ignore
(Table 4.8). The majority of farms, according to area, fell into the sma

TABLE 4.8 *Sample of reform farms by cropping zone, 1964–5*

Zone	*Farm size ha*	*Family size no.*	*S.L.U. Ha*	*S.L.U. farm*	*Gross return ha*	*Net return S.L.U.*
					'000s lire	
Irrigation:						
Metaponto and Brindisi	5·8	4·6	0·46	2·7	296	460
Tree crops and cereals:						
Foggia, San Severo	7·9	4·5	0·41	3·2	222	422
Cereals:						
Tavoliere	7·9	3·5	0·31	2·4	192	407
Fossa Premurgia	7·25	5·8	0·35	2·6	158	270
Mountains:						
Potenza	5·5	4·8	0·26	2·1	181	384
Salentine Peninsula:						
Lecce-Nardo	8·6	4·8	0·30	1·6	113	146

peasant class of 5–10 ha; but a third of them had to provide employme
for an excessive amount of labour, three or more standard labour unit
Only 46 per cent of them with between 1·5 and 2·5 S.L.U., approache
the ideal labour force for the family farm. Half the farms had attained

oss saleable production per hectare equivalent to the average for all the form zones, and approaching the national average, approximately £100 r ha. The other half exceeded this level, but only 13 per cent had tained the productivity characteristic of the more developed zones of ge-scale bonification. The effect of family size – 46 per cent had five or ore persons in the family – was to depress the per capita net income vel, so that in 80 per cent of the cases per capita income did not exceed 200 per annum. Classified geographically the influence of cropping ttern and environment was very apparent. The irrigated zones carried e greatest density of labour per hectare and returned the highest gross eld per unit of land and the highest net return per unit of labour. All her systems of farming represented a falling away from these standards. ut these geographical regularities ought never to hide the sociological stinctions; for there is little relation between the productivity of the soil d the size of family which has to be maintained. Within this new class small peasants there are quite considerable differences in living standards amongst families solely dependent upon farming for a livelihood; inevitable consequence of the necessity of having to fit the family to e farm, rather than the farm to the family.

In the mid '60s, now that the period of colonization is completed, the form areas are receiving less and less specific attention; their requirements are being integrated with the general programmes for agrarian and onomic development. The responsible office is no longer an *Ente di forma*, but an *Ente di Sviluppo* – an office for development. Emphasis is ing placed upon co-operation in working the land, in processing and arketing the produce. Co-operation in mechanization is limited by the adequate capital funds of the assignees themselves. Each local co-erative possesses an average of two tractors only. To provide the ser-cing of the machines which the local co-operatives cannot properly dertake themselves and to supplement the machine park a consortium s been formed with some eighty tractors of different sorts and other ricultural machinery. A high proportion of the machines are aged and e activities of the plant are dispersed over a very considerable area, from e Ionic coast to the region of the Ofanto, and amongst some forty-five parate local reform co-operatives. Consequently mules still provide most draught power throughout the reform areas. Greater strides have been ade with the promotion of processing plants, for wine, olive oil, milk, eese, spaghetti and pasta, to which non-reform farms may belong. As ble 4.9 indicates almost two-thirds of the assignees who received *poderi* e members – the proportion would be lower if those acquiring *quote* re included – but the degree of membership varies between one region d the next; as does the amount of capital per assignee. These industrial concerns are not burdened with the same problems as the general c operatives established in the reform settlements, where indiscipli recrimination, ignorance, shortage of money and diffusion of aims ha limited effectiveness. They benefit from considerable state aid, and bei market oriented and directed by a commercial and industrial cadre, th

TABLE 4.9 *Processing co-operatives Apulia-Lucania, 1964*

	Members				'ooos lire	
Province	*No.*	*Assignees*	*% of assignees receiving poderi*	*Non-Assignees*	*Capital*	*Capital/Assigne*
Bari	19	1,843	57	326	19,671	9·1
Brindisi	7	2,049	53	194	9,303	4·1
Foggia	49	6,584	88	498	77,827	11·0
Lecce	15	1,493	36	365	8,254	4·4
Taranto	11	1,493	67	93	12,030	7·6
Matera	33	3,981	77	111	66,444	16·2
Potenza	14	1,711	38	145	19,678	10·6
Campobasso	3	505	92	40	6,020	11·0
Total	151	19,659	63	1,772	219,229	10·2

stand a good chance of succeeding. Already the wine and cereal produ are widely marketed throughout Italy. Attractive cartons of reform wi are displayed in the A.G.I.P. motels, for instance; and in Apulia the *E* has established one of the rare lines of self-service stores to bring t products of the reform farms before the general public; and they do it we

The land reform in other regions

It is a great loss that so little detailed information is available on the refo in other regions, and what is available so often deals with the initial peri of colonization rather than the period of consolidation and success failure. For the Maremma there is Moschini's valuable investigation the socio-economic origins of the assignees and their attitudes to the r form and their budgets, but like the material on Calabria it deals with t situation of the '50s, as does Barbero's more general but informati economic survey.[20] What glimpses one can obtain of the execution of t reform in Sicily, where the privilege of regional autonomy appears have been used like a cloak to smother information, give rise to lit satisfaction. The evidence, it is true, is far from complete, a proper surv is lacking; but little has been brought forth to contradict what has be published. For English language readers the invaluable, but restricte

[20] Seronde (1960); Barbero (1961) and Rossi-Doria (1958): 177–234.

udies by Dr Loschiavo on Corlone and A. Ferretti on Capparinni are ailable in Danilo Dolci's *Waste*. In Sicily the expropriated land is attered from one end of the island to the other, predominantly through- ıt the zone of *latifondo contadino*, but in a too diverse range of ambients r these limited examples to be accepted as a basis for generalization. .me Rochefort's appreciation of the situation (and she knows the island thoroughly as any outsider), does nothing to disperse the doubts or :er radically the picture. For her the reform agency itself was an instru- ent to cripple the reform in thousands of ways.[21] Competent and devoted ronomists were a minority amongst a bureaucracy that increased in ımber with every election and professionally were indifferent, even ›stile, to the programme. Lavish in their expenditure upon the admini- :ative requirements – the main office building of E.R.A.S.* cost £480,000, e contract being let without calling for tenders – they were unsympathetic .d tyrannical towards the peasantry in their care. Inevitably hostile to e reform were the losers, the privileged titled classes, the large landowners d the *gabelloti*† who were able to subvert the law in numerous ways, pecially by recouping some of the expropriated land or obtaining a ıy on its distribution through some legal device or with a promise to troduce modern farming methods. By the end of 1958 the assignment of ,000 hectares of land had been delayed by these methods. Mme Roche- rt quotes three cases of the expropriated area being reduced by these eans from 3,679 ha to 412 ha, in the first case; from 3,557 ha to 1,654 ha the second, and from 2,000 ha to 219 ha in the third. In a sense these actices were facilitated by the failure and often the inability of the assign- s to occupy the land because of its distance from their point of origin, the sence of housing, drinking water, and electricity, and on occasions a easure of security. The environment itself imposed enormous difficulties on the execution of the reform. The interior of Sicily, more than any her part of the Mezzogiorno, fitted Rossi-Doria's description of the zone *latifondo contadino* – a concentration camp for the production of cereals. ne very shape of Sicily quarantines the interior expanse of arid hills and ountains against change. Nothing penetrates this fastness – this sea of ountains – the virus of development cannot take hold amidst such :rility. The incidence of expropriation displayed the usual capricious ıalities. The demand for land far exceeded the supply. The allotments :re small, in every province averaging little more than 4 ha. It was lculated that only one-third of the assignees received units of a size equate to support family farming.

* Ente per la Riforma Agraria in Sicilia.
† Bailiffs of the large estates often connected with the Mafia.
[21] Rochefort (1961): 109–17.

Assessment

The Italian land reform was the victim of its own timing. All previ agrarian reforms in Europe – whether they were called land reforms not – from the time of the French Revolution through to the inter reforms in Eastern Europe – had been inaugurated in overwhelmin agricultural states and their period had never coincided with a phase rapid and sustained industrialization. They were, very much, nineteen century phenonema in conception, outlook and intention. Opposed to monopolization of economic power by the landed classes these refor sought to rend the fabric of a tradition-fast society by redistributing means of production amongst a greater number of its members. Ar ments were brought forward, and they were sound ones, in support of economic and productive benefits that would arise with widespread own ship. But the reforms did not, and could not, change the essenti residual function of the peasant holding; neither did they alter the lab commitment. Their concern was the promotion of the peasant product system and this marked them as fundamentally conservative measures contrast to the radical collectivization of the Russian peasantry. In circumstances they could be little else, for until very recently an econo with less than 30 per cent of its labour force in agriculture has been c ceivable only under a set of highly restrictive conditions. When the p portion engaged in agriculture has exceeded this amount the interests social justice have ruled in favour of family farming. In 1951, 35·5 per c of the Italian active labour force was still engaged in agriculture, fish and forestry even in the most northern industrialized zones. The p portion for the whole country was 42 per cent and for the Mezzogiorno per cent; the highest provincial figure was 73 per cent, for the Basilic After a decade of remarkable industrial growth the proportion in agric ture for the whole country was still high – 29 per cent; and for the Mez giorno higher.

The Italian land reform carried all the marks of a nineteenth-cent reform: the removal of the injustices of a hidebound, degenerate, lan society; the creation of the maximum amount of employment; an incre in the consumption levels of the beneficiaries; investment in land rat than men, irrespective of the marginal character of much of the land; recognition of the residual function as the primary function of the ne established holdings. True, the lessons of the past reforms – the criti importance of credit facilities, co-operatives, post reform extension wor were taken to heart. Admittedly the fruits of the very latest in technol and science were available and made use of. And this made it an all better reform. But its timing, the industrial development of the Nor the demands of the French and German labour markets, the huge migration from the South, so radically altered the circumstances and the needs of the South, that the premises upon which the reform was founded were hardly relevant by the time it had been completed. For every individual who found in the land reform some relief from his economic and social

TABLE 4.10 *Proportion of active population engaged in agriculture, 1951–61*

Region	*1951*	*1961*
Italy	42·2	29·0
Mezzogiorno	55·3	43·2
Campania	46·4	35·9
Abruzzi and Molise	64·7	47·7
Apulia	58·2	50·3
Basilicata	73·1	57·3
Calabria	63·4	46·1
Sicily	51·3	41·0
Sardinia	51·0	37·7

Source: *SVIMEZ*

distress, three others, for whom very little preparation or expenditure had been made, found a solution to their problems in a massive migration to the north and beyond. Whereas those who remained, found themselves inadequately prepared for the life of a modernized peasantry in an industrialized society.

In 1960 I wrote: 'The severest problem which awaits the new settlements is the reappearance very shortly of agricultural overpopulation. For the *poderi* and the *quote* are small or minute, whilst the families are large and the adolescents are without any training to fit them for an urban and industrial existence.'[22] In Calabria Mme. Seronde observed that the farms originally created to feed five or six persons were often having to support eight or ten.[23] For Corleone, Loschiavo records a 27 per cent increase in the population of the reform area during the nine-year period 1950–9. Of the total population 53 per cent were under 18 years of age.[24] Over-population exists – the data for the sample of farms in Apulia-Lucania provides the evidence, but its character is not quite as simple as one imagined it would be in the '50s. Then it was assumed that the large number of young dependants would be forced to find employment on the family holding for want of alternative opportunities. It now seems that many of the young males when they have come of age have found extra-

[22] Franklin (1961): 347. [23] Seronde (1960): 133.
[24] Dolci, '*Spreco*' (1960): 223.

agricultural work or they have migrated, temporarily or permanently. This movement is leading to an increase of the dependant-worker ratio, as the very young, the women and the aged are left behind; or at best it is leading to no improvement in the ratio. The consequence is a degree of overpopulation associated with the genealogical structure of the family rather than with the character of the labour force. However the rise of earnings in the urban areas and amongst the more secure of the hired agricultural labour force, as in many other peasant regions, is making the returns to labour on small family holdings appear to be exceedingly low. In this respect overpopulation is to be seen as a function of technological and economic change rather than as a purely demographic factor.

Economically the reform has been a success. Considering what has been invested this constitutes a fulfilment rather than an achievement. The principal results are set out in Table 4.11. They indicate a considerable

TABLE 4.11 *Gross saleable production in reform zones*

	Milliard lire – current						
Ente	*1956*	*1957*	*1958*	*1959*	*1960*	*1961*	*1962*
Delta Padano	8·2	7·4	9·1	8·9	8·2	9·5	10·5
Maremma	13·5	12·7	15·8	16·1	15·7	17·7	22·4
Fucino	4·7	4·7	5·9	5·6	6·0	6·3	7·4
Campania (ONC)	3·4	4·2	4·2	4·5	5·1	5·0	7·1
Apulia-Lucania – Molise	11·3	14·3	15·7	19·8	16·9	23·7	28·5
Calabria	6·5	7·1	7·7	7·3	7·9	9·8	11·7
Sardinia-Flumendosa	0·17	0·14	0·15	0·17	0·21	0·25	0·3
Sardinia (E.T.F.A.S.)	1·4	2·7	3·8	4·0	4·3	4·4	5·0

increase in the gross saleable production over recent years and display th trend towards more intensive farming systems. For Sicily no returns ar made available – a fact that speaks volumes.

To establish the costs of the reform is not easy. Some of the expenditur was made in the North. Some of the charges for general works, irrigatio and roads, for example, in which the *Enti* had only a share are hard t apportion. By September 1962 a total of 620 milliard lire appears to hav been spent, with a further 17.75 milliard budgeted for the following yea Difficult though it is to be exact, there can be no doubt concerning th high cost of the venture, the considerable investment per hectare, pe family, per job – the statistical summary of the environmental imperative the sociological preferences, the political leanings out of which the refor was created.

To put the land reform into some perspective is not to argue that should have been conducted otherwise, that it should have never taken place, that it has been a flop. The trouble with land reforms is that, appealing to every proper and humanistic sensibility in man, they have to be implemented in a specific society, at a specific time, and in specific places. In the antinomy between their universalistic appeal and specific execution lies the cause of disillusionment, so often the principal legacy for the liberal minded observer. But in human terms – the day to day terms that one had to face up to in the tired eyes, the drawn faces, the peneplain of resignation to which unemployment had eroded the human spirit – the land reform brought relief and hope to the miserable and downtrodden. As a symbol it had importance, as the majority of its critics recognized. The interests that composed the Italian state could not in the early '50s offer any major relief to the poverty that was the lot of its citizens. No state can. What relief it did offer was hedged about with all sorts of limitations imposed by vested and particular interests, as will always be the case. But relief was offered. The symbol of a promise of better things to come was displayed, and it was accepted that the lot of the peasantry ought to be and could be improved. Another rent was made in the wall of indifference and obscurantism that tries to hide the facts concerning the effectiveness of collective action, and the beneficial effects and power of modern technologies when applied to the problems of society.

If there is one general lesson to be learnt from the Italian land reform it is related to the question of the context within which any particular agrarian programme is cast. The land reform was only one of the more recent attempts to develop the agrarian economy of the South. Travelling through the Tavoliere one sees the carcase of an earlier venture right alongside the embryo of another. Beside abandoned patches of intensive cropland established by the *Ente* there are private schemes under way with small tenant holders repeating the very same practices. Certain vantage points overlook abandoned homesteads of the interwar O.N.C. settlements as well as the occupied reform farms. Two or three kilometres from an earlier run-down scheme of private bonification one comes across a spanking new one in the process of establishment. In the Bradano valley too, over-capitalized and under-utilized large private *aziende* border the same highway as partially abandoned reform settlements. The obvious conclusion is that it is easier to initiate than maintain agricultural development schemes; and enough evidence could be collected from around the world to raise this to something of a maxim. What is less immediately obvious, and helps to explain the phenomenon, is the different contexts, economic, political and technological, to which these schemes have to conform during the course of their history. Each stage of development in the Tavoliere – in the whole of the Mezzogiorno – has followed the same pattern: the introduction of intensive tree and field crops, the fuller exploitation of water resources, the dispersion of settlement and the improvement of roading and other services. At times private initiative has prevailed, at others state schemes have been dominant. When state schemes have been in operation, continuity of programme and design have been favoured by a certain continuity of personnel; one reason why the reform settlements look like mini-versions of the O.N.C. settlements. But at one period the assumptions underlying the economic and demographic perspectives of the scheme have been those of an autarkic, lebensraum-minded, Fascist regime; at another, those of the reformist, new deal, anti-cyclical mentality of the immediate post-war era, and now the neo-capitalist, technological and Common Market outlook of the sixties. The general context of which the schemes have been part has evolved at a far more rapid pace than is possible for the schemes themselves. The inertia which characterises the agrarian programmes is not surprising when looked at in this respect; neither is the apparent failure to satisfy needs and conditions which in fact were not in existence at the time the programme was first formulated. Until social and economic engineering has reached an unheard of level of sophistication, agrarian programmes in the dynamic context of the modern world appear destined to finish serving ends for which they were never designed.

The next fifteen years, 1965–80

The Cassa's revised agrarian programme is the most recent attempt to modify agrarian development to fit the needs of changing circumstance. Thirty-eight per cent of the total planned investment is to be directed through the *Comprensori di Bonifica* to increase production in the *zona nuova bonifica e irrigazione*.

As an institution the *Comprensoria di Bonifica* is much closer to the agricultural traditions of the South than the *Enti di Riforma*. With successive legislative measures the Italian State since 1924 has committed itself to the financial support of private individuals and corporations in their efforts to increase the productivity of farming, principally in the lower coastal regions of the country. The State has been responsible for a large part of the land transformation costs, to which the members of the *consorzi* have contributed. They have been charged with financing the establishment of the improved farming methods, by means of credits raised with banks and other lending agencies, together with a contribution from the State for this purpose. As an arrangement this suited admirably the objectives and methods of the Cassa. Consequently the post-war period has witnessed a surge forward in the area of land undergoing transformation and in the determination to achieve results, despite

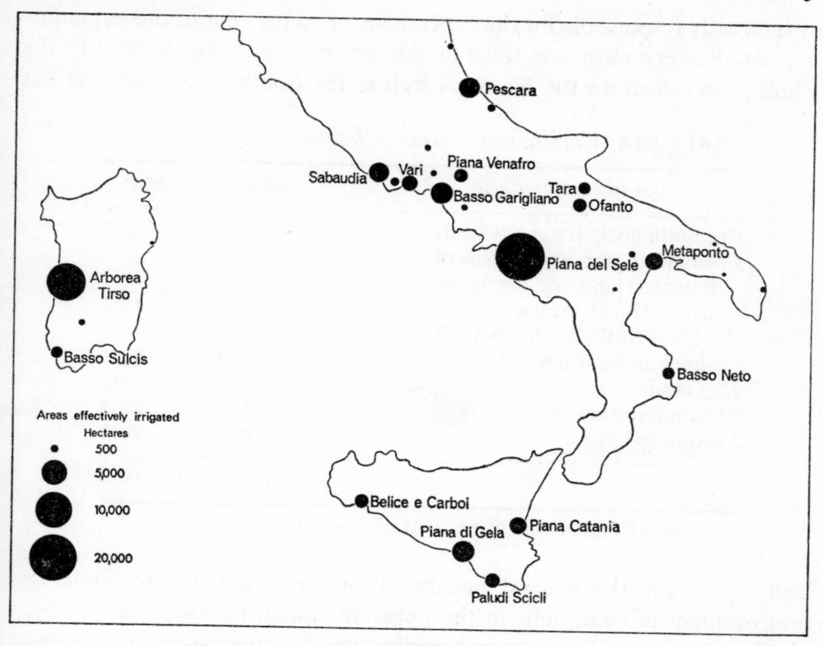

Fig. 4.5. Major irrigation comprensoria, 1961 (Cassa per il Mezzogiorno Dodici anni Vol. 2)

the knowledge that as a system of agricultural development and as a form of investing public monies, bonification has one great weakness, as its principal advocate and legislator, Serpieri, recognized from the earliest days:[25] it is difficult to ensure that the members of the *comprensoria* carry out their obligations once the work of the State is completed, especially when sanctions against backsliders are difficult to enforce. By 1929 2·0 million hectares of land in the Mezzogiorno were being treated under the legislation for bonification. At the end of the Second World War the area had doubled. Presently almost the whole Mezzogiorno is incorporated in some form of *comprensori*.

The political and class character of the programme for the South is apparent in the works of the Cassa as in those of the *Enti di Riforma*. Quite massive support has been offered to the land-owning classes since the war, and the effect of the new plan is to strengthen this already predominant trend. During the first fifteen years 15,507 milliard lire were invested in the Mezzogiorno, 18 per cent of it – 2,808 milliard lire – going to agriculture. Jointly the Cassa and the Ministry of Agriculture have been directly

[25] Bandini (1957): 134.

or indirectly responsible for the supervision of 72 per cent of this expendit-ure. At the very most one-third of this amount has been devoted to the whole land reform in the North as well as the South; the remainder has

TABLE 4.12 *Varieties of terrain affected*

Type of comprensoria	*'000s ha*	*area %*
Predominantly irrigated lands	322	3·2
Containing important areas of irrigated land and dry lands worth transforming	1,825	18·2
Predominantly dry lands with small areas of irrigation	1,313	13·1
Dry lands	1,516	15·1
Mountainous lands	2,140	21·3
Mountain basins	2,929	29·1
	10,045	100·0

Source: Comitato dei Ministri Mezzogiorno (1965).

been spent for the general benefit of Southern agriculture, upon the improvement of conditions in the upper mountain basins, or more spec-ifically upon irrigation works and bonification. It is impossible to apportion the expenditure in any strict fashion, but Tables 4.12, 4.13 and 4.14 provide what data is available in the most explicit form.

It was the experience with bonification on the right bank of the Sele that most influenced the thinking of the Cassa officials and rightly, for it provided a model widely suited to transformation schemes associated

TABLE 4.13 *Direct and indirect investment in the South, 1950–65*

Agency	*Milliard lire*		*Purpose*			
Responsibility of the Cassa	Direct	783	Irrigation	260		
	Indirect	530	Hydrology	114		
Ministry of Agri-culture	Direct	422	Bonification	954		
	Indirect	278	Mountains	238		
			Electrification	74		
			Sub-total	1,640	of which Land Reform	*c.* 361
			Land Reform	259		259
			Other	114		
Total		2,013		2,013		620*

* Includes Reform expenditure in the North.

ith river valleys and the construction of barrages, which incorporated onsiderable areas of unirrigated land. Before its conversion to more roductive uses the Sele plain, like so many of the coastal areas of the Iezzogiorno, was a desert of rough pasture, malarial at one time – a range or buffalo and cattle, extensively cultivated for cereals, the air of desola- on increased by the presence of those most moving ruins at Paestum.

ABLE 4.14 *Geographic distribution of global expenditure (A) and irrigation expenditure (B) and total agricultural output (C): Percentages*

Province	*A*	*B*	*C*	*Province*	*A*	*B*	*C*
azio	6·7	2·2	13	Basilicata	13·4	15·0	3
bruzzi Molise	12·4	4·1	9	Calabria	10·8	5·0	8
Campania	14·1	10·9	19	Sicily	12·8	18·7	21
pulia	16·1	15·5	20	Sardinia	13·6	28·5	7
				Mezzogiorno	100·0	100·0	100

ABLE 4.15 *Regional and commodity character of agricultural output, 1965. Percentages of gross saleable production*

Province	*Total output mill. lire*	*Total*	*Cereals*	*Vine*	*Olive*	*Fruit*	*Vegetables*	*Livestock*
icily	454	21	24	24	18	40	15	15
pulia	430	20	22	31	39	10	17	9
Campania	405	19	10	10	8	30	30	18
azio	272	13	14	13	7	4	16	17
bruzzi Molise	190	9	13	10	5	4	7	12
Calabria	167	8	6	4	17	7	7	9
ardinia	145	7	3	6	3	3	6	15
Basilicata	69	3	7	2	2	2	2	5
Mezzogiorno	2,132	100	100	100	100	100	100	100

The intensification of land use is recorded in the decreasing amount of and held in large properties (of 500 ha and over), and the increasing rea contained by 20–50 ha and 50–100 ha properties; the area contained n each category doubling in the period 1933–54. Nevertheless very large properties still contained 17 per cent of the total area, in 1954, and the 50–100 ha category contained 34·5 per cent.[26] Medium to large capitalistic farming, not peasant family farming, prevailed. Most of the land was worked by tenants who paid their rents in kind – so much quantity per hectare according to the quality of the land – little respect being paid to

[26] Cassa Mezzogiorno (1956): 301–18.

the laws attempting to enforce fair rents. A not inconsiderable proportion 42 per cent, of the land was operated directly by the landowners themselves but *compartecipazione* was the common form of organization. A large amount of additional work was supplied by day labourers, usually females working alongside a smaller contingent of annual wage labourers. The transformation of the land caused little alteration to the characteristic social and organizational features of southern rural life – though, admittedly, the amount of work per unit of land had increased and the remuneration was higher.

The provision of water allowed a considerable diversification of the cropping practices in the Sele plain. Higher yielding cereals replaced poorer varieties, though the fertilizer dressings remained light. Leys, or artificial pastures, made their appearance in the rotations, increasing the available forage and providing the basis of a small livestock sector. Tomatoes, sugar beet, maize tobacco were the really revolutionary crops, the principal cash earners and the raw material of the processing industries. Tree crops made their appearance. The result was a variety of holdings, in size ranging from as little as six to as many as 784 hectares; in gross saleable product per hectare ranging from as low as 88,000 lire (an extensive livestock holding of 127 ha), to as high as 475,000 lire (a six hectare fruit farm). The three principal types of farms were: very intensive fruit farms, industrial crop and livestock farms; an order that approximates to a decreasing scale of productivity per hectare.

By the early '60s the Sele scheme's 18,000 ha of effectively irrigated land, combined with the 4,200 ha of the Volturno scheme, made the Campania, followed by Sardinia (12,500), the foremost zone for barrage irrigation in the South. During the course of the next fifteen years the Cassa plans to raise the net irrigated area – a more generous measure – from the present total of approximately 250,000 ha to 600,000. If the proposals are fulfilled the result will be a marked shift southwards of the main irrigation zones. By 1980, Apulia, the Basilicata and Calabria will account for 36 per cent of the net irrigated area; Sardinia 19 and Sicily 16 per cent; whereas the Campania will be among the least important with only 14½ per cent.

These targets will be attained through the further development of schemes already in existence and the exploitation of resources in districts where large-scale irrigation schemes will come as an innovation. In the Abruzzi and Molise the works on the right and left banks of the Pescara will be extended further, whilst the Biferino, the Conca di Sulmona and the Piano di Boiano collectively are scheduled to supply a previously untapped 20,000 hectares of irrigated land. Existing schemes near Latina are already reaching a mature stage, so that an expansion of irrigated area in Lazio is to be obtained by a development of the Pontine Marshes and the course of the Liri. In the Campania the reserves of the Sele scheme are nearly exhausted, so it is from the Volturno and the Sannio Alifano that the new resources are to be won. Eventually the Volturno will be almost 50 per cent larger than the Sele development. The creation of more irrigated land in Apulia, the Basilicata and Calabria rests upon the intensification of work on schemes already in existence – along the course of the Ofanto, in the Metaponto, in the Plain of Sibari – but an enormous 67,500 hectare scheme for the Fortore, a fourfold expansion in the plain of San Eufemia and a doubling of the area in the Piano di Rosarno will add almost 100,000 hectares to the 45,000 hectares of the existing schemes. The future agricultural wealth of Sicily will be dependent on the completion of the Pozzillo-Simento works and the incorporation of the Jato and Ogliastro-Gornalunga schemes into the general framework. Additional areas of irrigated land will be obtained in Sardinia by the extension of the Flumendosa and Arborea schemes.

Out of a total 2,980 milliard lire set aside in the second fifteen year plan for investment in the Mezzogiorno's agriculture the Cassa plan to spend 1,145 milliard in the new irrigation zone, two-thirds of it being provided from public funds. In all 389 milliard lire, mostly public money, are committed to the completion of the physical works. Another 100 milliard lire is put aside for maintenance and 400 milliard lire, including half of the private outlay, is apportioned for the improvement and reorganization of individual properties; 160 milliard, mostly private money, will be used to provide working capital.

The Cassa displays great faith in its own works and in the goodwill of the majority of landowners who will be the beneficiaries. Already the organization has had to face up to the unanticipatedly high costs of the irrigation schemes, and it is admitted that for the major part of the territory to create an irrigated holding still signifies, more or less, the creation of the holding from nothing. Seventy to eighty per cent of the work in the new irrigation zones, the Cassa reckons, has still to be done. The success of the programme will depend heavily on that much despised element in the South, the human factor; and at every level too, from the co-ordinating committees at the inter-departmental level, to the field worker. A prop for the landowners who will be responsible for the most critical phases of the programme is being fashioned in the form of extension centres, one for every 3,000 hectares; better trained labourers, one for every 6 hectares; and 4,000 technicians with university qualifications.

Already evidence is accumulating of the failure to intensify farming once water becomes available, of the tendency to persist with mechanized, monocultural farming. A remarkable example of this can be seen in the

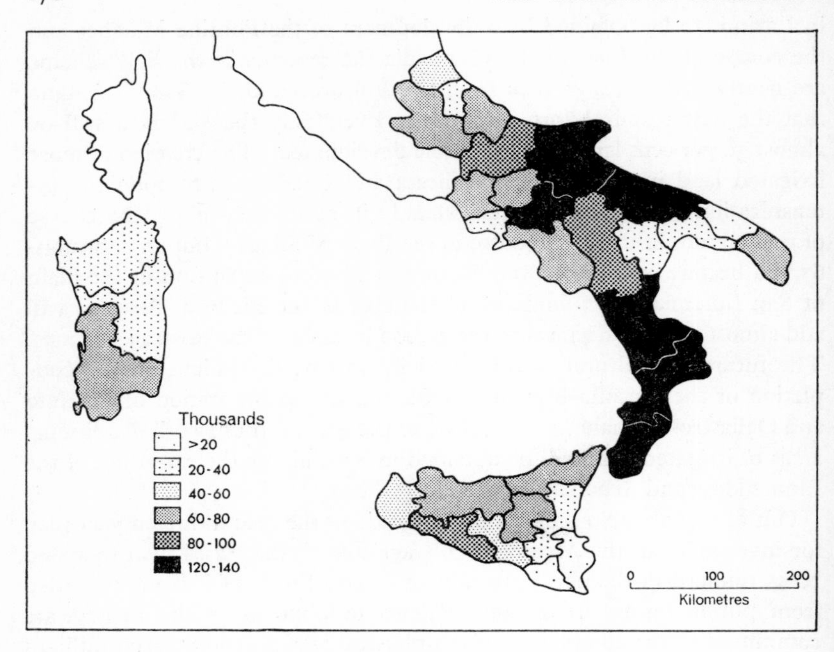

Fig. 4.6. Volume of migration 1951–61
(SVIMEZ No. 38–9, 1964)

valley of the Bradano, in the Basilicata, where modern *aziende* provided with stalls and silos and water from the San Guilano dam, designed to carry livestock, still produce mostly cereals. In the Tavoliere the large farms have been slow to use irrigation waters. Calabria has long been the cemetery of public works.[27] From Sicily comes the best documented study of wasteful investment to date. English language readers can read it for themselves in Dolci's *Waste*, pp. 338–47; but they will miss the outstanding land utilization map which accompanied the original version in *Spreco*. All the same, Michele Mandiello's stunning conclusion is there: the remedies to the situation are all normal practices in land transformation schemes, and ought to have been incorporated in the original programme.

These most recent decisions of the Cassa have been taken in the full knowledge of the high capital output ratios that have accompanied the previous investments in the agrarian sector.* For the period 1951–60,

[27] Rossi-Doria (1958): 168–9.

* It is difficult to assess the effects of the Cassa's investments in private farming during the period of the first fifteen year plan. The Campania, Apulia and Lazio, which produce the greater share of the South's agricultural output (Tables 4.14 and 4.15) all returned high rates of growth. After Liguria and Emilia-Romagna, the

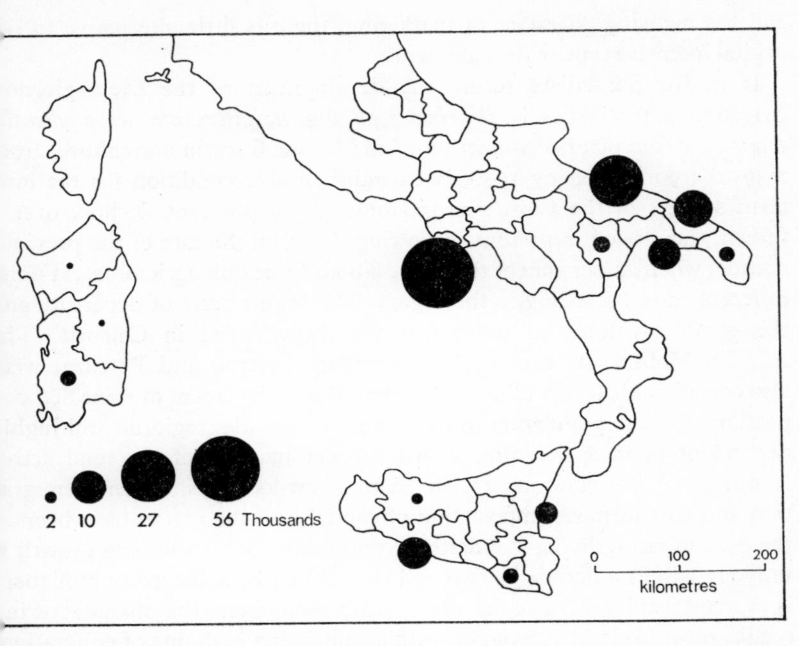

'g. 4.7. Net increase of active labour force, 1951–61. (All remaining areas registered a decline during the decade) (Census of population 1961)

hen charges for public works investments were apportioned between the arious sectors, the incremental capital output ratio for agriculture was 7·91, for industry, 4·60. Without these charges the ratios were smaller, ut the difference still high, 11·99 and 3·75 respectively. Comparative gures for the North were 8·61 and 2·51, excluding charges for public 'orks.[28] Nevertheless within the cadre of a Common Agricultural Policy,

ampania remains the third most intensively farmed and highly productive rovince in the whole of Italy, and the level of productivity in Apulia and Lazio ith respect to the Campania has improved during the period. Whereas the other rovinces have only just maintained their relative standing, and in some cases – icily and Calabria – have fallen back. However the Cassa investments relative to ıe total value of agricultural output have been lower in these three provinces than lsewhere, with the exception of Sicily, where output has been slow to rise. In ardinia the rate of growth of agricultural output has been high, and in the Abruzzi-Iolise and the Basilicata it has been satisfactory, but in each case the contribution) the total value of agricultural production in the South is small. In Calabria which as received a large volume of Cassa funds the growth of agricultural production has een slow and erratic. In general it would seem the Cassa's investments were more roductive in those areas which were already advanced in their development along ıe very lines which the Cassa sought to promote.

[28] Cassa Mezzogiorno (1962): Vol. I, 328–38.

and the evolving character of marketing, there is little alternative to th capital intensive type of development.

If in the immediate future the development of the Mezzogiorno' irrigation potentialities is '*il primo e pui urgente intervento nel quadro d piano* . . .' the planned reduction of the labour force in agriculture, fro 2·59 to 1·90 million by 1980, is an indispensable condition for the lon term success of the Cassa's programme. A 29 per cent decline, over fifteen year period, represents a slowing down on the rate of the previou decade, when 24 per cent of the active labour force quit agriculture, at quit different rates according to the region. The highest rate of departure an the greatest volume of movement was experienced in Calabria. Th Abruzzi-Molise, the provinces of Avellino, Salerno and Potenza, wer also considerable foyers of out-migration. But a movement of some 860,00 peasants left the population in most areas of the Mezzogiorno still highl dependent upon agriculture, whilst the net increase of the total activ labour force was slow and restricted to a few localities. General emigra tion and an enormous importation of capital into the region have been a the base of rising living standards in the South. Self sustaining growth i unlikely within a decade or two and then it can be achieved only if ther is a remarkable increase in the contribution from the manufacturin sector, most likely in association with a continuing high rate of emigration The chosen perspectives for agricultural development will remain realisti only so long as these two conditions are likely to be fulfilled.

'Terroni in Citta'*

Hindsight and all, was there an alternative to the programme of the pas fifteen years? The assumption of the late '40s was that agriculture mus provide the employment and the programmes were drawn up accordingly Faith in the recuperative powers and dynamism of capitalism was limite in those days. It is doubtful if any influential group would have been abl to effectively sustain different assumptions – or if such a group existed i Italy at that time. In the light of the widespread acceptance of thos assumptions one must agree in general with the measures adopted, they were designed to provide more work. Any argument over the manner i which the schemes were implemented is to take the different and almos universal topic of management and efficiency, a field where there is eve room for improvement; and a particularly intractable field in the environment of the South.

Circumstances may have rendered the assumptions acceptable at the time, but an acceptable assumption is not therefore a tenable one. Considering how modest the achievements of the agricultural sector have been,

* The title of Compagna's book (1959) on migration from the South.

ι very favourable conditions, can anyone believe that in totally adverse rcumstances agriculture could have found work for an additional uarter or half a million people? The continuity of the Cassa's programme oes not lie in a continuity of assumptions. Currently the success of its rogramme for the next fifteen years is predicated on the very inverse of ιe earlier assumption: that there will be a continuing decline in the gricultural labour force.

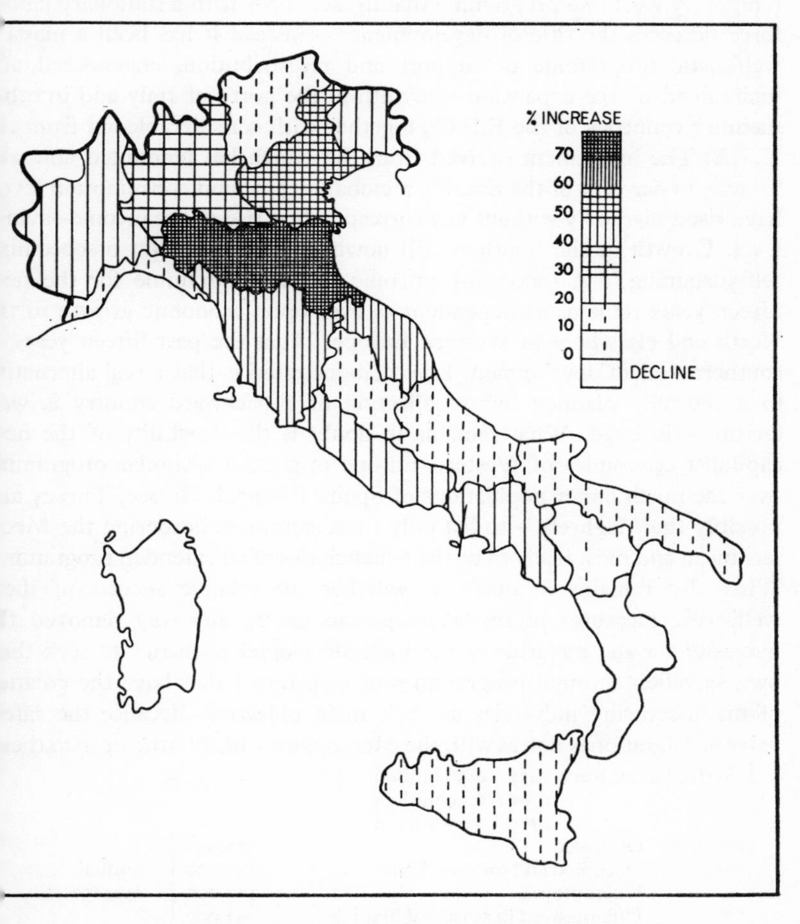

Fig. 4.8. Industrial employment in Italy, 1951–61

Because the Agriculture-Employment thesis was ultimately untenable, ιe alternative thesis of Industrialization would not as a consequence ave been any easier to put into practice. A full-scale drive towards industrialization might easily have foundered in the social and politic morass of the Mezzogiorno that constituted the objective condition which any programme of reform and development ran the risk of slo strangulation. In fact given the state of the South and its politically d pendent status the choice between either thesis was never a real one.

What in fact has been executed in the past fifteen years has not been t implementation of a programme of economic development – in the co temporary world no programme that in fact copes with a stationary labo force deserves the title of development* – instead it has been a massi welfaristic programme of support and redistribution, engendered a maintained by the expansion of wealth in the north of Italy and in oth member countries of the E.E.C., together with considerable aid from t U.S.A. The investment derived from the North has amounted annual to over 20 per cent of the South's regional income and consumption leve have risen markedly without any corresponding rise in the income-savin level. Growth in the South is still nowhere near the point of becomi self-sustaining.[29] A successful outcome to the programme for the ne fifteen years remains as dependent as ever upon economic growth in t North and elsewhere in Western Europe. What the past fifteen years southern Italian development have demonstrated is that a real alternati to a centrally planned industrialization of a backward country is we farism writ large. What remains in doubt is the capability of the ne capitalist economies of Western Europe to sustain a similar programn over the much larger populations of Spain, Portugal, Greece, Turkey ar possibly the Maghreb, – to list only those countries bordering the Med terranean and most likely to be the beneficiaries of an extended programm What also remains in doubt is whether the relative success of the welfaristic measures in the Mezzogiorno has in any way removed t necessity for the majority of the underdeveloped countries to seek the own salvation through programmes of investment that have the creati of manufacturing industries as their main objective. Because the safe valve of migration is not, as with the Mezzogiorno, likely to be open to the

* Active labour force 1951 6·56 million
1961 6·39 million
1965 6·20 million

of which:			
	Occupied	5,971,000	annual average
	Occupied and on short time	146,000	
	Unemployed	137,000	
	Unemployed in search of first job	93,000	

The net effect of the first fifteen year programme was to leave the South with active labour force of approximately the same size as in 1951, but without so mu unemployment and under-employment. Most development programmes have reduce under-employment and unemployment and find jobs for the newcomers labour force. In effect migration solved this problem for the South.

[29] Campolongo (1962): 76.

; PEASANTS IN THE E.E.C.:
ame plot – bigger screen

'he agreement on the financing of the Common Agricultural Policy
:.A.P.) reached by the Council of Ministers in May 1966 was widely
:cognized as the cementing in place of the arch-stone of the Common
Iarket. It constituted a commitment on the part of the other five members
) a policy which the French deemed to be particularly vital to their
ıterests and the success of the Community; a viewpoint that coincided in
large measure with that of the Commission of the E.E.C. itself. However
esirable for France a common market might be politically as well as
ıdustrially, without a C.A.P. it would lack a real economic foundation.
'rom the beginning it had been recognized that access to the growing
rban markets of Federal Germany for the increasing volume of French
gricultural produce was an indispensable condition for the economic
uccess, and hence electoral and political success, of the E.E.C. amongst
section of the French population. Walter Lippman went so far as to call
ıe Common Market a bargain between French agriculture and German
ıdustry.

As these two countries were the most influential of the partners, and
'ithout their agreement no union was possible, agricultural matters
cquired predominantly Franco-German overtones. Although some sec-
ions of the agricultural community in each member state are likely to
ain certain competitive advantages following the establishment of com-
ıon prices – Holland's highly efficient and productive livestock industry
; favourably placed both geographically and economically, the producers
f Mediterranean crops in Italy are afforded a natural protection against
ther competitors, except those in Bas-Rhône-Languedoc – basically
ierman agriculture has always stood to lose the most from the imple-
ıentation of a common agricultural policy, whilst French agriculture has
een expected to gain the most.

But if the Common Agricultural Policy – a policy that awaits a final
ormulation – has introduced some novel elements to the West European
gricultural scene they are of secondary importance only. The principal
ffect of policy making so far has been to strengthen trends already extant
'ithin each of the member states. There has been a growing recognition

of the fundamental similarities of the agricultural problems facing indi-vidual countries and an increased desire to explore them jointly; but there has been a positive reluctance to create the necessary executive powers for their solution at a Community level. A marked, one might say, inevitable tendency has appeared for the internal electoral interests of the member governments and peasant organizations to prevail upon and strongly influence Community decisions.

The policy makers have maintained the high level of protection against foreign competitors by the use of the support price, the variable import levy and the *montant forfaiture*. They have pursued at the supra-national level the national policies of maintaining farm incomes by supporting and when necessary raising prices with little regard for the debates or doubts similar policies have created in member states. The eventual abolition of intra-Community tariffs will stimulate competition within the heavily protected walls, but the most beneficial effects of competition from the consumers' viewpoint have been nullified, or their consequences retarded, by the adoption of common prices that reflect the conditions of the higher cost producers. The consequences of this decision are manifold. Immediately and in general the high price levels will tend to retain people in agriculture. Lower ones would have forced them off the land more quickly. In the longer run, within any one member state the high price level will favour the more efficient producers with a quasi-rent, and this will promote further the differentiation of the peasantry already underway. At a Community level there will be a concentration of these effects within certain favourably located or naturally endowed agricultural regions – the capitalistic zone of the Paris Basin is a leading example – which will tend to become the principal source for surpluses of farm produce. The high price level will tend to create regional and social imbalance within the farming community, which the less favoured peasantry will seek to reverse by demands for more and more assistance, their electoral weight remain-ing relatively significant because of a failure to adopt a price policy that would have speeded their departure from the land. In the west of France the realization has quickly spread, and it has been accompanied by a growth of anti-European feeling, that only the capitalist regions of France are properly geared to take advantage of the new situation; that a C.A.P. does does not mean a walk-over victory for French farming, or ensure the survival of the family sized farm. The peasants of this peripheral region have become disillusioned with the policy and with their leaders who have championed it.

An enormous amount of energy was consumed in the establishment of a price policy at the Community level, and even more, it seems, will be required to formulate a structural one. In principle the need for a structural policy has long been accepted, and the limitations of a price policy alone understood both in ministerial and community circles. But the consideration of a structural policy has exposed two politically awkward requirements. First, the need to treat E.E.C. agriculture in terms of two or three 'agricultures' as C.E.N.A.G. advocated for France (see above, p. 104), and to adapt policies accordingly. Secondly, the need to award priorities in a geographical sense to those regions, irrespective of their national location, where structural reforms have the best chance of success; of planning, as Dr Mansholt suggested in the latter part of 1967, at a Community rather than at a national level. These requirements are in fact similar to those which have emerged in the individual countries; and as one might imagine, difficult to implement in a national context, they were rejected outright in a supra-national one. For once applied they might create a politically impossible situation that might involve, as one commentator foresaw, the French minister of agriculture bombarded with eggs by the irate peasantry of Brittany, having to request Brussels, not Paris, to approve subsidies which might relieve his personal distress and the political embarrassment of the French government. These structural measures not only lack political support at the ministerial level, none of the national agricultural confederations agree with them. Speaking against Mansholt's proposals the German representative at the Council of Ministers, October 1967, invoked the spirit of Stresa, and re-affirmed that the enterprise of the future should be the family farm.*

Thus for all the documentation, the burning of the midnight oil, the squabbling over pfennigs, the complexities and intricacies of the 'réglements', the realities of a 'Green Europe' are little more than the national problems of the member countries projected on to a larger screen; their solution at the supra-national level no easier because the deficiencies in national policies exist also at the Community level. Nevertheless some real advantages have accrued already from the C.A.P., notably, the

* In the preface to the documents of the Agricultural Conference of the E.E.C. held at Stresa in July 1958 Dr Mansholt summarized the main preoccupations of the delegates as follows: (i) 'la nécessité de résoudre le problème que constitue la détérioration relative des revenues agricoles'. (ii) 'l'orientation de la structure de notre agriculture vers une exploitation familiale rentable'. (iii) 'la recherche d'un équilibre, d'une part, entre la production agricole de la Communauté et des importations agricoles de pays tiers, et d'autre part, les possibilités de débouchés aussi bien à l'interieur de la Communauté que vers d'autres pays.' In *Le Monde*, 19 October 1967, F.-H. de Virieu wrote, 'M. Mansholt est convaincu que les difficultés de la petite paysannerie des régions déshéritées de l'Europe ne pourront pas être résolues par la politique d'organisations des marchés et la politique de prix, qui ont jusqu'à présent été l'alpha et l'oméga de la doctrine communautaire.' Mansholt referred also to 'le gaspillage de deniers publics que peut représenter aux Pays-Bas la poursuite d'une politique de remembrement qui aboutit à créer des exploitations de 15 hectare, manifestement dépassées par le progrès technique.'

expenditure of a formidable volume of E.A.G.G.F.* monies to dispose
the French and other countries' surpluses, and the very promising tren
in the trade in agricultural products between member nations which h
appeared before the final abolition of tariffs (Table 5.1). At the same tin

TABLE 5.1 *Percentage increase in the value of E.E.C. trade in all farm products,* 1958–65*

	Imports		*Exports*	
	From E.E.C. members	*From non-members*	*To E.E.C. members*	*To non-members*
Germany	154 (1,614)	50 (3,841)	147 (262)	114 (385)
France	269 (468)	6 (2,462)	325 (924)	54 (1,039)
Italy	238 (435)	103 (2,169)	140 (516)	23 (438)
Holland	148 (317)	53 (1,255)	129 (1,166)	30 (749)
Belgium-Luxemburg	116 (489)	46 (850)	183 (473)	50 (194)

1965 totals in millions of dollars are set in brackets.

* Includes food, beverages and tobacco, hides, furs and skins, oilseeds, cru
natural rubber, wood and cork, natural textile fibres, crude material, oil and fats.

the Common Market encourages not only a concurrence of agricultur
interests, but the chance for industrial interests to concert their efforts
modify, resist or deflate a policy which may be too inflationist, conserv
tive or discriminatory for their liking. The disquiet of the industri
sector was carefully voiced by a counsellor of the Belgian Federation
Industries in the monthly review published by the French Ministry
Agriculture. He cited the experience of the Belgian coal industry, ar
implied that in agriculture, too, it was possible, 'sous prétexte de tra
sition, on a pratiqué un conservatisme coûteux', detrimental to th
interests of the consumer. He considered it an error to hinder the econom
progress of the Community by fixing the guaranteed agricultural prices
such a level that it would retain in agriculture people whose labour wou
be more profitable to society if it were engaged in other sectors. Amo
other points he acknowledged the necessity of the variable import levi
(prélèvements) for the cohesion of the E.E.C., but added that the i
dustrialists joined third countries 'pour dénoncer certains excès

* European Agricultural Guidance and Guarantee Fund. (F.E.O.G.A. in Franc

systeme des prélèvements'. He added 'L'inconvénient des systèmes trop logiques est d'être aveugle et de manque de souplesse.'*

How long it will be before the operation of the Market produces a new agricultural geography of Western Europe is a matter for conjecture, even doubt. There are four major productive nodes which are most favoured as poles of agrarian development. In the Mezzogiorno lies the emerging node for the production of specialized Mediterranean crops. It is balanced in the north-west by a node centred about the Rhine delta, where intensive vegetable and livestock farming is concentrated. The capitalist zones of the Paris Basin and the North Italian plain could quite easily become the great granaries and the important livestock zones for the E.E.C. Aquitaine and the west of France are two zones whose future importance remains problematical. The remaining areas of France, large sections of Appenine Italy, seem destined to lose whatever importance they once possessed. Certain areas of specialized farming in Germany will undoubtedly retain their competitive advantages; but at present a significant concentration of cereal, fodder and livestock production occurs in Germany, and specialization within the E.E.C. ought to induce a shift away from this country. This is one hypothesis. There is another outlined over a decade ago by Niehaus, and it may in the end prove to be the correct one.† 'The persistence of institutional factors proceeding from historical causes leads me to the thesis that European integration will come about the lines of least resistance, i.e. with the maximum retention of existing locations and demographic distributions.'

* *Revue française de l'agriculture*, summer 1966.
† International Labour Review, 1958.

6 SELJACI I CHŁOPI: the peasant sector in the socialist state: Yugoslavia and Poland

Twenty years of Communist rule have left the peasantry of Poland and Yugoslavia intact; not unchanged, but retaining the physionomy of an ideal type and, it follows, retaining most of the characteristic problems of the peasantry: low productivity, over-manning, structural inadequacies and organizational deficiencies. Both societies display certain common features which have arisen out of the policies of the immediate post-war years or are associated with the progressive industrialization of the economy. Land reform had the double effect of creating a socialized sector in agriculture, having little connection with most of the peasantry, and of establishing a fairly homogeneous class of small and medium peasantry. The big private estates, the large peasants and the rural proletariat that figured so prominently in the pre-war scene disappeared in the process, along with rural indebtedness. The abandonment of collectivization institutionalized, or confirmed, the dual structure of the agrarian sector. The socialized sector now utilises 13 per cent of the arable area in Poland and only 15 per cent in Yugoslavia, and employs even smaller percentages of the total agricultural labour force. The contribution to the total output of agricultural produce is, however, proportionately greater, in part because of the preference received in the allocation of goods and investment. Though the socialized sector is the more capital intensive sector, compared with western conditions it remains very labour intensive, using a lot of low productivity, mostly female, labour. The private sector is even more labour intensive in character, almost wholly unmotorized, and still performing many of the residual functions of peasant farming. However it now performs those functions in the context of a dynamic and industrializing economy. This has meant primarily that the proportion of population dependent upon agriculture has declined markedly without, however, reaching the level of 40 per cent, which is indicative of the society reaching the stage when it is reasonable to refer to it as an industrial rather than as an agrarian society. Consequently the population of the rural areas remains a youthful one and the ageing effects which become marked during the later stages of industrialization have not fully manifested themselves though they are in existence. The second major effect of industrialization has been to stimulate the growth of the worker-peasant class, a process which has a more immediate and beneficial effect upon the living standards and socio-economic conditions of the rural classes than upon agriculture itself. Peasant agriculture has been required to meet not only a growing demand from industry for raw materials but also a growing demand from both the urban and rural populations for more and qualitatively better food. It has been willing to meet this demand primarily because it has been offered the incentive of better prices and secondarily because of a growing investment of materials and techniques in agriculture. The important consequence for the peasant population has been a rise in income and an improvement in levels of consumption. The areal impact of all these developments has been far from uniform, so that the regional diversity of the rural areas, which already bear the imprint of both environmental contrasts and varied histories, is becoming more accentuated.

The abandonment of wholesale collectivization as an objective left the regimes with the need to formulate an alternative policy. The burden which the cost of agricultural imports has imposed and still imposes in Poland, the high demand elasticities for foodstuffs, now officially acknowledged, the relatively low level of agricultural output, the size of the agrarian population, and the demonstration effect which agricultural development in the West is having – all these items indicate the sort of issues an agrarian policy must deal with if it is to be operatively successful. At the same time, if it is to be ideologically correct, that policy must also produce a socialist transformation of the countryside. Kardelj has argued that the superiority of socialist measures in agriculture will be recognized only if their economic results are better than those on the private holdings; that the achievement of better results is dependent upon more investment and the establishment of effective institutions for promoting, without forcing, co-operation amongst the peasants. Both regimes have sought to propagate suitable institutions, the General Agricultural Co-operative in Yugoslavia, the Agricultural Circle in Poland, and with a variety of measures they have sought to bind the peasant producer to the socialist agrarian sector, with probably a greater degree of success in Yugoslavia than in Poland. Vertical integration, followed by horizontal integration, best describes the more cautious process by which they now seek the transformation. In both countries it is recognized, '. . . the provision of employment for a large part of the population will remain the most important function of agriculture for a long time to come'. But in Poland it has been argued, '. . . as far as the choice of techniques is concerned the structure of output, that of working capital investment outlays etc. – our future socialist agriculture will approach more closely the Dutch rather than the British or American-Soviet model'.[1] Kardelj rejects both the Western and the Soviet model for Yugoslav purposes. He separates the peasant problem into a sectoral and a social issue, and finds the solution in a geographical and institutional concentration of effort. For him, '. . . the problem of the socialist transformation of agriculture, as a branch of the economy, would be largely solved in practice if about 30–40 per cent of the arable land were farmed by large-scale production methods with high yields and high productivity of labour'. When this has been achieved the peasantry as a social rather than an economic problem will come to dominate rural affairs, and in these circumstances the state must be willing to maintain, '. . . the necessary social, cultural and other services in the village, independent of its productivity'. But it will not, as in the West, '. . . keep and support his (the peasant's) small property illusions artificially with subsidies'.[2]

YUGOSLAVIA

Socio-economic character of the labour force

In 1961 a little under half of a total population of eighteen and a half million persons were classified as actively engaged in or dependent upon agriculture. Of the actively employed in agriculture – 4·6 million persons – about 250,000, at that time, were engaged in the socialist sector. The latest figure has now reached a sum of 285,000, so that the overwhelming proportion of the people remain within the private and peasant sector of agriculture. It is only in Slovenia that the proportion of the active labour force engaged in agriculture has fallen below 40 per cent, and only in two other republics, Croatia and Montenegro, have less than the national average engaged in agriculture. In the autonomous region of the Kosmet (Kosovo and Metohija) 67 per cent of the active labour force remains in agriculture.

The peasantry is divided between two main socio-economic groups, the class of small and medium full-time family farmers, and the worker-peasant or part-time family farming class. Holdings of 2 ha and above display the features that one has come to expect of the classic type of peasant holding. About half the labour force is provided by full-time males, a quarter by full-time females and a further quarter by part-time females, all drawn from the family. Very little hired labour is used and about one-third of the holdings have an excess of labour. The majority possess their own ploughs and draught animals. Most families, and this must be a reflection of the land reform and the ceiling imposed on the size of holdings, consist solely of a married couple with children. Two generation families, however,

[1] Tepicht (1966): 33 and 36. [2] Kardelj (1962): 119, 182 and 181.

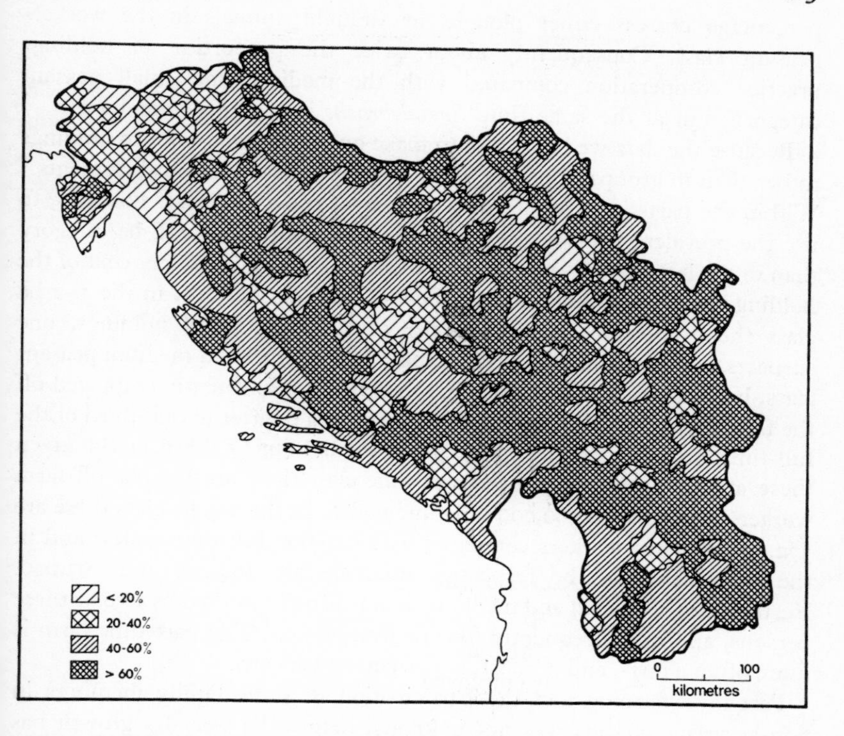

Fig. 6.1. Percentage of population active in and dependent upon agriculture, 1961

are not absent, and in the 5–8 ha category a quarter of the holdings are worked by families in which the parents are residing with a married son. This category is the most typical of the full-time peasant class. At either end of the spectrum other characteristics become more marked. Over 8 ha for instance, and particularly over 10 ha, under present conditions a greater proportion of the farms are deficient in manpower and it is rare to find even one member of the family permanently engaged outside agriculture. Towards the tail of the agrarian structure a greater percentage of farms display characteristics more common amongst the part-time class. Whereas the ratio of family members permanently employed off the farm is 0·20 in the 5–10 ha class, in the 2–3 ha class it is 0·49. This ratio approaches and eventually surpasses unity in the holdings of less than 2 ha. Thus off-farm incomes become progressively more important, the contribution of male full-time labour declines and the bulk of the farm work is provided by part-time family females as the part-time class is entered. Only 40 per cent of the 2–3 ha farms possess their own draught animals and a very low percentage possess either ploughs or draught animals in the worker peasant class. Consequently about twice the proportion of holding practice co-operation compared with the medium and small peasan category; but at the same time *Sozialebrache* is also more common.

Because the data we have used to make our distinction refer to holding rather than to groups of people, each division contains atypical elements. Within the part-time class there is a body of full-time dwarf holdings, t use the prevalent pre-war phrase, more important in the 1–2 ha categor than in the less than 0·5 ha category. Even here, however, 28 per cent of th holdings derive the bulk of their income from agriculture; in the 1–2 h class the proportion rises to 50 per cent. These dwarf holdings, on suspects, are often old-persons holdings. In the small and medium peasan class, holdings in which at least one member is permanently employed of the farm are not uncommon; they account for a quarter to one-third of th full-time farms, depending on the size of the holding (Table 6.1). But give these atypical elements, in the part-time class there are 543,000 off-farn workers compared to 460,000 full-time males. In the 2–5 ha class there ar 372,000 off-farm workers compared with 976,000 full-time males; and i the 5–10 ha class, the respective numbers are 164,000 and 793,000 Furthermore the small and medium farm is usually worked by two or thre persons, and quite frequently four or five persons. The part-time farm i more often a one-, and at most, a two-person concern.

Part-time farming and the participation of some family members i non-agrarian pursuits was not unknown before the war. Its growth ha been accelerated by the post-war expansion of industry, whose regiona distribution it tends to reflect. Slovenia, as one might expect, has th highest proportion of part-time holdings, 48 per cent; and Montenegr and Serbia proper the lowest but far from insignificant proportion o 31–32 per cent. *Pendelwanderung* has thus become a feature of rural lif in Yugoslavia too; though unfortunately the most detailed statistical dat available is now ten years out of date.[4] Fig. 6.2 reveals the widesprea existence of worker-peasant households throughout the Republic. Th influence of the major poles of development and of the local large administrative centres is easily discerned. The impact of developments in th Sarejevo-Zenica zone upon the social structure of the surrounding rura communities is very apparent. However, there are many regions in the upland and mountainous areas and some in the richer lands of Slavonia where the part-time element is of far less importance.

By comparison with the population dependent upon agriculture alone for its livelihood the worker-peasant element is markedly younger: 28 per cent of the farm population are over 50 years of age in contrast to 13 per

[3] *Statistički Bilteni:* various dates. [4] *Statistički Bilteni* (1957)*:* No. 101.

TABLE 6.1 *Socio-economic character of the Yugoslav peasantry*

	Dwarf holdings and part-time holdings	*Small and middle peasant holdings*			
	< 2 ha	*2–5 ha*	*5–10 ha*	*> 10 ha*	*Total*
PERCENTAGE:					
of holdings	35	36	22	7	100
of agricultural land	8	29	35	28	100
of agricultural population	29	36	25	10	100
of permanently employed outside agriculture	48	33	14	5	100
FAMILY LABOUR '000S					
Males – full-time	460·4	976·8	793·4	301·6	2,532·2
Females – full-time	242·2	482·0	371·2	147·8	1,243·2
Females – part-time	560·2	671·6	423·6	153·3	1,808·7
Permanently employed outside agriculture	543·6	372·0	164·6	55·9	1,136·1
Total	1,806·4	2,502·4	1,752·8	658·6	6,720·2
PROPORTION OF HOLDINGS IN WHICH:					
Bulk of income is derived from agriculture	42	63	73	73	59
One or more family members work outside agriculture	41	33	25	25	33
All family members work permanently outside agriculture	12	2	1	1	5
Without manpower	5	2	1	1	3
	100	100	100	100	100
AGRICULTURAL POPULATION (MILLIONS):					
Full-time holdings	1·4	2·7	2·1	0·6	6·9
Part-time holdings	2·1	1·6	0·7	0·2	4·7
Non Peasant holdings	0·8	0·02	0·008	0·003	0·8
Total	4·4	4·4	2·8	0·8	12·6

Source: Statistički Bilteni: 263,352,370

cent of the worker-peasant element. Likewise 46 per cent of the farming population are between the ages of 20 and 39, compared with 65 per cent of the worker-peasant population. It is in Slovenia, predictably, that the aging of the farm population is most advanced, 43 per cent are over 50 years of age; whilst in Bosnia-Hercegovina, Macedonia and the Kosmet, the over 50s account for 17–20 per cent only of the active labour force in agriculture.

Manufacturing is far from being the only source of employment for the

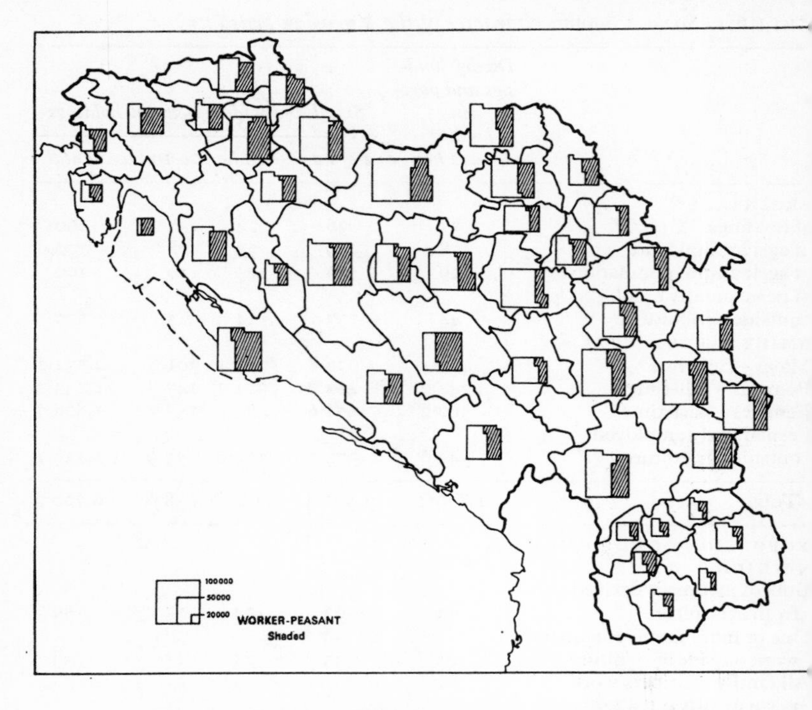

Fig. 6.2. Peasant and worker-peasant households, 1961

worker-peasant class. In both Macedonia and the Vojvodina about on
third of the worker-peasants find employment in the socialized sector
agriculture. In the Kosmet, the building industry, arts and crafts ar
socialist agriculture outrank manufacturing in the provision of emplo
ment; and the structure of the worker-peasant employment in Monteneg
– 17 per cent in administration, 24 per cent in building industry and 23 p
cent in manufacturing – has all the marks of a development programn
highly dependent upon net imports of capital and far from self-sustainin
However, in Bosnia, Croatia and Slovenia one finds the more characterist
pattern of manufacturing, the building industry, mining and transpo
providing the main avenues to incorporation of the peasantry in the moder
industrialized sector of the economy. The majority of worker-peasan
participate – at least they did ten years ago – in a diurnal pattern of mov
ment between work place and residence; but in Bosnia, Macedonia an
the Kosmet more than a quarter of the people were absent for periods
longer than a week. Belgrade, Zagreb and Lubljana, in 1957, drew mo
than 10 per cent of their daily migrants from settlements more than

ilometres distant. Zenica's commuters (62 per cent) came mostly from ithin a radius of 5–15 kms. Banja Luka was in an intermediate category ith 54 per cent of its daily migrants travelling between 10 and 25 kms om residence to place of work. Until another survey is made available it ill be impossible to judge what influence the greater provision of housing the industrial settlements, or the somewhat improved supply of bicycles nd motor bikes, has had upon the extension or restriction of the com- uting areas. Certainly as in Federal Germany in the past, the immediate nd visible results of the apppearance of the worker-peasant class in the small ervicing settlements has been the creation of a few plate glass windows in hops displaying a modest range of basic consumer goods. And though fter work traffic on the roads recalls images of a decade ago in Germany, he Yugoslav five o'clock farmer remains wholly unmechanized and his illage displays few indications of a marked improvement in amenities. Neither has the dispersion of industry to the village level reached anything ke the degree attained in Germany.

Periodic migration in search of work, the derivation of income from non- arm sources – building, crafts and transport – none of this is completely ovel to peasant life in Yugoslavia. It is the volume of population involved, nd its high rate of growth in the dynamic context of industrial develop- nent that constitute the new and impressive features.

ncome, expenditure and differentiation

For the past decade the majority of peasant households have enjoyed ising incomes in both nominal and real terms. The rise in private farm roduction has made a greater quantity of food available for autoconsump- ion, and since agricultural producer prices have nearly trebled during a eriod when industrial producer prices have risen by not more than a hird, the exchange rate has favoured the peasant producers. Since a rowing volume of produce has been marketed at a higher price, cash ncome earned from the farm has risen faster than farm income in kind, nd during the '60s it has risen at about the same rate as off-farm cash arnings. Ignoring structural and socio-economic as well as regional ariations within the peasant community, between 1956 and 1964, nomin- lly, total income per household rose almost threefold, cash farm income ose a little more than threefold, and off-farm income rose almost exactly hreefold. All farms do not, of course, derive their income from the same ource in equal proportions. Worker-peasant farms draw more of their otal income from off-farm cash earnings; some full-time farms market a reater proportion of their output than others. But because there has been nly a slight difference in the rate of growth of income from the principal ources, it is difficult to detect any variation in the growth of income according to size of holding between say less than 2 ha farms where worke peasants are more common and the farms of more than 8 ha with a great marketable surplus. More conspicuous are the variations according region, with the rate of growth in income being above the average in t Vojvodina, Serbia proper and Croatia.

About half the holdings (48 per cent) have annual incomes of betwe 240 and 560 thousand dinars. A smaller group, 14 per cent, have incomes less than 240 thousand and a larger group, 38 per cent, have incomes excee ing 560 thousand dinars. The distribution of all holdings between these thr income categories most clearly matches the income distribution of farms the 3–5 ha class and in this sense they constitute the most representati group of holdings. Farms of less than 3 ha have a somewhat higher percen age in the lower income bracket in contrast to those of more than 5 which have a greater percentage in the higher income brackets. Incon figures, unfortunately, are not as meaningful as at first they might appea for the average size of family in the 8 ha class is 50 per cent larger th the average size of family in the less than 2 ha class. Hence the distributi of farms according to per capita income levels does not fit too well t distribution according to total incomes. But it would be fair to assume fro the available data that in general terms the disparities in per capita incom and, consequently, levels of living are not all that great between farn of different sizes – regional differences apart. In the recent past, levellir processes have prevailed amongst the Yugoslav peasantry.

A more immediately meaningful classification of private farms may made according to whether they are primarily subsistence farms or wheth they produce sufficient to provide a net marketable surplus. Farms of le than 5 ha tend to be in the first category, and of more than 5 ha in t second category. Half of all private farms, it is estimated, are net consume of agricultural produce; whereas 7 per cent of private holdings produ 43 per cent of the marketable output. As a rule a marketable surpl appears only when the total sale of agricultural produce surpasses 100,0 dinars. On this basis it is apparent that some regions have a concentrati of farms in the net surplus class: the Vojvodina, Slovenia and Macedoni together with the richer parts of Croatia (Slavonia) and Serbia prope In the mountainous zones of Bosnia, Hercegovina, Montenegro and t Kosmet, the farms are, on balance, net importers of agricultural produc Families in these circumstances tend to meet the deficiencies in the supp of agricultural produce by accepting a lower standard of living, which t regional figures for per capita incomes crudely reflect. Food requiremen then constitute a proportionately heavier charge upon total resources, an often the food itself is of poorer quality. On average cereals supplie two-thirds of the calorific intake of peasant families in 1960, but in t ıountainous areas that figure exceeded 70 per cent and rose as high as ı per cent, and maize flour alone supplied a fifth or more of the total ıtake. In the Vojvodina, Croatia and Slovenia, the intake of protein-rich ɔods was proportionately greater and in absolute terms the per capita onsumption was much higher. However the territorial pattern of net sale nd net consumption of food was influenced by the distribution of the vorker-peasant class. Off-farm earnings reach a maximum, 45 per cent f total earnings, and contribute the bulk of the total cash earnings, 72 per ent, in the less than 2 ha category. These worker-peasant farms are in a etter position to afford the purchase of food than either the dwarf peasant r the small peasant family farms which tend to concentrate in the 2–5 ha lass.

The increasing marketable surplus of the medium peasant farms ought ɔ be working to the disadvantage of the smaller subsistence holdings with ttle to sell; it ought to be the basis of a greater socio-economic differentia- ion amongst the peasantry. Any such trend has not made itself evident ı the household income figures, as we have already observed. An inspec- ion of the manner in which these increased incomes have been expended of no great assistance in this matter either.

The first impression and one borne out by investigation is that the eeds of the household and consumption have taken priority over the eeds of the farm and in particular the needs for capital investments. On verage more than half (59 per cent) of the cash expenditure goes on ousehold requirements, food alone taking almost one-fifth. On the vorker-peasant holdings only 30 per cent of the cash expenditure is llotted to farm expenses and food purchases absorb one-quarter. On he larger full-time holdings somewhat more (51–5 per cent) is allotted ɔwards the expenses of running the farm and less is spent on food. ːxpenditure on farm expenses has grown at the same rate as expenditure n the household but the proportion of income devoted to capital invest- ıents varies little between the different size categories. This means that the roductive capacity of the full-time farms has been somewhat retarded in heir growth and the socio-economic differentiation implicit in the produc- ve character of the agrarian structure has had little chance to manifest self. The incidence of agricultural taxation, what is more, is three times reater on the full-time farms than on the worker-peasant farms.

Though it may be impossible to demonstrate statistically, and though it ıay be too early to permit any assessment, there can be little doubt that ifferentiation is under way within the Yugoslav peasantry, despite the npression of homogeneity left by the analyses of incomes. The distinction etween the worker-peasant and the full-time peasantry is clear, and ocumentation exists. The difficult trend to assess is the one towards the emergence of a 'middle' peasantry. Since 1949 the number of holdin of less than 2 ha and of more than 8 ha has declined, whereas the numb of holdings in the 2–5 class and the 5–8 class has risen by 11 per cent an 14 per cent respectively. Land purchase and the leasing of land within th private sector are the means by which holdings are being enlarged. Th 1960 Census of Agriculture revealed that full-time holdings were on ave age taking in more land on lease than they were letting out. The differen amounted to an average of only 0·04 of an hectare, however. Between 19 and 1959 full-time holdings had on average made a net acquisition of property to the extent of 0·10 hectares of land. Those holdings with a n agricultural surplus included a higher percentage of holdings whic leased extra land (*c.* 15 per cent), and which purchased land (*c.* 23 per cen than subsistence holdings. Their acquisition in the period 1954–9 had bee on average 0·35 hectares of land compared with the national average of 0·19 hectares of land.

Whatever aspect one looks at, production, income, expenditure, in th present circumstances geographical contrasts within the agrarian secto are more obvious than the socio-economic ones and they follow th pattern already extant in the prewar period. Per capita incomes of peasan households in Slovenia are 50 per cent above the national average an twice the Macedonian level. The Vojvodina and Croatia are the only oth regions where incomes exceed the average. Together the three region stand out because of their proportionately above average expenditure of cash upon farm expenses, their proportionately higher than averag earnings from livestock production, and their lower than average cas expenditure upon food purchases. In terms of capital investment however, they do not greatly distinguish themselves.

The expansion of agricultural production

Post-war increases in agricultural output have fed a growing and somewh richer industrial population, as well as supplying raw materials to th factories and improving the consumption levels of the peasantry them selves. The private sector has been responsible only in part for thes achievements and then largely because of an increasing degree of co-opera tion with the socialist farms. Before taking up a discussion of this emergin relationship, and its significance for the future of the peasantry, it is neces sary to describe and account for the increase in agricultural productio itself, for the measure of success achieved here has been very influential i determining the regime's attitude towards the private sector and its futur

The war losses were enormous and the trials and difficulties associate with collectivization delayed the attainment of pre-war levels of productio until about 1955. Since that time the volume of production has increase by almost a half. The growth has not been regular or even; consequently the overall growth of the national income has been advanced or retarded by the variations in agricultural production. 1959, 1963 and 1964 were relatively good years; 1958, 1960, 1961 and 1962 were relatively poor years. Thus wheat production rose from 2,450,000 tons in 1958 to 4,130,000 tons the following year; but not until 1963 was that figure surpassed. Likewise the 1959 tonnage for maize production, 6,670,000 was not surpassed until 1964. Using 1955 as a base year (100) by 1964 – a good year – the index of agricultural production had risen to 145. The index of agricultural production of the socialist sector had risen to 411; for the private sector it had risen to 129. The socialist sector had received preferential treatment with respect to the provision of investment and services, and it was concentrated on the better lands. In 1964 it received three-quarters of the total investment in agriculture and its share was subsequently increased. Its tractor park more than doubled in the last decade, whereas the private sector's increased only slowly, and not at all since 1960. Eighty per cent of the fivefold increase in the fertilizer consumption between 1955 and 1965 was absorbed by the socialist sector. The private sector shared some of these benefits through co-operation and, in addition, it benefited from an increasing volume of credit being made available. The system of subsidies and guaranteed prices worked largely in favour of the socialist sector, but both sectors benefited from the continuous and fairly high increase in producer prices, which must be counted as one of the major stimuli to increased production. During the decade 1952–62 producer prices for agricultural commodities rose at an average rate of 6 per cent per annum, compared with a rise in producer prices for industrial goods of only 1·1 per cent. Previous to 1952 the increase in industrial prices had been the faster of the two and agricultural produce had been relatively underpriced. After that date agricultural prices commenced their sharp and continuous rise, which shows no sign of abating. The effect upon production was most marked. A decline in the prices of some industrial commodities has mitigated the effect of rising food prices upon urban living standards so that nominal incomes have kept pace with a rising cost of living, and real incomes have continued to rise, though of late rather slowly. A continuing rise in producer and retail prices for agricultural commodities at immediately past rates is certain in the future to affect adversely the real incomes of the urban and industrial populations.

Together with deep ploughing and the use of certified seeds, increased inputs of fertilizers have been largely responsible for the higher yields. At the same time the area under cultivation by the socialist sector has expanded considerably, and consequently its total production has risen appreciably. So has production in the private sector, but not in suc a spectacular fashion, and without much of the material and technical ai afforded the socialist farms. Bigger harvests have been recorded throughou the country during the '60s, but they have been concentrated largely i the rich plains of the Vojvodina and Croatia. The effect has been not onl to widen the gap between the performance of the private and the socialis sectors but also been between the performance of the Vojvodina and it adjacent areas and the remaining republics. In the period 1947–56 whea yields in the Vojvodina were 20 per cent above the national average; in th period 1955–64 they have been 42 per cent higher. For maize they wer 42 per cent greater in the earlier period; more recently they have been 5 per cent greater; and this during a period when average wheat yields hav almost doubled, and average maize yields risen by almost two-thirds.

The acquisition of a marketable surplus as well as the increase of tota output has been of particular concern to the regime, and in this matter i cannot afford to ignore the private sector, for in terms of value it supplie over half (56 per cent) of the marketable output. This percentage is not, c course, indicative of the sector's contribution to total food supply; i neglects the production of food for subsistence purposes, which stil remains the principal activity. Although it is losing out in relative impor tance to the socialist sector (in 1960 it contributed 65 per cent of th marketed produce) the rate of growth of sales is impressive. With 1959 as base year (100), the index for sales from the private sector stood at 268 i 1965; the index for the socialist sector was 450. That sector provides major share of the cereals, the industrial crops, sugar beet especially an milk products, whereas the private sector provides mostly livestock pro ducts; though its contribution of cereals and industrial crops – basicall tobacco – is not negligible. Most of the vegetables, the fruit, the eggs skins, hides and timber which is marketed also comes from the privat sector.

The geographical origins of this contribution are, however, highl concentrated. Jointly, the Vojvodina, Serbia proper and Croatia suppl 70 per cent of the private sector's output. The Vojvodina alone supplie 28 per cent. The marketable surplus from Bosnia, Montenegro and th Kosmet is negligible. Tobacco accounts for more than half of Macedonia' marketed output, and nearly a quarter of Slovenia's sales are accounted fo by timber. Only in the Vojvodina is the volume of cereals marketed of an great significance. In the socialist sector the pre-eminence of the Vojvodin is even more apparent; alone it produces 44 per cent of the marketabl output, more than thrice the output of any other republic. The importanc of the Vojvodina when the output of both sectors is joined is, of course overwhelming. With 21 per cent of the total arable area it produces 3 er cent of the marketable output. Given this pre-eminence, it is not urprising that the degree of co-operation between the private and the ocialist sectors should be most advanced in the Vojvodina, and the djacent plains of Slavonia. There the productive achievements of socialist griculture are best displayed and, therefore, following the logic of Kardelj, he attraction exerted by the socialist sector ought to be at a maximum.

he socialist sector

)ne can have little measure of the significance of the co-operation between he two sectors without having some idea of the weight and importance of he socialist sector itself. Far from homogeneous, it is concentrated geo;raphically in the plains of the Vojvodina and Slavonia, approximately '50,000 ha of arable land out of a total 1·1 million ha, and hence its impact n the peasant sector is far from uniform.

In 1965 the socialist sector farmed one-tenth of the cultivated area arable, meadows, vineyards, orchards), one-seventh of the arable land nd gave employment to only 4 per cent of the active agricultural labour orce. Half the cultivated area belonged to the state farms (P.K.D.F.).* Most of the remainder was invested in the hands of the General Agricul-ural co-operatives (O.Z.Z.),† which in addition to the farming carried out n socially owned land, engaged in trading and manufacturing, and acted s the principal vehicle for co-operation with the private sector. The npopular 'collectives' (S.R.Z.)‡ now possess only 22,000 ha of land. Since he wholesale quittance of this institution by the peasantry after 1953 he land remaining under their control has been absorbed by the other two ocialist forms. The state farms are enormous concerns, conforming in very respect to the popular image, even more so with the trend towards oncentration evident since the beginning of the decade. In 1959 there were 559 farms utilizing 662,000 ha; by 1964 their numbers had been early halved and the area worked almost doubled (1,383,313 ha) so that he representative farm is today more than 5,000 ha in extent, and the tate farm of less than 1,000 ha has become a rarity. The density of ermanently engaged labour per 100 ha of cultivated land has fallen below 10; but in 1959 this labour force was supported by a seasonal labour force of approximately the same size and a temporary labour force, again of pproximately equal dimensions, made up of females and other family nembers. It is clear that mechanization has not yet circumvented the xtremes in the demand for manpower which the highly seasonal character of the agrarian year imposes.

* Poljoprivredni Kombinati, Dobra I Farme.
† Opšte Zemljoradničke Zadruge.
‡ Seljačke Radne Zadruge.

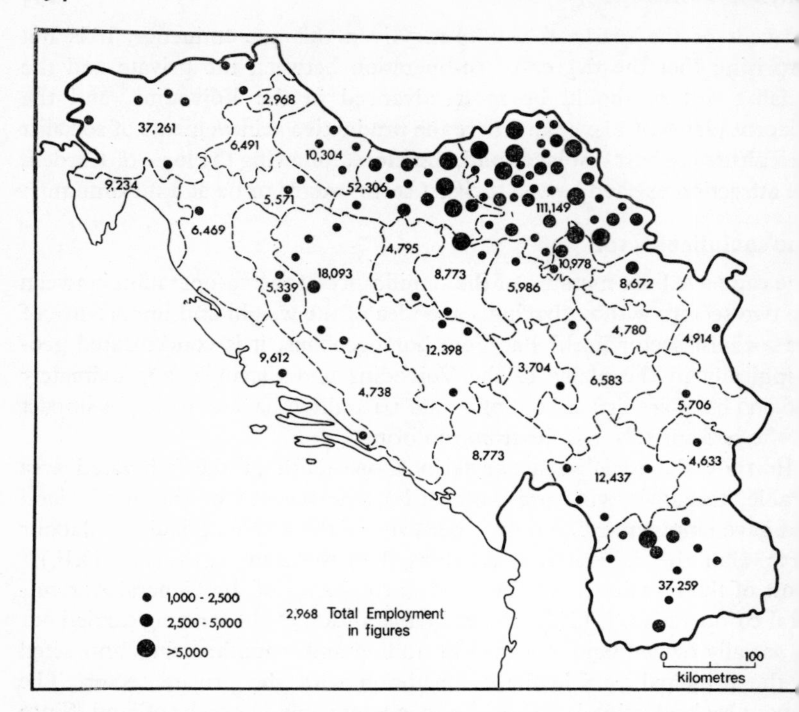

Fig. 6.3. Employment in the socialized sector in agriculture and forestry, 1

A trend towards concentration is also evident amongst the Gen Agricultural Co-operatives, but almost one-third of them are less than ha in extent, and in 1959, at least, they displayed exceedingly high densi of labour per unit of area, 35 permanently employed workers per 100 Currently farms of more than 1,000 ha control 62 per cent of the cultiva area, compared with only 19 per cent in 1959; and correspondingly area operated by the less than 50 ha holdings has fallen to negligi proportions.

The enormous expansion undergone by the area of the socialist sec in recent years, combined with the higher yields, is the principal rea for the sector's considerable growth in output. It has also been the princi factor in the relationship of the socialist to the peasant sector, one mi add, in the euthanasia of the individual holding. It is difficult to establ anything more than approximate figures for this growth. The inclusion two and a half million hectares of poor pasture in any consideration of socialist sector's importance is misleading. One must concentrate upon cultivated area, and best of all the arable area. In 1954 this amounted

752,000 ha. The transference of land to the private sector consequent upon the relaxation of the collective drive, and the fallowing of land because of administrative and economic difficulties, together reduced the arable acreage effectively worked by as much as 100,000 ha during the mid-'50s. By 1959 the arable area had regained its former extent and since that date the total arable area in the socialist sector has increased by approximately 50 per cent, by some 360,000 hectares; 124,000 ha were located in Croatia, 94,000 ha in the Vojvodina, Macedonia and the Kosmet gained 69,000 and 31,000 ha respectively. A fair proportion of this increase has been acquired from the private sector. At first the practice was to lease land. In 1960 a maximum of 187,000 hectares was leased. More recently the area has been reduced to 60,000 ha; approximately a half of the total has always been located in the Vojvodina. Latterly more preference has been given to the outright purchase of private land, by means of credits advanced by the agricultural banks and at prices ranging from 120,000 dinars per ha for the better grade land, 90,000 dinars per ha for the lower grade land. In the period 1958–65 a total of 411,000 ha has been purchased – not all of it arable land – mostly lying in the Pannonian plain.

Co-operation

These enormous predial changes outrank in significance any of the advances made in the degree of co-operation between the two sectors. After some setbacks, some reshuffling and readaptation, three principal types of co-operation between the socialist and private sectors are in the process of development. A common and widespread arrangement is the provision of services, particularly tractor work, and the sale and purchase of commodities by the General Agricultural Co-operatives to and from the private sector. At this level co-operation is widely diffused. The relationship is a temporary though renewable one which keeps the productive integration of the holding with the co-operative at a minimum. The significance of co-operation at this level is not easily assessed, the number of co-operators alone hardly being a fair guide. About 2,080 co-operatives, distributed throughout the Federal Republic, maintain contacts with some one million peasant households. In 1965, for instance, 914,349 persons were reported to be co-operating in crop farming. In 1960 the permanent male labour force in the private sector had numbered about 2·5 million. On this basis one could argue that approximately 40 per cent of all farmers in the private sector were co-operating. However the total area in the private sector ploughed and deep ploughed in 1965 amounted to 1,036,000 ha, representing an average of 1·14 ha per co-operator. Given the distribution of holdings according to size categories, this means on some farms the area worked co-operatively must have been exceedingly small. Certainly this was so in 1960, a year for which detailed figures are available, whe 425,273 holdings had a total of 455,130 ha ploughed by co-operativ services. On 11·5 per cent of the farms less than one hectare in extent, th average area ploughed was 0·37 ha. On a further 35 per cent of the farm of between 1 and 3 ha, the average area ploughed was 0·87 ha. On th remaining 53·5 per cent of the farms, the average area ploughed wa 1·36 ha. At this level, economies of scale must be near minimum. In th harvesting of wheat, maize and sugar beet a considerable increase in th area worked co-operatively has been reported since the beginning o the '60s. Only with sugar beet, however, has it become the rule for a hig proportion of the the private land to be co-operatively harvested: 80 pe cent. For wheat and maize, depending on the year, between 25 and 30 pe cent of the area is worked jointly.

During the period 1957–60, as an encouragement to co-operate, som co-operatives guaranteed the yields of private farmers who entered int joint production agreements, usually for maize, wheat and sugar beet The co-operative provided the seeds, chemical fertilizers, machinery an expert advice; the farmer provided the land, labour and bore part of th production costs. In operation these agreements produced their own cro of organizational, economic and ideological difficulties. All risks, fo instance, were borne by the co-operative, and economically the contribu tion of the farmer was overvalued. The application of mechanized method to what was virtually monoculture severely reduced the amount of labou which in all practicality the private farmer could contribute. His status wa very close to that of a landlord. From an organizational viewpoint th structure of the farm became the inverse of *colonia parziaria non appo derato*. Instead of one large property being farmed by a large number o tenants, none of whom had holdings in a contiguous block, as used to b the case in Southern Italy, in Yugoslavia it was the case of the dispers strips of a large number of landowners being farmed by one large tenant In response to the problems created by this type of arrangement tw original solutions have been formulated.

When it has been practicable under the system of long-term leases private land has been consolidated into larger blocks, if possible favourabl located with respect to the ground plan of the organizing co-operative With engaging historical innocence the Yugoslavs refer to this develop- ment, in their English language publications, as 'enclosures'.[5] To circum- vent the under-utilization of the peasant families' labour, produced by th application of machinery to much of the arable farming, the co-operative and socialist farms are stimulating the development of more labou intensive activities, fruit and vegetable growing and livestock production.

[5] Ilijin (1965).

In most instances the socialist farm or co-operative provides the individual farmer with some animals and accepts interest in the form of additions to stock – an arrangement which is open to abuse and grave risks. This particular scheme is only another variation of a simple contractual relation between the two sectors and accountably it has become the most common type of arrangement for co-operation with livestock. Under these schemes the rise in poultry deliveries from the private sector has been phenomenal; from half a million birds in 1960 to nine million birds in 1965. During the same period deliveries of cattle have risen from 139,000 to 318,000 and pig deliveries have fluctuated between three-quarters of a million and a million and a half. Deliveries of sheep have fluctuated widely. More integrated schemes, however, have been instigated in which the labour resources of the peasant households are concentrated on an enlarged livestock sector (the buildings provided by the co-operative), that draws its fodder from the fields belonging to the co-operative, and sells the produce to the co-operative at contract prices, at the same time receiving the expert advice and benefit of the co-operatives' expert management. By vertically integrating the peasant households at a much larger scale of organization, the co-operative hopes to raise their income level to the point where the ownership of land and the income derived from it lose their previous significance. Going a stage further the process seeks to alienate the peasant producer from his individual status by offering security of employment as a full-time member of the socialist sector. The success of this project will depend ultimately, of course, upon the elimination of the under-utilized and surplus labour in the socialist sector and the establishment of competitive wage levels.

The most consistent achievements in co-operation have been obtained with the continually increasing volume of certified seeds, fertilizers, anti-parasite products, fodder concentrate and thoroughbred animals supplied to the private sector. However, as with all aspects of co-operation, the highly localized geographical incidence of these innovations and arrangements is of equal importance for any assessment of their significance. Thus the Vojvodina with approximately 20 per cent of the arable area, and 12 per cent of the total agricultural area, has 43 per cent of the area co-operatively ploughed, 48 per cent of the area co-operatively sown and harvested, 37 per cent of the people co-operating in livestock production, and it absorbs 26 per cent of the fertilizer supplied to the private sector.

The geography of socialist transformation

In the final analysis a geographical treatment of the Yugoslav agrarian situation is necessary and the classic regions still suffice for this purpose. Agriculture is of least significance in Slovenia, though productivity per head is higher than elsewhere. The more advanced stage of industrialization, the closer settlement and denser lines of communication have aided the evolution of the worker-peasant class. Central European in many ways, a German-like solution to its peasant problems appears to be an obvious if not inevitable course. Matching the Slovenian industrial diamond of Rijeka, Ljubljana, Maribor and Zagreb, is the Pannonian diamond of Belgrade, Kikinda, Subotica and Sombor, agro-industrial rather than

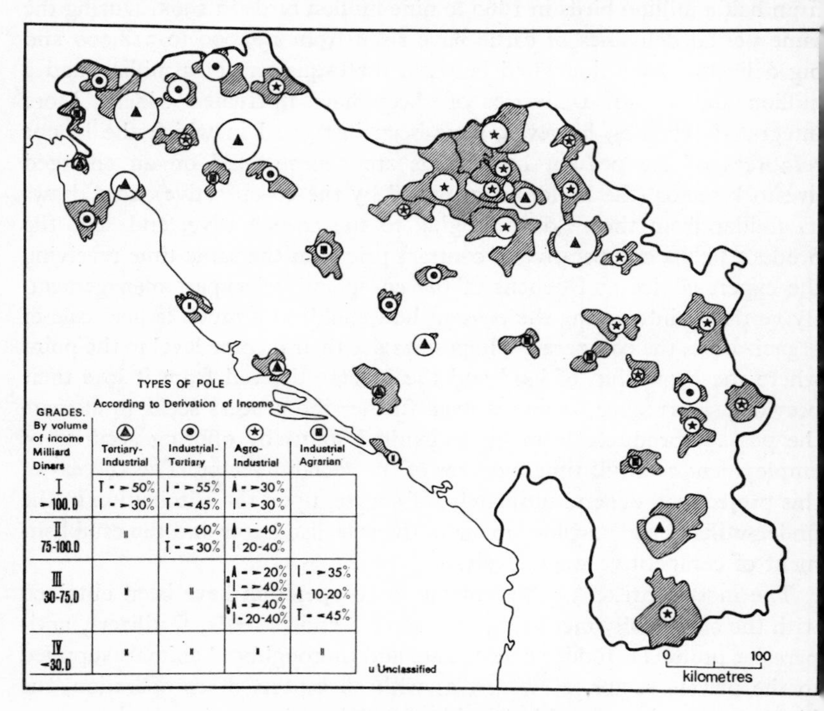

Fig. 6.4. Poles of development, 1966

mainly industrial in character. With its large-scale state agrarian sector, its high and increasing level of productivity, the advanced degree of co-operation with the peasant sector, the evolution of the worker-peasant class and the chances which exist for further vertical integration, it represents the major zone for future agrarian development. At both poles the rapid creation of jobs in the non-farm, non-peasant sectors provides the fundamental condition for the resolution of the agrarian structural problems, whilst for the rich agricultural communes of Slavonia vertical integration offers the prospect of relatively high standards of living amongst a predominantly agricultural population.

The prospects for the upland and mountainous areas to the south of Slovenia, Slavonia and the Vojvodina are far less promising and the solutions to their problems even more remote. In the main the conditions or factors which make for economic progress in the north are either absent or poorly represented. The majority of the communes are agricultural ones and impoverished into the bargain. Forty per cent, often more than sixty per cent, of the population is still dependent upon farming for a livelihood. The impact of industrialization is restricted to a relatively few communes, and it obtains nothing like the effects of concentration achieved to the north.

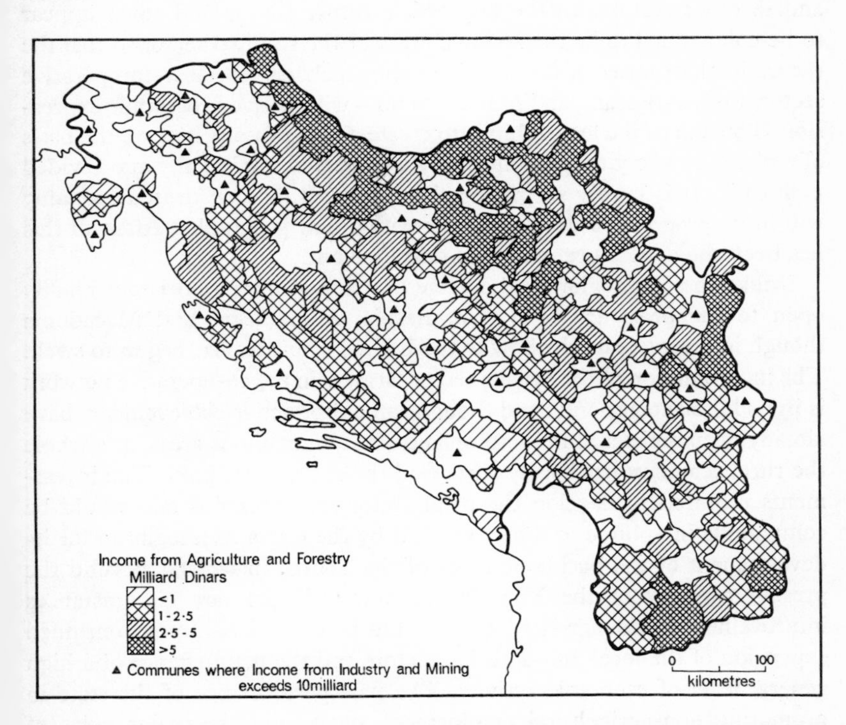

Fig. 6.5. Agricultural communes, 1965 (Agriculture provides the largest single contribution to income)

Predominantly agrarian areas displaying marked emigration and declining populations are to be found in those parts of Croatia near to Slovenia, in the eastern regions of Serbia proper, and to the south-west of Belgrade around Titovo Uzice and Valjevo. Throughout most of the upland areas the population has continued to increase since the early 1950s. Migration, vocational and geographic, can be the only final solution to the problems of living standards in an environment comparable with and in places worse than the upland areas of the Mezzogiorno. This environment offers few of the immediate and spectacular chances of success which the socialist farms achieved in the richer lowlands. There are fewer plums to be picked, and one has the general impression that already in these zones the state has acquired some of the best, as well as some of the worst lands. For socialist farming to become generalized a much lower density of population than the prevailing one would be an indispensable requirement, while the costs of development could only be enormous in volume and lower in profitability relative to the investment opportunities in other regions and in other sectors. In the foreseeable future the upland zones appear to be condemned to be the residual areas of the residual sector so that the theoretical categories of the agrarian policy makers – socialist-co-operative sector, worker-peasant, and peasant sector – will receive geographic expression. The aim of the leadership is to create a non-peasant state on the basis of a peasant society that was formerly fragmented territorially and divided politically. It is hardly surprising therefore that a reconstituted economy will in its progressive development create a new geography. After all this has been the experience of Italian development.

Unlike the Mezzogiorno, the valve of external migration is not readily open to the peasantry of Serbia, Bosnia, Montenegro and Macedonia though in recent years the flow to the E.E.C. countries has begun to swell. The incorporation of the private sector farmers in the co-operative network is in its initial stages only, and though some productive achievements have already been registered in these upland and mountainous areas, as a whole the rural economy has hardly surpassed the subsistence level. The investments required to develop the rural sector are enormous and would be comparable in volume to those required by the Cassa Mezzogiorno for its development of the backbone areas of the South; in fact far beyond the present capacity of the Yugoslav economy. Under any circumstances improvement in the agrarian sector would be conditional upon continued expansion of the local non-agrarian sectors and the maintenance of a high general level of economic activity. The past performance of the state in promoting non-agricultural employment away from the major poles of development has been remarkable. The rate of increase in the Kosmet and Macedonia has been higher than in all the other republics, with the exception of the Vojvodina; and the Bosnian rate of development has kept pace with the Slovenian. At the major poles of development, however, the rate and volume of natural increase of population has been slowing down and diminishing, whereas in the excessively agrarian zones the rate of natural increase of population has been retarded only slightly – in the Kosmet it has risen – and the volume of natural increase has remained fairly constant. Non-agrarian employment in Bosnia and Slovenia, for instance, has grown at the same rate and in similar dimensions. The average annual increase in employment, 1952–65, outside of agriculture has been of the order of 18–20,000, but in Bosnia the natural increase of population has been of the order of 68–78,000 annually; in Slovenia it has been only 12–18,000. Currently the natural increase in the Kosmet is of the same order as in Serbia proper, *c.* 30,000 per annum. In the early '50s the natural increase of population in Serbia proper was 60,000; in the Kosmet it was only 20,000. Between 1952 and 1965 about 50,000 new

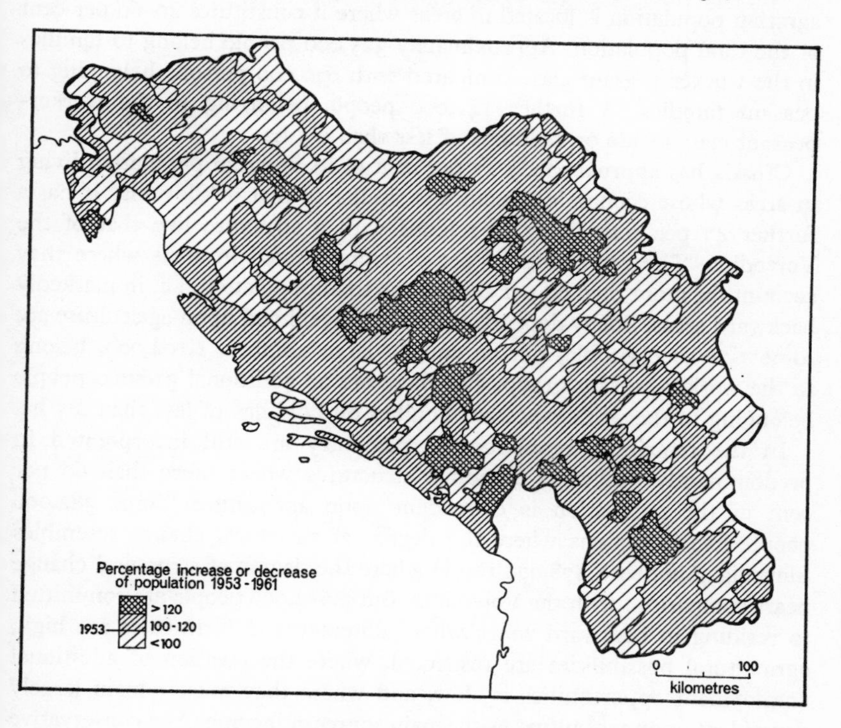

Fig. 6.6. Variation of population, 1953–61

jobs were created in the Kosmet in contrast to the creation of about 450,000 in Serbia proper. To stay where they are, it appears, the residual peasant areas must run faster in future.

Peasant society in Yugoslavia is caught up in that complex situation which we call change. In Slovenia and the adjacent areas of Croatia the transformation of economic structures has reached the furthest point. Almost half of the agricultural population is located in regions where it constitutes the minority, where less than 40 per cent of the population is dependent upon agriculture for its livelihood. Some 313,000 people live in families with holdings of 0·5–15 ha in which part of the income is derived from outside of agriculture. By contrast only some 275,000 people belong to families who are dependent upon agriculture as their main source of income. In addition there are another 152,000 people living on holdings of less than half a hectare who were principally dependent upon non-agrarian sources of income.

Structural change is not so advanced in the Vojvodina. The bulk of the agrarian population is located in areas where it constitutes 40–60 per cent of the total population. Approximately 325,000 people belong to families in the worker-peasant class compared with 640,000 persons belonging to peasant families. A further 141,000 people belonging to the worker-peasant class reside on holdings of less than 0·5 ha.

Croatia has approximately 17 per cent of its agrarian population living in areas whose economic structure is similar to that of Slovenia. It has a further 47 per cent living in regions with a structure like that of the Vojvodina. The remaining 36 per cent are located in areas where they account for more than 60 per cent of the total population, i.e. in markedly backward areas. Solely dependent for their livelihood upon agriculture are some 1,269,000 people, but an equally large number, 1,104,000, belong to the worker-peasant group, and there are an additional 316,000 people belonging to the worker-peasant families on holdings of less than 0·5 ha.

In the remaining republics the peasantry are still incorporated in predominantly backward economic structures where more than 60 per cent of the population is dependent upon agriculture. Some 382,000 people live in regions where the degree of structural change resembles Slovenia. Another 1,878,000 reside where the degree of structural change bears comparison with the Vojvodina. But 3,654,000 people are committed to residing in backward zones where illiteracy and birth-rates are high, agricultural possibilities are restricted, where the creation of additional employment opportunities is slow, and where they must remain largely dependent upon agriculture as the main source of income. At a conservative estimate, about one-fifth of the total Yugoslav population is existing at the residual stage so characteristic of peasant farming at its most elementary level.

POLAND

Almost sixteen million people, half of the total population, still reside in the Polish countryside. Fourteen million of them are, in some way, still dependent upon agriculture for their livelihood. Since 1950 the proportion of the population living in rural areas has declined by 10 per cent, though the actual number has hardly varied; which has been a cause of some concern to the Poles. Most of the natural increase has been absorbed by the towns whose population has risen from nine to fifteen and a half million since 1950. On the basis of the surveys undertaken by the Institute of Agrarian Economics in Warsaw it is possible to sketch the socio-economic character of this rural population, though necessarily the proportions one uses have only an indicative value.[6] A little less than half (42 per cent) of the population in some way dependent upon agriculture is occupied in full-time farming; another 17 per cent are part-time farming families who draw as much as 60 per cent of their total income from non-agricultural sources. Jointly, with the very small class of capitalist farmers still in existence, these two groups form the peasantry, ranging in character from the small and part-time holders through to the medium and large peasantry. A second major social category, accounting for 18 per cent of the total, is composed of the worker-peasant class, who draw more than 60 per cent of their income from outside of agriculture, but who retain agricultural holdings, the majority of which are between 0·5 and 2 ha, the remainder being of 2–5 ha. If one chooses, one can join the part-time farming group to the worker-peasant group, and argue, with some justification, that the part-time sector accounts for approximately one-third of the agricultural population. The remaining 23 per cent of the rural population, in some way dependent upon agriculture, which we have still to account for, is not of immediate relevance to this analysis, though it represents a fair chunk of the rural population. One of its segments, and a small one, is associated as hired labourers with the socialist sector of agriculture. The biggest segment has either holdings of less than 0·5 ha – there are 347,000 of them – or no land whatsoever, and it is employed mainly in industry or to a lesser extent as hired seasonal labour in agriculture. A third and socially significant group (5 per cent of all people dependent on agriculture), entirely without land, or possessing only very small holdings, is composed of aged people, a high proportion of the chefs, 46 per cent, being women.

By adopting the customary terminology of small, medium and large peasant holdings one may all too easily overlook the fact that at present the Polish peasantry are a fairly homogeneous group, that the greatest differentiation is to be sought between the peasantry and the worker-peasant class rather than within the peasantry itself. There are 2 million holdings of between 2 and 10 ha; and 2·8 million holdings, out of a total of 3·24 million, between 0·5 and 10 ha. The small peasant farm is the characteristic farm, and without too great a distortion of reality one may delineate its general outlines.

[6] Gałęski (1966).

TABLE 6.2 *The agrarian structure of Poland, 1950–60*

INDIVIDUAL HOLDINGS '000S

Ha	*1950*	*1960*
0·5–1	206·5	306·9
1–2	415·1	523·0
2–3	375·5	427·0
3–5	616·3	664·9
5–7	477·5	475·7
7–10	499·0	462·0
10–14	246·3	283·6
14–20	92·7	66·6
20 +	39·9	34·5
Total	2,968·8	3,244·2

AGRICULTURAL POPULATION '000S

		Size of holding						
		<2	*2–5*	*5–7*	*7–10*	*10–15*	*15+*	*Total*
Total	1950	1,181	3,269	1,934	2,178	1,138	621	10,357
	1960	1,354	3,164	1,776	1,921	1,297	478	10,081
Active	1950	770	2,042	1,175	1,285	673	386	6,349
	1960	951	2,011	1,060	1,091	711	268	6,098
Family labour	1950	319	1,142	709	794	428	255	3,658
(full-time)	1960	241	961	587	631	428	167	3,020

Source: *Rolniczy Rocznik Statystyczny 1945-65*

Most peasant families are nuclear conjugal families composed of four or five persons. Joint family holdings are rare and three generation households are common only amongst the larger peasant households. The majority of farms consequently have two or three active people, though a quarter have as many as four or five. The chef provides the principal source of male labour, the females supplying the remainder on a full or part-time basis. The average age of chefs is high; half of them are over 50 years of age, compared with 40 per cent in the worker-peasant class. There can be little doubt that a tendency towards the feminization of the labour force and an aging of the male labour force already exists, though its full development is probably impossible at the present stage of economic development reached by Poland. Amongst the very small and part-time farms, however, the feminization of the labour force has already reached an advanced degree. On most small peasant farms, most of the family labour is absorbed by the holding itself and what little off-farm employment or income is obtained comes principally from working on neighbours' holdings or in the socialist agrarian sector. In the case of the part-time farms, the principal source of off-farm earnings becomes factory work, and in contrast to the worker-peasant families, largely unskilled factory work. Usually the married couple are rural people by birth and in about a quarter of the cases they originate from the same village. Their socio-economic origins are not so uniform.

One in eight of all chefs are derived, strictly speaking, from non-peasant households; they come principally from the families of hired hands, or from the working class. Amongst those of peasant origin two opposing trends are apparent. In the smaller farms of 2–5 ha chefs originating from larger holdings are in the majority, whereas on the bigger farms chefs originating from smaller properties preponderate. In addition to the normal dynamics of a peasant population – the rise and decline of individual families – this data indicates a trend towards the establishment of a fully fledged middle peasantry, and also a leaching away of the peasantry by 'demotion' through the stages of small farm, part-time farm, and worker-peasant holding. Anna Szemberg's studies point to the same conclusion: '. . . a clear sign of the "medium holder" tendency', assisted by the chance to lease or purchase land from the State Land Fund and from migrants to the town or from worker peasants willing to reduce the areas farmed by themselves.[7]

The typical full-time farm is about 6 ha in extent, most of it under arable-cereals, potatoes, and a few industrial crops, sugar beet principally – and pasture. One horse, four cows (milkers and heifers), five pigs and about eighty fowl constitute the livestock and produce half of the global output. The basic equipment consists of a plough, a harrow, a four-wheeled cart and perhaps a mowing machine; tractors are a rarity. The global income of the average farm in 1964–5 amounted to 88,400 zlotys. The deduction of production costs, taxes and other charges left the disposable income (in kind and currency) at 43,400 zloty, and expenditure on food, clothing and services left a reserve of 5,200 zl. In recent years the single biggest charge on the running of the farm has been the costs of animal feed. Fertilizer, seed and depreciation are the other principal costs. Food, of course, is the major item of expenditure for the disposable income, 54 per cent, with clothing and household goods being the other main items. In recent years, 1955–6–1963–4, the increase in real disposable income has been largely the outcome of a competition between the costs of animal feed, the growth in output of animal products, and the market price for these commodities, which rose markedly after 1955. With larger incomes the proportion spent on food has declined, but owing to a shift to qualitatively

[7] Szemberg (1963): 10.

better and often purchased foods – meat, sugar, oils and fats, wheaten bread – the decline has been relatively small; 5 per cent only. Hence the relative increase in the consumption of other articles has been limited. Though net reserves have also increased, they have not increased in as regular a manner as disposable income and consequently expenditure upon productive investment has not risen greatly. Cautiously the peasant has invested, first of all in housing (this is a most conspicuous feature of the Polish countryside), and secondly in farm buildings, neither of which are easily expropriated. Ten years ago housing took 46 per cent of the private sector's total investment. In recent years, despite a doubling of the amount invested, it still absorbed over a third; and jointly, housing and farm buildings now absorbed 60 per cent of the total – though it needs to be added, the share expended upon machinery and the improvement of the land has increased progressively.[8]

One might expect this increase of wealth to act as a stimulus to the socio-economic differentiation of the peasantry. M. Czerniewska's survey reveals a very strong correlation between the amount of land per family member, the volume of disposable income and the level of consumption.[9] In general the greater the size of the holding, the larger is the per capita amount of land, and it follows that the middle and large peasantry represent the wealthier segments of their class. But currently the differentiation is expressed in terms of levels of living, the expenditure upon food and consumer durables, rather than in terms of investments in reproductive capital. Perhaps for this very reason the universal increase in the value of output from peasant farms, according to Anna Szemberg, has in recent years tended to retard rather than accelerate stratification.[10] Certainly, geographical contrasts are at present more apparent, if not more significant, than socio-economic ones amongst the peasantry. In the province of Bialystok, for instance, the average disposable income for the large as well as the small peasant farm falls below the national average: whereas in the province of Poznan average income per farm for all categories of farm is above the national average. In the western provinces of Wroclaw, Zielona Gora, Poznan, and Bydgoszcz, average incomes as a whole are above the national level, though the difference between the small and the medium and large farms is considerable in Wroclaw. In the east and south-east parts of the country all incomes, whatever the size of the holding, tend to bebelow the national average, whilst in the central and northern parts the bigger farms have average incomes above, and the smaller farms have average incomes below the national level.

Poland's regional diversity is more a reflection of the country's history than its physical geography. The Regained Territories because of their

[8] I.E.R. (1966). [9] Czerniewska (1963). [10] Szemberg (1965): 26.

history have much in common, though eventually one must distinguish between the Baltic, or nothern zone, and the Oder-Neisse or western zone. To begin with they contain almost two-thirds of the socialist sectors' land. Structurally they are far less dependent upon agriculture than most other regions. Since the end of the war the rate of natural increase in the rural areas has been high, but nevertheless in the private sector the man : land ratio is above average. Participation in the Agricultural Circles is higher than elsewhere. With 29 per cent of the total arable area, these territories contribute 30 per cent of the total marketable output and 28 per cent of the global agricultural output. These broad figures disguise, however, the influence of the Oder-Neisse lands – the provinces of Wroclaw, Zielona Gora and Opole – which together with only 12 per cent of the arable land produce 15 per cent of the marketable output. What is more the private sector is more prominent in these two provinces – in Opole especially – and therefore this considerable contribution to the commercial output cannot be attributed alone to the presence of a large state sector. In fact in the Baltic area the presence of a large state sector is associated with less than proportional contribution to the commercial output.

The remaining parts of Poland constitute peasant Poland. This becomes increasingly true of the south-eastern regions beyond Lodz and Warsaw, towards Lublin, Kielce, Krakow and Rzeszow. The Centre-West region – the provinces of Poznan and Bydgoszcz – partly for historical reasons, display some similarities with the Regained Territories; it contains areas with a long standing reputation for higher farming standards. The socialist sector is not so extensive, but 17·7 per cent of its total acreage is located in the region, which contains 18 per cent of the total agricultural area. It produces about one-fifth of the total marketable output and almost a third of the sugar beet production. As a whole it is the richest and most productive of all the agricultural regions and, it is of interest to note, the region contains the largest single concentration of privately owned tractors in the country. Together with the Oder-Neisse lands the Centre-West region account for 57 per cent of the privately owned tractors, compared with 38 per cent of the tractors possessed by the Agricultural Circles; numerically there are approximately 11,000 private tractors compared with 16,000 tractors belonging to the Circles.

The Centre-East region – the provinces of Warsaw, Lodz and Bialystok – to quote once more the words of Anna Szemberg: '. . . is a region of indigenous owners of medium-sized farms, who are generally held to be the most conservative in their opinions and the most backward in their methods of farming.'[11] The greater part of the region is still at a low level of economic development, which is due both to the legacies of the capitalist

[11] Szemberg (1965): 27.

period and to the fact that the region has so far profited little from such social and economic changes as agrarian reform and industrialization. Without distortion, or a denial of some internal differences, one can extend this description of the Centre-East to include the South-East region – the provinces of Krakow, Kielce, Lublin and Rzeszow. In these two regions the man : land ratio reaches its lowest degree. There are only two hectares, sometimes less, of agricultural land per member of the labour force, in contrast with the three and a half hectares in Poznan and the five hectares in Szczecin. The dependence upon agriculture as a source of livelihood attains its highest level: 66 per cent of the labour force in the province of Lublin. The productivity of land is low in some areas, in Bialystok and parts of Kielce for instance. Elsewhere it is only a little above average. Small full-time holdings predominate; the application of fertilizers is low; participation in the Agricultural Circles is at a minimum. In short, peasant farming in all its residual aspects prevails. But jointly the two regions are responsible for 50 per cent of the country's global agricultural output; 47 per cent of the marketable output. They contain 50 per cent of the total arable area, 58 per cent of the cows, 49 per cent of the pigs, 59 per cent of all individual holdings and 49 per cent of the medium and large peasant holdings. Only 12 per cent of the socialist land area is located there. In productive as well as social terms the agrarian problems of Poland are centred in her historic provinces, and a study of immediate and past trends provides one with no grounds for anticipating that a solution to the productive issues, at least, may be sought as in Yugoslavia, by means of a geographic shift in emphasis.

Ranked according to net agricultural output per holding the list of provinces reads inversely to the list of provinces ranked according to net agricultural output per unit of land. The least productive group of provinces are the Regained Territories of the Baltic; the most productive are those of the South-East. However, given the large difference in the average size of holding, in terms of net output per holding the Baltic provinces rank high with the Wroclaw-Oder-Neisse zone and the Centre-West region. The South-East provinces rank low with the Centre-East and Bialystok region. Thus the two parts of peasant Poland reflect the old historical division between the Prussian and the former Russian and Austrian parts. Once the income from non-agricultural sources is included, and total income is expressed on a per capita basis then a more nuanced regional structure is exposed. In the provinces of Zielona Gora, and Katowice, and in the Carpathian zone the contribution of non-agrarian sources reaches a maximum. In the Baltic provinces the size of family is appreciably higher than elsewhere. Thus on a per capita basis the richest areas are those with a favourable combination of environment, size of holding and size of family:

the Oder-Neisse lands, the Poznan-Bydgoszcrz region, and the industrialized zone of Katowice. The Warsaw-Lodz provinces and the Baltic provinces are in an intermediate position; low productivity is balanced by larger holdings, but in the Baltic area larger families act as a detraction. The South-East region, Bialystok, and the Carpathians are the poorest of all regions, their per capita income being only 85 per cent of the national average.

Looked at in a more dynamic context, about 1·9 million people dependent upon agriculture are located in low income, structurally very backward zones, in Lublin and Bialystok along the frontier with the U.S.S.R. Five and a half million persons are located in areas where 40–60 per cent of the population still depends upon agriculture, where industrialization is confined to a limited number of fairly large towns. Three million, three hundred thousand peasants are located in areas where 20–40 per cent of the population are dependent upon agriculture; that is in areas where the degree of industrialization is advanced; but only a very small number, one-third of a million, are located in highly industrialized zones, Katowice principally. This province alone is responsible for one-fifth of the country's total industrial output. Along the Krakow-Katowice-Wroclaw axis 45 per cent of the total industrial output is concentrated. The only other important industrial zones are associated with Lodz and Warsaw and the lesser 'poles' of Poznan, Bydgoszcz and Gdansk. Reference to them only serves to emphasize the contrast already drawn between the western and eastern parts of the country.

Worker-peasants

It is no easy matter to estimate the size of the worker-peasant force in Poland. In part it is a question of definition, never easily settled; in part it is a question of the adequacy of the statistical data. A broad interpretation of the term permits one to argue, as pointed out above, that approximately one-third of the population dependent upon agriculture may be classed as part-time. Maria Dziewicka, working on a more restrictive definition, estimates that a quarter of the farms of 0·5 ha and more belong to the worker-peasant class of farms; and she states that one-third of the farms of 0·1 ha and more belong to this class.[12] Between 1·6 and 1·7 million workers employed in industrial establishments are either the owners of farms, of 0·1 ha or more, or members of farming families. Again this is equivalent to one-third of the estimated labour force engaged in private farming. A degree of indeterminacy does not prevent one from making the point that the worker-peasants represent a substantial element in the present agricultural population. Though found in many parts of the

[12] Dziewicka (1963).

P

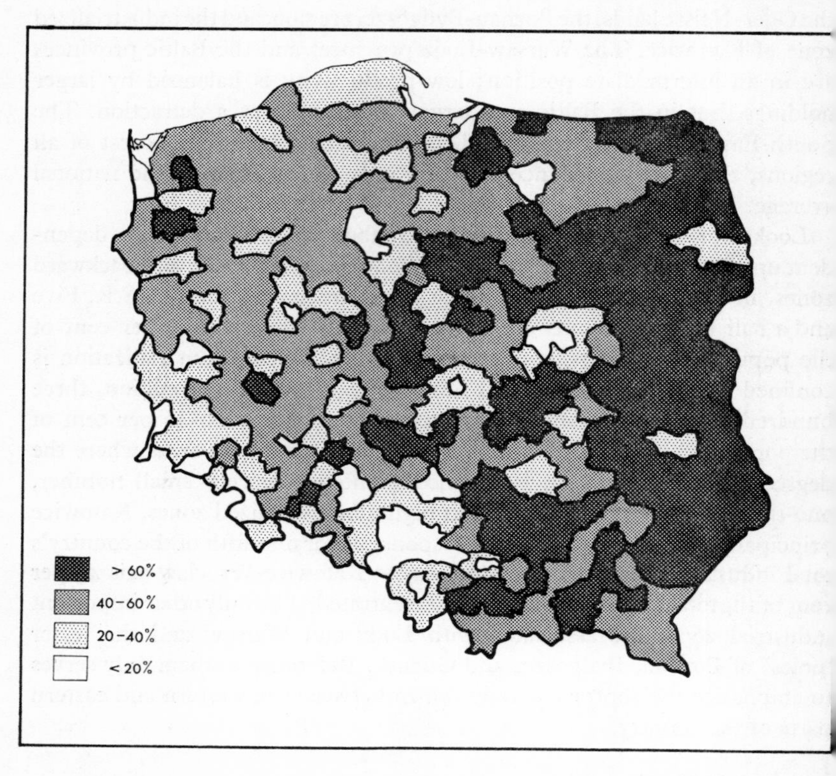

Fig. 6.7. Rural population as a percentage of total population, 1960

country, the worker-peasants are concentrated particularly along the Opole-Katowice-Krakow axis (unfortunately Dziewicka excludes Katowice and Krakow, as well as Gdansk, from her survey), more generally throughout the territories of the Oder-Neisse and the Centre-West region; but they are limited to a smaller number of restricted zones in the remainder of the country. Dziewicka's data reveals that a very high proportion of the 0·5–4 ha farms in the Western part of the country belong to the worker-peasant class, whereas in the Centre-East (Warsaw and Bialystok) and the South-East (Kielce, Lublin and Rzeszow), about a third of the holdings in this category, and particularly those in the 2–4 ha group, are full-time holdings. Given the right opportunity it is highly likely that family members from these farms would be willing to seek more regular and permanent employment in the socialist and non-agrarian sector.[13]

[13] See the two useful maps in Golachowski (1967): 26–7.

Worker-peasant, as a term, is reserved for those families in which the chef, in the main, or other family members work in the socialist sector, in manufacturing, building and construction, transport and communications principally; or as artisans: tailors, carpenters, smiths, masons, coopers, tanners, carters and basket makers. Compared with full-time farms of a similar acreage the worker-peasant farms return higher per capita incomes and higher levels of living. Off-farm earnings constitute the bulk of the earnings but it is of interest to note that on most farms of a comparable size, and in most regions, the contribution of farm earnings on the worker-peasant farms is on average never more than 20 per cent below the level of total income of the full-time farms. As a consequence for 2–3 ha farms, per capita income on the worker-peasant holdings is greater than per capita income on full-time holdings by as much as 50 per cent in the Opole Province, and by as much as 40 per cent in the South-East region. Productivity per hectare and the production of a marketable surplus are lower on the worker-peasant holdings than on the small full-time holdings, but the differences are no greater than 20 per cent. The worker-peasant furthermore is not loath to invest in buildings, in the dwellings rather than farm buildings, and in livestock rather than machinery. It is significant that worker-peasant families tend to be headed by younger men, which no doubt enables them to bear the strain of a twofold occupation.

The emergence of a worker-peasant class is not a solely post-war phenomenon, though the industrialization of the economy has accelerated its growth. Maria Dobrowolska refers to a third generation of worker-peasants employed in the steel plants and coal mines of Upper Silesia and Opole, and associated with the chemical works of Tarnow.[14] In the Krakow Province a system of *Pendelwanderung* has been in existence since the early part of the century, including skilled workmen too. She recognizes the opportunity to find work as the main factor stimulating the development of this class, but is not prepared to let the matter rest there. On the one hand the 'specific character of production' itself, and accessibility, influence the extent of commuting. Some coal mines have as much as 80 per cent of their workers commuting – even some of the older mines possessing large housing estates. Quarries, lime kilns, plants producing building materials, those which use a lot of unskilled labour employ many commuters, as do many construction sites. Branch factories paying low wages, and manufacturing plants of a seasonal nature attract the worker-peasants. On the other hand pressure to find work because of the prevalence of dwarf holdings acts as a strong stimulus to commute. Since 1931 the numbers dependent upon agriculture in Krakow Province have increased by 66 per cent and the average size of holding has declined from 4·9 to

[14] Dobrowolska (1961).

2·4 ha. Stefania Mańkowska perceives a strong correlation between the prevalence of a very low average size of holding and a high frequency of *Pendelwanderung*.[15] The Krakow-Katowice area has strong similarities with the German pattern of worker-peasant evolution, and for obvious reasons. The geography of industrial development inevitably concentrates commuting in this region. But in other and sometimes less historic zones, the phenomena of *Pendelwanderung* is readily observable; on the periphery of Lodz and Warsaw, and around a town like Radom, for instance. The industrialization of a city like Kalisz and the large-scale rebuilding of a town like Kielce creates both employment and the diurnal movement of workers between the town and the villages, which becomes a conspicuous feature of the local traffic flow. In the Zakopane region tourism rather than manufacturing has provided an additional source of income and employment, with obvious effects on the standard of rural housing rather than on the pattern of commuting. One long-established zone of worker-peasant existence is located in the Lysa Gora in settlements like Suchedniow close to the railroad. There the farming is intensive, very intensive in comparison with areas further north, but the minuteness of the holdings inhibits agronomic and institutional innovation which the secondary importance of the farming in the total economy does little to advance. The existence of worker-peasant farming does not necessarily detract from the standard of farming or, as other writers point out with reference to the dwarf holdings of the south-east, prohibit the production of a small but significant marketable output. But as we have remarked previously and in the same context, the development of a worker-peasant class solves the problems of the agriculturalist rather than agriculture.

The presence of industry in the countryside undoubtedly effects changes in rural and village life. It introduces, as Polish rural sociologists have asserted, a change in the valuation of the peasants' labour whether it is hired out or applied to their own plots. Because of greater economic stimulus it also induces an increased productivity of work and its better organization. It widens the view and alters the mode of life, assisting in the establishment of the urban way of life as the model generally aspired to in the village. But it does not put an end to the structural problems of agriculture as Szemberg recognizes. Above all the industrialization of the countryside is not the same thing as the industrialization, through vertical integration, of agriculture, when, for instance, the establishment of a fruit and vegetable processing plant leads to higher productivity and higher returns to the farmers, promotes the acceptance of better farming techniques and co-operation as well as a greater interest in scientific methods, in addition to social and psychological changes.[16] It is to this sort of

[15] Mańkowska (1961): 217. [16] Turowski (1964).

innovation that the Polish agronomists and economists are turning their attention, in an attempt to overcome the production problems of Polish agriculture.

The growth of agricultural output

Polish writers who deal with the topic of agricultural output and its growth concern themselves, most of the time, with two basic issues: the need to put an end to the importation of basic agricultural produce, together with the need to meet the increased demand for food consequent upon the higher incomes and a greater degree of urbanization; and the more controversial issue of what means and methods are best suited to achieving this objective. The production issue is dominated by the fact that 82 per cent of the marketable output is derived from the private sector and any reversal of this situation is inconceivable in the immediate future. True the contribution of the state sector has increased during the past 15 years from 8–18 per cent, but the Yugoslav alternative is not easily imitated; partly for geographical reasons, most of the highly productive land being concentrated in the old peasant zones, not the Regained Territories, and mainly because the experience with the state farms has been discouraging. Yields for the four major cereals in the state sector fall below those of the private sector. Potato yields hardly surpass them and sugar beet yields fall below, despite the application of fertilizers per hectare at twice the rate of the individual sector. Even in the richest zone of the Oder-Neisse lands state farming has not been able to demonstrate a clear superiority. The improvement in agricultural output which has occurred since the mid-'50s has been due largely to the efforts of the private sector which now bears the major responsibility for the projected changes: increased fodder and grain output; the development of cattle breeding, milk and beef production with less emphasis than previously on increasing the output of pigmeat; and a rise in the production of industrial crops and more specialized labour intensive crops.

To the present time the increases in output have been achieved by raising prices and offering additional incentives of a monetary nature; by increasing the inputs into agriculture: machinery, fertilizers, certified seeds and improved livestock, and by experimenting with resurrected institutions, the Agricultural Circles principally. The Circles are much more favoured in the western and Regained Territories than elsewhere, which indicates an immediate need to increase participation in the populous peasant areas, and in addition, a need to define more closely their mode of organization and method of operation. Initially the Circles were composed of and operated by the peasants themselves, but the necessity for a minimum degree of specialization in some tasks has led to the creation of full-time, paid, situations. This step has raised the question whether the Circle might not be developed as an enterprise conducting its own business with its membership on the basis of contracts, services and purchases. Already contracts with the producer co-operatives have become a common feature in the production of sugar beet, milk, meat and vegetables and the whole trend has been recognized by some observers as a move towards vertical integration between the state, co-operative and private sectors in agriculture. However, for one critic, the attitude of the regime, for another, the peasant character of farming, constitute obstacles in the path of this type of development. Though investment funds have been made available through the Circles they have not been fully spent, in Tepicht's opinion due to an inflexibility of attitude on the regime's side as to what constitutes productive capital investment in agriculture.[17] Mechanization, he argues, remains for them the spearhead of investment and hence change. He would prefer a more diversified scheme of investment that recognizes the cumulative effect of a variety of small, less conspicuous, efforts; he cites the value of associating the spare labour of the village community with investment funds to improve local access roads. Above all he wishes to see the so-called preceding and subsequent industrial branches treated at least on a par with enterprises concerned with the provision of tractors and other farm machinery. Contractual relations he regards as being the main propellant for the development of the whole agrarian system, in part because vertical integration proceeds at a faster rate and on a larger scale than the horizontal integration of farms.

Collectivization may be out of fashion in Poland – it is a shibboleth for Gałęski,[18] it cannot be a fundamental vehicle for Hunek[19] – but the socialist transformation of the countryside is not; even though the Restriction on the Division of Farms Act has introduced the principle of land belonging to those who make their living from agriculture and who are genuinely interested in good farming. Anna Szemberg whilst describing the dynamic character of the contemporary agrarian structure and the trend towards the consolidation of a 'middle' peasantry points out that, 'A decisive breakthrough in the socio-economic structure of the rural areas as well as in the purely agrarian structure can be accomplished only by a socialist transformation.'[20] But Hunek is himself sceptical of the immediate prospects for transformation offered by vertical integration because of the impediments created by the essentially peasant character of Polish farming. He argues that the multiplicity of small peasant production units creates considerable organizational and managerial problems for the linking industrial branches. The non-specialization of production

[17] Tepicht (1966): 37–8. [18] Gałęski (1964): 31. [19] Hunek (1963): 16.
[20] Szemberg (1965): 12.

on the peasant farm, an outcome of the peasant chef's labour commitment, is another detrimental factor. Given the large reserves of labour in agriculture, he suggests advanced specialization on one or two items only aggravates the labour situation, a point, if not true in general, which might be relevant to the immediate Polish situation. Besides, continues Hunek, and at this point he becomes utterly ambiguous, vertical integration in developed countries perpetuates the individual holding, it does not bring about horizontal integration, and if the socialist transformation of agriculture is to be seen 'in the form of integration at the village level (horizontal) of the basic factors of production (land, labour and capital), then . . .' Collectivization is out, but horizontal integration it would seem is not.

That a transformation of the village is already under way is indisputable: the outmigration, the impact of the worker-peasant class upon the social structure, the disappearance of the old classes, the penetration of the urban family as a desirable model, the rise in output, income and consumption, and the diversification of consumption; if this does not qualify for the epithet, socialist, it does in anybody's language constitute transformation. Equally indisputable is the growing participation of the peasantry in contract, credit and service agreements with the state. So is the need to provide the preceding and subsequent links. For want of abattoir facilities in the Bialystok province 67 per cent of the livestock in 1960 had to be transported to other provinces for slaughtering, some as far as Katowice, 500 kms distant. From whence it was reshipped for cool storage to Bialystok until it was finally supplied to Upper Silesia.[21] Why some of the Polish writers attach so much weight to the issue of the scale of operation alone, given the circumstances of their agriculture, is easiest explained as an ideological hangover. But Hunek himself recognizes that the expansion of state farming would be economically expensive, reducing the contribution made by peasant accumulation and burdening the state with a relatively high and fixed wages bill irrespective of the performance of the work force – in addition to the cost of land purchase and expropriation. At the same time he fears the prospect of industry having to support agriculture; which it does already, in the sense of having to supply industrial exports to pay for agricultural imports, a situation which can be circumvented only by the investment in agriculture of capital largely industrial in origin. Of course the policy of self-sufficiency in agriculture may be the wrong one for peasant Poland at this stage in the evolution of her economy. The importation of cheap foodstuffs and fodder concentrates may, given the prevalent small size of holding, be the most economical way of raising output and productivity in the livestock sector and of allowing for specialization in other sectors. To ask a primarily peasant agriculture to provide

[21] Chiczuk (1962): 156.

for absolute national self-sufficiency as well as rising standards of consumption is to ask for something which has rarely been achieved. As one soon appreciates after contemplating the figures for the rising importation of animal feed into the peasant economies of late nineteenth-century Western Europe.

The formulation of an agricultural policy without apparent internal contradictions will depend, it seems, upon the final rejection of a few dearly held beliefs, a more flexible attitude towards policy making, and the re-evaluation of a few obvious facts. Given the size of the agricultural population and the structure of holdings, given the amount of time which will be required to reduce the proportion dependent upon agriculture to the levels current in post-liberation France, the value of the residual function of peasant farming ought not to be underrated. It has the merit of providing some sort of work and some sort of security for a great number of people, and under present conditions maintains them in a far from hopeless, miserable or immobile condition, without the disadvantage of presenting for solution all of their problems at one instance of time, as is the case with collectivization. In the opinion of some critics this may constitute a reprehensible sort of socio-economic limbo. As Golfin puts it, perhaps the peasantry are eternally condemned to live outside the walls of the socialist city.[22] One may respond, this has been the prime condition for the construction of the capitalist city.

Tepicht acknowledges the necessity for agriculture to provide employment for a large part of the population for some time to come. If during this period of time the peasantry is to prosper then accumulation in the private sector must occur, and by the sensible and imaginative use of state investment funds it can be stimulated. Is it, one is forced to speculate, this fear of accumulation, and hence capitalism in the countryside, that so grievously perturbs the ideologues? If it is, then do they not underestimate the import of their own achievements in the construction of a socialist society? In Lenin's time, surely, capitalism in the countryside could have meant only one thing – capitalist labour relations which formed the basis of exploitation and hence the creation of capital in certain hands. With the expansion of the socialist sector and the creation of a wage earning class the Communists have created a situation where the labour utilized or purchased for the peasant holding must now be evaluated according to a higher and foreign standard. The existence of an industrial wage level, and the opportunity for employment outside of agriculture will mean in Poland, as it has in Western Europe, that hired labour will be too expensive for the private sector to afford. To combat this change the farmer will invest singly or co-operatively in machinery. Accumulation will take place and the

[22] Golfin (1961): 39.

capital resources of the individual farmer must increase; but no Marxist ought to argue that by increasing the capital investment per worker one is creating capitalism, or a capitalist mentality. True enough, in Communist eyes, unless a greater degree of incorporation in a co-operative sector occurs, certain vestiges of capitalism or a capitalist mentality may persist in the countryside which may be deplorable in terms of their value system. But by the creation of socialist industry and employment in the socialist sector the Communists have established the essential condition for the socialist transformation of the countryside. It could be objected that this is insufficient, that the transformation under way in the Polish countryside will produce conditions too closely resembling the conditions produced by the transformation of the West European countryside, and therefore the agrarian sectors will come to resemble one another as closely as the industrial sectors have every appearance of doing. Only collectivization, it could be argued, has so far produced a transformation of the countryside without parallel in the West – a point to which, given the irony, one would have to assent.

Conceivably, under two conditions, capitalism could re-emerge in the Polish countryside: if the socialist sector became incapable of expanding its non-agrarian employment opportunities, and this condition became chronic; if the process of differentiation under way within the peasantry at the moment led to the creation of a latent capitalist class, who would reveal their existence in these circumstances by hiring the labour unable to find employment in industry. Such circumstances might justifiably arouse fears; but a persistence of the condition essential to such a state of affairs – a chronic failure to expand industrial employment – would be tantamount to the failure of the socialist economic system itself. For surely the aim of socialism is to provide that security of employment, but at a higher material and cultural standard of living, which, unaided, the peasant farm has supplied for so many centuries.

7 PEASANTS: park-keepers, proletariat and paysans évolués

In the post-war world peasant farming has become more capital intensive and as a consequence, more productive; the eastern and southern European countries trailing behind those in the north-west as they did in the inter-war period. Not only has the volume of capital invested increased, its character has changed; land has become relatively less, and the products of modern industry and science relatively more important. The modern *chef d'entreprise* needs to supply himself and his family labour with an amount of capital per worker that approaches and often exceeds the ratios in manufacturing, in order to achieve a level of remuneration somewhere within the range received by the factory worker. The necessary capital resources are often beyond his individual capacity to acquire; or they impose upon him such heavy charges that his consumption standards are slow to rise. His earnings are jeopardized by the fluctuations in market prices which reflect the ever increasing amount of produce his new productivity supplies. The prices of land remain high. True, there are less people earning a living from farming, but the competition for land amongst farmers desirous of enlarging their scale of operation, and between agricultural and non-agricultural uses, as well as the attractiveness, in the West, of farm land for urban investors, all maintains a seller's market in properties. Without reiterating all the problems of the peasant farm, one can say, despite its remarkable capacity to adapt, to incorporate new technologies, to modify the composition of its labour force, despite its capacity to survive – its survival in the coming decades is not assured; basically for two reasons. First, the amount of capital per unit of labour has become so enormous and costly that the peasant chef cannot for very much longer accept responsibility for the labour commitment which is fundamental to his enterprise and social system. When land and labour were the major factors of production, then within what were often elastic limits it was feasible to provide work and income for all members of the family. When it becomes necessary to invest in the farm at present standards, in order to remain competitive within the farming industry, then it is often beyond the capacity of the majority of chefs to supply sufficient capital for all members of the family labour force. Unless the chef is prepared to withdraw from the circuit of economic existence and disregard contemporary materialistic standards – an attitude more attractive to a type of urban rather than a type of rural mentality – he is forced eventually to consider his labour supply from the point of its productivity and in terms of profit and loss common to industrial society. As the pressure increases for him to accept this form of economic accounting so does the necessity to free himself of his labour commitment. Fortunately, at the very time the chef's capacity to meet the labour commitment of the peasant enterprise has diminished, so has the industrial system removed the necessity for the existence of the peasant economy – the second fundamental reason why its survival is unlikely. The evolution of industrial society has created, or is in the process of creating, a situation where an unheard of degree of security of employment, and income, at high and progressively rising levels of living can be provided for the vast majority of the population. In these circumstances the labour commitment of the peasant enterprise has lost or is losing much of its historical and social significance.

Peasant society has entered a phase in the century old crisis induced by the appearance of industrial society which in all probability will conclude with the final disappearance of the peasant economy – in the sense we have chosen to understand it. The significance of the past two decades is that during this period general, long-term, economic growth has become a certainty for the future. Whereas in 1910, or 1920, one could not assume that secure employment could be guaranteed by the non-agricultural sector for the mass of the population, in the 1960s not only is the assumption a reasonably safe and commonly accepted one, it has been widely accepted as a primary aim of national economic policy. The retention of the peasant economy is not only unnecessary in the long run, it is also liable after a certain stage of economic development has been reached to delay the achievement of the desired ends; and some of its characteristics, for instance the close association of the kinship and economic orders, inhibit the full development of an industrial society. The principal doubt concerns not the final outcome of the process, but the length of time that will be required for its completion. Some future, as well as certain past actions of the state, may have the effect of delaying the result. Peasant society is not without means to defend what it considers to be its real interests. At certain times it is in the immediate interests of the state to take advantage of certain features of the peasant economy. Though the conclusion may appear to be a simple and obvious one, there are no grounds for assuming the process itself will be either simple or direct.

How the final phase in the long crisis of peasant society will work itself out will be influenced by the varied character of the different socio-economic groups that compose the twentieth-century peasantry. Four groups are common to all the peasantries of Europe: the elderly peasants and those with marginal full-time holdings constitute the first two, and they are not always clearly separable from one another. In future they may come to be recognized jointly as the park-keeper element. The worker-peasant class constitutes the third group. In future I think it would be advantageous to reserve this term to those who are employed as salaried or wage workers in manufacturing or tertiary industries. The term 'part-time' could then be reserved for those who run an additional business as well as a farm. The distinction lies in the preservation of managerial functions by the part-time farmer and the loss of those functions by the worker-peasants when they participate in the secondary and tertiary sectors. The tendency is for the worker-peasant to assimilate to a form of industrial labour, the proletariat; whereas the part-time farmer – in the West – acquires the characteristics of the petite bourgeoisie. It is a misnomer to refer to chefs who engage seasonally in off-farm, but agricultural work, as either part-time farmers or worker-peasants. They never leave the agricultural sector; their future will most likely be determined by the evolution of that sector, particularly the capitalist or socialist part. They could be referred to as the 'labourer-peasant' class, and could conceivably, whilst remaining within the agricultural sector, undergo a process of proletarianization and assimilate to the permanent wage labour force of either the capitalist or socialist branches.

The fourth group consists, of course, of the full-time family farms – the paysans évolués – the group that will strive to stay in farming at the price it is assumed of shedding all the basic characteristics of the peasant enterprise. Before one forecasts the shape of things to come amongst this group, it is advisable to consider further the evolution of the other two groups – the park-keepers and the proletariat – because the policy adopted by the state towards the full-time farmers will in part be influenced by the policy it adopts towards the others. Furthermore it should be made clear that the forecast is built around the French example, because at its present stage of evolution it falls approximately mid-way between the more advanced stage of north-west Europe and the more retarded stage of southern and eastern Europe. Once placed within a regional context the forecast must be varied accordingly.

The problem of the elderly in agriculture will persist for another generation or more without any doubt. There are at present a large group of chefs in their forties and over committed to farming because of investments and the lack of vocational adaptability that comes with age. For humanitarian reasons the collectivity must, and for electoral reasons the state will, support their level of living. Over the decades their relative importance should decline, and any uneasiness that persists in the liberal economic minds of the western dirigists concerning the propriety of maintaining them can be assuaged by regarding them as park-keepers of a cultural heritage; a role which they will share with the class of marginal full-time farmers located in the more isolated but, fortunately, often the most scenic areas. The economies of these peripheral regions, and their demography, can only be restructured by a policy of industrial revival and decentralization. Basically, as the French have come to recognize, these regions will in future fall within the scope of the portfolios of the Ministry of Industry, or the Department of Regional Development rather than the Ministry of Agriculture. But of course it is primarily to the budgets of the Agricultural Ministry that the peasants will continue to look for succour, for it is there they will be able to exert maximum political pressure.

In certain fortunate areas the possibility will exist for the park-keeper class to merge with the part-time class by entering the tourist trade. However, capitalistic features are becoming more evident in that industry, and the competitive position of the *Fremdenzimmer** in the era of the package tour is reduced. Already some of the old farmhouses are being purchased by urban dwellers as summer or winter retreats; a trend which reflects the changing function of the countryside in an urbanistic civilization. But such developments can be of only marginal significance to the future of the agricultural classes, though they are far from unimportant to the future of the countryside.

Because of the social and economic needs of the aged and park-keeper group, continuing state intervention will be inevitable, and whatever the real intention of the administration may be, their actions will have the effect of preserving the characteristic and ancient structures of peasant farming. It will be difficult therefore to resist the goose and gander argument, and on past evidence one will have good grounds for assuming that the paysans évolués will use the measures intended for the park-keeper element to protect and preserve some of the rigidities within their own structures. What is more, the ranks of the park-keeper group are likely to be swollen by the drop-outs from the modernizing groups as the threshold of viability is successively raised in terms of technology and capital. In reality the apparent interests of the évolués will not be so different from the interests of the other groups as the classification implies.

In the chapter on Federal Germany the factors accelerating and retarding the proletarianization of the worker-peasant class were discussed and it was stressed that there is little novel about the existence of a binary

* A sign which often stumps the monolingual novice in German speaking areas; it offers bed and breakfast, sometimes more, like the cottages of the Lake District.

economy in rural areas, as a reading of Deffontaines' historical geography of the Middle Garonne will convince one. The original features of the economy in this century are that it allows the peasantry to participate in some of the latest scientific and technological developments of the industrial age; it enables them to participate in some of the growth industries and thereby engages them in the process of economic development so that they can assist themselves to overcome some of their backwardness. It increases the taxable capacity of the community, and the possibilities of its investing in its own future by building schools and improving community facilities, housing and water reticulation for instance. It raises material living standards and introduces the population to a new educational and vocational perspective. It renders possible a transition from one type of society to another without necessarily de-rooting the population, and in a variety of ways it provides the basis of a more independent and personal life less cramped by the irritations, the arbitrariness, the insensitivities, the restrictions and restraints of a familial existence. What the expansion of the binary economy does not solve are the structural problems associated with the agrarian side of the enterprise.

From both a regional and economic planning point of view the expansion of the worker-peasant class retards the concentration of the population in the metropolitan areas, it assists in the retention of the young people in the countryside, and it helps to modify in a favourable manner local or regional demographic structures. It reverses the simplification and agriculturalization of the rural economies which has been widely associated with the establishment or penetration of the capitalistic mode of production by recreating the more varied economic structures of the rural areas in the pre-industrial revolution era. Encouragement of an expansion of the binary economy must be considered as a means of raising living standards amongst the park-keeper class. Furthermore it is to be expected that an inflow from the full-time farming class will help in maintaining numbers within the binary economy. In Denmark, a country with almost only full-time farmers, dual employment is on the increase, though at most only 3 per cent of the agricultural labour force is concerned. However, the considerable achievements of the binary economy in Germany, its appearance in the East, its adoption in the schemes for the Mezzogiorno, are no guarantee that if it is promoted it will necessarily be successful.

One of the outstanding characteristics of rural industrialization in Baden-Württemberg is the long-standing support and encouragement it was given by the state, especially during the first half of the last century, when there was never any doubt about the inapplicability of the Manchester School of economic reasoning to this particular case. Another feature that has bearing upon the success of this Swabian venture lies in the structure – and structure in the Levi-Strauss sense – of industry in Baden Württemberg. Despite an apparent diversity and lack of similarity in the products of the region there is a basic similarity of organizational arrangement, manufacturing processes and skills which has permitted to a remarkable degree the transference of learning and skill, imitative adaptation, differentiation from a common core, a wide range of variation upon a dominant theme.

The Baden-Württemberg model encourages the diffusion of industrialization throughout the rural areas and it is not the only pattern of decentralization available. Industrial growth can be, and has been, centred at chosen nodes and poles, with the surrounding rural population being drawn into an industrial system composed of the branches of national, even international, firms; in any case consisting of rather large plants located on industrial estates. This pattern is naturally suited to a centralized and dirigist form of administration, whether it be of the Cassa or East European type. The more centralized system is likely to overlook the variety of opportunities and sources of materials and labour which entrepreneurs in a diffused pattern can more easily discover. Diffusion can mean that the benefits of the industrial systems reach the village level more rapidly than with a system under centralized direction, and many of the differences, if not antagonisms, between town and country are genuinely wiped out. But a diffused pattern of industrialization does pose real as well as ideological difficulties for the dirigist as well as the centralised bureaucracies.

Although a modernized peasantry has been the accepted aim of Western policy makers and statesmen for the last two decades, and a somewhat similar aim has been adopted, a little reluctantly, in Poland and Yugoslavia, what constitutes a modernized peasantry remains an unanswered question. The term itself is thoroughly ambiguous. Paysan évolué represents at best a forecast, at worst an aspiration, and its specifications can be laid out according to various degrees of satisfaction depending on the hopes of the planner.

It is unlikely that as a class the paysans évolués will attain parity with comparable industrial earnings. For the '60s the O.E.C.D. experts 'did not expect full income parity to come about . . . rather a maintaining of the present income-parity ratios was assumed'.* This would be an equally safe assumption for the '70s. It is easily forgotten that the whole discussion of parity is conducted in averages, that in fact there are already an undetermined number of family farms which have reached or exceeded income parity. Farmers as a group always prefer to deal in averages; it helps to

* All quotations in this chapter are derived firstly from O.E.C.D. Documentation in Food and Agriculture 67, 'Problems of Manpower in Agriculture', and later from Kardelj 'Problems of Socialist Policy in the Countryside'.

maintain the illusion of the poor underprivileged country dweller. Perhaps more peasants will enter the more fortunate category in the coming decade, but it is highly doubtful that the whole class of family holdings will gain entrance to this chosen state. There is every indication that the threshold of viability for the full-time class will rise. Not only have France and Germany a surplus of labour in agriculture; so have more agriculturally advanced countries like Holland, Denmark, Sweden – even the U.S.A. and probably New Zealand. To think in terms of a certain size of farm, with a certain capital loading, as the farm of the future is probably quite misleading. Past experience would indicate this. To project in terms of a lower percentage of the labour force being engaged in agriculture and most of it employed in a modernized family farming may be a more enlightened approach, but the exercise serves only to remind one of the enormous changes which must occur to achieve such an end; and in the process one is forced to consider whether in fact the family holding is the best choice for the future – particularly when one reads in the same O.E.C.D. report, 'The increasingly family centred character of the Dutch farm industry may be regarded as one of the chief problems for a continuing adjustment to changing economic and technical conditions.'

If an indeterminacy surrounds the modern peasant holding from the viewpoint of the size of holding and the attainment of income parity – one assumes a rise in real and nominal income – this emergent type can be defined by other attributes. A progressive shedding of the peasant enterprises' labour commitment is a prime condition for its successful development. In the process the dual role of *chef d'entreprise* and *chef de famille* will be replaced by one that is equally dualistic but more specifically economic: worker-manager. Probably the best indicator of the break up of the peasant enterprise will be the disappearance and dissolution of the two-generation household, and particularly the assumption of the entrepreneurial functions by the chef at a much earlier age than has been customary. One assumes the chef will take over the running of the farm according to his managerial capacities and capital resources, rather than having to wait upon the parents' decision to relinquish control. For this to happen will require a degree of security and assured income being available to the retiring chef; it may also involve a vacating of the farm dwellings by the parents for a second dwelling located on the farm, or more likely, in the near-by town. It could be achieved by the son acquiring control of a second and not parental farm before the retirement of his father. Either alternative presupposes a much higher level of income and productivity than exists at present and an unheard of degree of mobility within the land and mortgage market.

Instead of being content to see his family housed, fed and clothed as a result of their joint effort, the chef of the modernized holding will adopt a more individualistic attitude to the enterprise. He will expect a return for his manual and intellectual efforts at a level related to some urban rates of remuneration. As a manager he will come to judge his operations in terms of the yield upon the capital invested. His whole production programme will be decided from the beginning by the needs and demands of the market. Manpower problems will remain, but they will be of a different nature to those posed for his predecessors. It will be a long while before even modernized farmers will be able to dispense with some of the work provided by wives. But one must assume, given the penetration of urban attitudes, that the amount of work will have to be reduced and its nature lightened – otherwise farmers will find it hard to get wives. The character of the relationships between the conjugal pair will change, making the married couple one of the principal items of sociological research in future. The children's contribution of labour will be reduced on account of their longer period of schooling, and because the majority will quit the agricultural sector upon entering the labour force.

The chef of the future will have to obtain his labour supply either through some form of group co-operation, or by hiring labour, or by utilizing contractors; perhaps some combination of all three. Group co-operation is considered by some experts to hold considerable promise for the future. One will have to wait and see, but the magnitude of the problems which it raises are undeniable. To attract and retain hired labour, the chef will have to meet wage rates comparable with those in urban areas, and working conditions will have to reach higher standards than those which prevail at present. Agricultural contractors usually operate successfully only if agriculture itself is prosperous, and there is some degree of specialization. In order to modernize the peasant chef must rid himself of the old historic labour commitment. In order to be successful the chef of the future must solve quite original labour problems. Whether he can do this within the limits imposed by that somewhat magical entity – the two-man unit – must be regarded as a matter for doubt.

To set down in cold prose some meaningful description of a modernized peasantry is to map the enormous gap which separates even this modest model from reality. It does have the value of reminding one that for all the discussion and documentation concerning the modernized family holding, it was only accepted recently as an objective of social policy. That for all the current spate of reports and papers the formulation of a policy to achieve this end is only in its infancy. That the majority of problems remain unsolved, and very little that is new has in fact been attempted on any considerable scale. It can be summed up by saying that it took the first half of the century to pose clearly the problem of the family holding in a modern industrial and European civilization; leaving the second half of the century in which to formulate and implement a solution. In the meanwhile the greatest single aid to the solution of the problem has been the massive, unorganized movement of labour out of the agricultural sector, made possible, fundamentally, by the dynamic state of the industrial economy.

L'ordre éternel des champs?

One of the most impressive contrasts to be observed in Europe is the contrast in field patterns between the capitalist or socialist sectors and the peasant sector. Perhaps the most memorable case, because one is least prepared for it, is the contrast between the Czech and Polish sides of the Bohemian border. The immobility of peasant agrarian structures which this parcellated field pattern reflects is oppressive, because it expresses in a physical manner the magnitude of the problem which restructuring involves. It is to be compared with the environmental and socio-economic problems created in urban areas by the progress of the industrial revolution, so costly to redevelop, so inhibiting to change. Decades will pass before this urban heritage is finally demolished, before industrial society can bear the full costs. One can only assume it will be even longer before the costs of redeveloping the heritage of an older and lengthier civilization can be borne. In Bohemia and Moravia especially – in parts of Hungary and Yugoslavia also – to observe the total erasure of the strip system has an almost surgical effect. In one enormous crude gesture a wholesale geographic and cultural change has been produced. Perhaps time and familiarity soften the effect of a similar process when one travels across the capitalistic areas of the Paris Basin. There, however, one knows that hidden beneath the pattern of large fields there is, or was until recently, a quite morcellated pattern of properties. This is true of some parts of the Vojvodina, where the practice of enclosure has brought the small property of the small peasant within the organizing control of the socialist farm. Is agricultural progress possible, one is forced to reflect, without the acceptance of a more fluid concept of property and holding, without less ideological attachment to either big or small scale, without the substitution of capital per man for acreage as the measure of bigness? In America a highly varied structure is receiving wide acceptance. 'It is characteristic that the largest and most efficient farms at present tend to be of mixed tenure, part-owned and part-rented. The even larger holdings of the future may require some innovation in mode of tenure or financing.'

It is doubtful how soon in Europe large scale and small scale can be divorced from their historic and ideological context. Small scale for some sections of the community in the West is synonymous with family property and individualism. It can be used on different occasions in both an anti-capitalist and an anti-socialist context. It is often difficult to divide agricultural issues and the production of food from social matters, questions of economic democracy and individualism, though the relationship is more historical than logical. Therefore it is very difficult amongst some sections in the West to discuss the future of agriculture in anything but a family farm context. Yet it seems highly improbable that an agrarian structure basically oriented towards family farming can achieve the degree of fluidity which a highly technical and productive level of farming demands.

In the West the expression, large scale, can have either a feudal or collectivist connotation. There is a reluctance to admit that the free world brand of industrial society is itself a type of collectivist society, in which many economic and social problems are solved by the adoption of collectivist measures. It is therefore rather anomalous to disregard a capitalist and large-scale solution for agrarian problems in the West and somewhat of a confusion to associate large-scale farming solely with the communist form of collectivism. In the East, by contrast, an ideological reluctance persists to accept a small-scale solution to the agrarian problem, because of the confusion in farming of small scale with capitalism and large scale with socialism! Yet the small-scale peasant farm solution appears to be the best suited for the economies of Poland and Yugoslavia given their present stage of economic development.

If ideological rigidities have been slow to disappear from public debate and conference,* in practice both in the East and the West, a varied

* To remind the reader of the sort of context within which peasant farming has been discussed in the West, the following quotations are reproduced. The first is from a speech delivered to a conference of agricultural economists; the second is from an article by an Austrian minister of agriculture. It is only fair to add that other persons concerned with agriculture reject such attitudes:

'Neither the Catholics nor the Protestants are against communal life entered into freely, but they refuse to see, as do the Hutterites, a propertyless existence as the necessary basis for eventual salvation. They are not of the belief that within the context of the family peasant farm and of the peasant family all social and economic problems are solvable, but, however, they see in the family peasant farm a form of economic and social existence in which mankind thrives and grows and in which an indestructible community and community life can be realized, and which is capable also of providing a moral basis to that life. In the modern community the churches intercede in favour of the family peasant farm on ethical and social grounds. They will not settle for a pressurized and subversive extermination of the peasant economy.'

'Western culture has sprung from a peasant basis. No culture can thrive if it loses its roots. We live during a vast and disturbing crisis. Crises can be final or a new beginning. In one that goes as deep as this, then must the life force draw if it can upon the original sources.

'Dialectical materialism will be overcome if we can subdue our own materialism. Because the communists are systematically destroying their peasantry we have agrarian structure has emerged, and has been accepted explicitly as a geographical phenomenon. An agrarian structure that includes a capitalistic, a socialistic, an advanced peasant co-operative and a residual peasant sector is not inconceivable, illogical, or very far from the facts in some countries. In Algeria for a brief period after independence all four forms were in operation at one time – though the circumstances were exceptional. The political antagonism between the capitalist and the socialist forms tends to make life impossible for one of them; but either one can exist alongside the remaining two. In France and Italy, particularly in the Mezzogiorno, and Yugoslavia, the state has given expressed support to this type of geographical evolution. The Polish position has been less positive, but in actuality the situation is very close to that in the other countries. In Czechoslovakia the refusal to accept a varied structure and a geographical solution has entailed the abandonment of land in some areas, or its under-utilization in others. On close examination the socio-economic farming zones are never as homogeneous as one might wish for; their principal significance is that they are inducing an unusual degree of flexibility into state planning, and the design and administration of agrarian programmes. The execution of a geographically differentiated programme can only result in a greater differentiation of the regions within a country. Initially this is going to make the elimination of differences in regional standards of living rather more difficult; and initially the effect will be to produce different economic structures and socio-economic geographies rather than homogeneous ones. Already economic growth has produced in the West, and is producing in the Mezzogiorno and the East, quite marked geographical shifts in emphasis. Regional policy it would seem needs to be conceived in the context of phases or stages of economic growth as much as does agrarian policy.

What effect this type of development will have eventually upon the general character of agrarian policy can only be surmised. But it is not unlikely that success in the socialist zones of Yugoslavia will be used as proof of the superiority of the socialist measures, which might lead to a heavier emphasis upon the promotion of the socialist sector. Whether the rapid advances that are likely to be made in the capitalist areas of farming in the West will advance official support for this type of enterprise is problematical; for the electoral strength of the peasant areas, though slowly diminishing, will still be a factor to contend with.

In what manner the Yugoslavs and the Poles will respond to the latent political pressure of their peasantries during a period which will most

therefore every ground for maintaining our own. From a spiritual standpoint the maintenance of a peasantry in an industrial society is unquestionable and this fundamental decision has to be taken.'

probably see some increased degree of political participation is for the moment a matter of speculation. However it is not rash to assume that the socio-economic evolution of the peasantry in the East will be similar to that outlined above. It seems likely that the worker-peasant group will continue to distinguish itself from the remainder of the farming population; proportionately its importance will most probably increase. Amongst the full-time peasantry, the process of differentiation which is rather difficult to trace at the present, will, no doubt, lead to the emergence of the elderly, the marginal and the economic units, with the latter strengthening their economic position in society. Kardelj has made it quite clear that the state will not pander to private property ambitions; neither does it 'intend to keep and support (the peasants) small property illusions artificially with subsidies'. He does, however, recognize the working peasant as 'one of the pillars of our political system' and that 'to maintain and strengthen the peasant population's actual political support for our socialist force' constitutes the second immediate aim of agrarian policy. Primarily he believes the peasant question will be solved 'through the industrialization of the country by the movement of the greater part of the labour force from the villages into industry and other branches of the economy'. And while recognizing the persistence of a large residual peasant population for some time to come, he assumes that it 'represents only a remnant from the past and a social problem which will be gradually solved by the process of economic and social development'. A viewpoint which on the basis of Western experience is rather too sanguine if not actually delusive. Very indicative of trends likely to emerge more fully at a later date were the elements of a structural programme very similar to those in the West which the Poles produced in late 1967. It included remembrement, pensions to speed the departure of the aged, and a good farming law which threatened confiscation of land that is poorly farmed. It is too easy to say that these two countries in the relations with the peasantry will follow a course close to that followed in the West. They will nevertheless, find it impossible to avoid confronting many of the same issues, and to avoid meeting some of the economic and political demands that arise from a modernizing peasantry.

An inherently labour intensive system

In a sense the Poles and Yugoslavs have been forced to debate the old issue of the disadvantages and advantages of peasant farming, an issue that will come up for debate again and again in many underdeveloped countries. It is not a subject upon which one wishes to expand within the framework of the book, except for two arguments arising from the material presented: that the most significant characteristic of peasant farming is not its backwardness, but its labour intensiveness: that to adopt this characteristic as the basis on which to formulate a development programme is not always advisable. Two arguments which help to give definition to a further argument – investment in industry or agriculture? – that needs considerable definition itself before it can be developed in a productive manner.

The labour commitment of the peasant enterprise constitutes a positive advantage for Yugoslavia and Poland at their present stage of development; it provides work and security for a mass of people for whom no ready alternative exists. The capacity of the peasant enterprise to absorb and adapt modern technologies and scientific knowledge to a basically labour intensive system is a further advantage. At the phase of development reached in the West these virtues appear to be vices. The problems of peasant farming, one may say, are a reflection of the problems of the larger economic system, its stage of development, of which the peasant economy is a part, frequently the major part. Peasant societies, when they are backward, are backward because the society to which they belong is backward; because only a certain stage of technological development has been reached; because the society consists of a partly decimated population and destroyed culture lorded over by a foreign, landed, ruling class; because of the dependent or colonial status of the whole society during a period of rapid demographic growth. Some persons may like to think of peasant farming in the West as a backward sector; but bearing in mind the remarkable adaptations it has made since the war, and the extraordinary performance of the industrial sector during the same period, it is obvious that the term can be applied in only a highly relative sense. There is little that is inherently backward about peasant farming itself, though it has been designed primarily to satisfy an autonomistic type of society usually at a far lower level of material existence than prevails in the present industrialist-collective society. The peasant economy is, however, an inherently labour intensive system. Given the eco-system and the technological level, it seeks to find work for as many hands as are available. The majority of countries throughout the world, with large or small peasant populations, will be planning to achieve some degree of economic development and structural change in the coming decades. What they ought to consider is not so much the pros and cons of peasant farming – most of them for political reasons will have to favour peasant farming anyhow, and if they do not then they will run the risks of economic setbacks. Rather they should bear in mind that in a developmental situation the rationale of of the peasant productive system – the creation of as much work as possible – can be misleading. As it was in the Mezzogiorno. In those countries where agriculture is considered to be successful, in New Zealand and Denmark for instance, it is successful, and this is not the least important reason amongst many, because the export trade provides the farming industry and its entrepreneurs with a yardstick against which decisions, investment decision especially, can be assessed. Agriculture is cast in a framework of economic rationality that is not self engendered. When emphasis is placed on industrial expansion in a development programme, then agriculture is provided with a similar sort of yardstick. But when agriculture itself is preferred, in many underdeveloped countries this is tantamount to deriving the priorities for investment from a productive system that is predicated on a largely non-economic basis; to adopting a framework of rationality that is self-engendered and self-referential.

One does not wish to advocate the industrial case of the Industry *v.* Agriculture argument. The post-war experience in Europe leads one to the conclusion that the real question which an investment programme must answer is not whether the money should go to Industry or Agriculture, but to what sort of agricultural investment and what sort of industrial investment. And, most important, what stage or phase of economic development will have been reached at the end of the investment period. Agricultural investment should not always be designed within the context of the present stage of development. It should have regard for the likely stage of development that will be reached. Otherwise as in the Mezzogiorno one may end up with abandoned farms and inadequate marketing facilities; or as in Holland, with modernized farms already outdated by new circumstances.

The European experience has clarified the importance of the preceding and subsequent links in the agro-industrial complex. The Polish, Yugoslav and Mezzogiorno experience has indicated at how early a stage of development these links become significant. The West European example has indicated their long-term and continuing importance at a much later stage of development. In effect both the eastern and the western countries are saying that they hope to overcome the disadvantages of peasant farming by linking the farms through a regulated or centralized marketing system where non-peasant modes of production prevail. At one time it was thought that the introduction of the tractor would be the means by which peasant farming was revolutionized or destroyed. To the contrary, peasant farming adapted the tractor to its own ends. It brought about changes but they were never as far reaching as expected. Along a similar line of reasoning might not the association of the peasant holding with the preceding and subsequent branches have the effect of helping to maintain rather than change the peasant enterprise? It must be acknowledged that generally the degree of vertical integration attained is not high, only for certain products has a complete level been achieved. Generally there is still a long way to go before integration becomes a common feature of agriculture. Integration is advocated as a means of helping the family farmer to overcome his difficulties, which is not quite the same thing as saying it will help to preserve the peasant economy. Compared with tractorization, vertical integration is a far more pervasive phenomenon. It attacks the polycultural basis of peasant farming. It requires the coordination and programming of the farm operations to the requirements and rhythms of the other sectors. It puts an end to the anarchy of marketing procedures and replaces outright individualism with co-operation and discipline. It brings capital into the agricultural sector, not to the level of the farm it is true, but it creates the conditions where investment at the farm level may become more attractive. Perhaps the basic reason why vertical integration is most likely to produce radical changes is that it finally reduces the peasant economy to the status of a dependent system, integrating it to a quite foreign system, socialist or capitalist, from whose own logic the stimulus for reform will be derived.

Both in the East and the West the weight given vertical integration in the '60s constitutes a recognition, not necessarily explicit, of the importance of tertiary services in the modern world. On both sides a degree of economic fundamentalism has prevailed which has lead to the over-emphasis on directly productive activities, agricultural or industrial: growing wheat, ploughing land with tractors, making steel or concrete. The attitude towards tertiary services has been conditioned by their association with precarious forms of employment; odd-jobbing and petty trading, professional and bureaucratic employment. Consequently the new technological and scientific branches of the tertiary sector and their influence upon agrarian development have been underrated. It amounts to this, that in future and with respect to the stage of economic development, programmes of agrarian investment ought to have in mind the market situation towards which the economy is evolving, and the type of industrial investment best suited to achieve that end. European experience stresses that a varied agrarian structure both economically and geographically has much to recommend it, so long as the variations are politically enforceable or acceptable. If there is the chance of redistributing land without granting a permanent title, the opportunity ought to be seized, to avoid the immense costs of remembrement which may arise at a later date. European experience leaves one in no doubt whatsoever that only in the context of a dynamic economy moving towards a collectivist and industrial solution can any general solution of low rural living standards be found. But given the general validity of this point there is the essential qualification that the requirements and aims of an agrarian programme must vary according to the character of the prevailing stage of economic development and the immediately succeeding stages.

In the interwar period when the concept of economic growth had only limited diffusion, when the desire for growth lacked its present urgent and politically unavoidable appeal, then agrarian programmes were tailored for a redistribution of wealth and the maintenance of the peasantry as a sort of economic and cultural enclave. Only the Russians seem convinced of the necessity to liquidate them – the British having achieved this very thing at a far more convenient historical period. Now growth has become the master principle for all economies and it has been recognized that the peasantry must participate and assist in this growth. In Poland and Yugoslavia it has been accepted that an anti-peasant programme retards growth. In the West it is recognized that too large a peasant sector restrains growth, but at the same time it is acknowledged that some mitigation of the unfavourable effects of growth must be sought. Strong attachments to particular forms of property and to particular scales of operation are somewhat less common than previously among certain sections of the administrators, though a considerable rearguard remains to fight a series of last stands. Agriculture itself is now treated as part of the whole economic structure, related to and influencing other sectors and other opportunities. There is a refreshing willingness to adopt a more nuanced, less doctrinaire, more eclectic attitude towards agrarian problems and their solution. This constitutes real progress.

Indicative of which way the wind is blowing are the titles of books dealing with agrarian problems. In France, for instance, immediately after the war one could call a book simply '*Les Paysans*'. In the mid-'50s it was obvious that something had to be done about agriculture. It was a case of '*Exode ou Mise en Valeur des Campagnes?*' By the end of that decade some writers still believed in the '*Vocation Agricole de la France*', but others caught the militant and resistant mood of the peasantry: '*La Révolte Paysanne*' and '*Les Paysans contre le Passé*'. The events of the '60s produced a more decisive, final, sort of title. Suddenly it was, '*Une France sans Paysans*', '*La fin d'une agriculture*', '*La fin des Paysans*' – titles which in no way influenced the choice of sub-title for this volume, but encouraged one to stick by the original decision.

It will be at least a decade or two in the West, longer in the East, before people looking like the peasants in the photographs of this book no longer populate the rural landscape. What the traveller of the future must remember is that many of them will be for most of their time factory workers, some will be evolving towards a type of economic and cultural existence not so different from his own, whilst many, especially in those rather isolated and backward areas that are likely to attract the urban holiday-maker, will be little more than wards of the welfare state.

Over the centuries our thinking has been conditioned and confused by the occlusion of food production with the family labour unit, and we have called this agriculture. This industry has been required to fulfil two main functions, to supply food and material for manufacturing – the societal function; to provide work for the large bulk of the population – the social function. At low levels of material existence food, clothing and shelter – all agricultural products – have constituted the bulk of a person's income. So the equation which has dominated the existence of the peasant enterprise, work = income, has approximated closely to reality. Around the central theme of work, most of the variations of peasant existence have been woven. We have yet to create a society, as opposed to a class, whose existence is not built around this theme. But in the developed world a society structured around leisure now appears to be a not too distant prospect – at least it is comforting to believe this. If this sort of society becomes a reality then the need to confuse the provision of food with the need to create work will no longer exist, and the peasant enterprise and economy will have reached a point where their historical and social purpose will have quite disappeared.

REFERENCES

CHAPTER 1

BARBERIS, C., 1963 'La femme dans l'agriculture italienne', *Études Rurales*, 10, 50–67.

BARBICHON, G., 1964, 'Le devenir du paysan hors de l'agriculture – Recherches récentes', *Études Rurales*, 13–14, 194–211.

BICANIC, R., 1956, 'Occupational Heterogeneity of Peasant Families in the Period of Accelerated Industrialization', *Trans 3rd World Conference of Sociology*, 4, 80–96.

BOURDIEU, P., 1962, 'Celibat et condition paysanne', *Études Rurales*, 5–6, 32–135.

CHAYANOV, A. V., 1966, *Theory of Peasant Economy*, Illinois.

DEBATISSE, M., 1963, *La révolution silencieuse*, Paris.

——, 1966–7, 'Le monde paysan et les instutions politiques', *Paysans*, 63, 7–18.

VAN DEENEN, B., *et al.*, 1964, *Materialien zur Arbeitswirtschaft*, Forschungsgesellschaft für Agrarpolitik und Agrarsoziologie e. V. Bonn, Band 153.

FRANKLIN, S. H., 1962, 'Reflections on the Peasantry', *Pacific Viewpoint*, 3, 1, 1–26.

——, 1965, 'Systems of Production: Systems of Appropriation', *Pacific Viewpoint*, 6, 2, 145–66.

KARDELJ, E., 1962, *Problems of Socialist Policy in the Countryside*, London.

NIEHAUS, H., 1954, 'Lage und Aussichten der Kleinbauern in der gegenwärtigen Wirtschafts – und Gesellschaftsordnung', *Bericht über Landwirtschaft*, Sonderheft, 160, 40–59.

Polish Perspectives 1963, 'Against Fragmentation of the Land', 6, 10 October, 56–8.

RÖHM, H., 1957, 'Die Vererbung des landwirtschaftlichen Grundeigentums in Baden-Württemberg', *Forschungen zur Deutschen Landeskunde*, Band 102, Remagem.

SHANIN, T., 'The Peasantry as a Political Factor,' *Sociological Review* 14, 1, 5–27.

VINCIENNE, M., 1965, 'Un aspect de l'exode rural: l'image de la ville chez les immigrés', *Études Rurales*, 18, 79–100.

CHAPTER 2

BECKHOFF, J., 1963, *Wandlung der Lebensverhältnisse in zwei ursprünglich kleinbäuerlichen Taunusgemeinden unter dem Einfluss der sich wandelnden Sozial-, Wirtschafts und Agrarstruktur*, 139, Forschungsgesellschaft für Agrarpolitik und Agrarsoziologie e. V. Bonn.

VON BERGHES, F., 1961, 'L'évolution d'une region économiquement pauvre illustrée par l'example de l'Eifel-Hunsruck', *Documents de la Conférence sur les Économies Régionales*, E.E.C. I: 165–82, Brussels.

BERGMANN, H., 1958, 'Der Einfluss der Mechanisierung auf Produktivität, Einkommen und Kosten landwirtschaftlicher Betriebe', *Berichte über Landwirtschaft*, 36, 3: 502–44.

Bundesministerium für Ernährung, Landwirtschaft, und Forsten, Bonn, *Landwirtschaftliche Buchführungsergebnisse*, annual.

Bericht der Bundesregierung über die Lage der Landwirtschaft (Grüner Bericht-Green Report), annual.

Die Verbesserung der Agrarstruktur in der Bundesrepublik Deutschland, 1964–5.

1966, 'Struktur- und Investitionspolitik Soziale Sicherung und geistige Förderung der Landwirte', Heft 124, *Landwirtschaft-Angewandte Wissenschaft*.

Bundesministerium für Wohnungswesen, Städtebau und Raumordnung, Bonn, *Erster Bericht der Bundesregierung über die Raumordnung* (Raum-ordnug Bericht), 1963.

BUSCH, W., 1936, *Die Landbauzonen in deutschen Lebensraum*, Stuttgart.

VAN DEENEN, B., 1963, 'Wirtschafts- und Erwerbsstruktur als Bestimmungsgründe der Tragfähigkeit'. *Forschung und Planung in ländlichen Entwicklungsgebieten*. 147, Forschungsgesellschaft für Agrarpolitik und Agrarsoziologie e.V. Bonn, pp. 27–36.

——, 1965 (A) 'Die Aussagekraft einer Gemeindetypisierung für regionale und agrarstrukturelle Entwicklungsmassnahmen', *Die Verbesserung der Agrarstruktur in der Bundesrepublik Deutschland. 1964-5*, Bonn, pp. 24–30.

——, 1965 (B) Karten (maps), Die Gemeinden der Bundesrepublik Deutschland nach der sozialökonomischen Struktur und Funktion; A. Die Gemeinden nach der Unterhaltsstruktur der Bevolkerung und nach der Standortfunktion 1961; B. Die Gemeinden nach der landwirtschaftlichen Betriebsgrossenstruktur und nach der sozialökonomischen Funktion der landwirtschaftlichen Nutzflache 1960, Forschungsgesellschaft für Agrarpolitik und Agrarsoziologie e.V. Bonn.

VAN DEENEN, B., MROHS, E., *et al.*, 1964, *Materialien zur Arbeitswirtschaft*, 153, Forschungsgesellschaft für Agrarpolitik und Agrarsoziologie e.V. Bonn.

——, 1965, *Materialien zur Alterssicherung in der deutschen Landwirtschaft*, 158, Forschungsgesellschaft für Agrarpolitik und Agrarsoziologie e.V. Bonn.

FARHI, L., 1962, 'Monographie de la grande région agricole C.E.E. No. 15, (Allemagne)', *Études Agricoles Régionales à l'échelle de la Communauté Économique Européenne*, E.E.C. Informations Internes, cyclostyled, Brussels.

FRANKLIN, S.H., 1964, 'Gosheim, Baden-Württemberg: A Mercedes Dorf', *Pacific Viewpoint*, 5, 2: 127–58.

HARTKE, W., 1956, 'Die "Socialebranche" als Phänomen der geographischen Differerenzierung der Landschaft', *Erdkunde*, 10, 257–269.

HESSE, P., 1949, *Grundprobleme der Agrarverfassung*, Stuttgart.

——, 1965, 'Der Strukturwandel der Siedlungskörper und die Landesentwicklung in Baden-Württemberg zwischen 1939 und 1961', *Jahrbucher für Statistik und Landeskunde von Baden-Württemberg*, Neunter Jahrgang, Jahresband, Stuttgart.

Hessisches Statistsches Landesamt, Wiesbaden.

1960, *Hessen im Wandel 1860–1960*.

Monthly: *Staat und Wirtschaft in Hessen*.

HISS, D., 1966, 'Faktorproportionen und Faktormobilitat als Probleme der westdeutschen Agrarpolitik', *Agrarwirtschaft*, 15, 5: 159–63.

HOFFMAN, H., 1935, *Landwirtschaft und Industrie in Württemberg*, Berlin.

HÜFNER, W., 1964, 'Das Bruttoinlandsprodukt der kreisfreien Städte und Landkreise in der Bundesrepublik Deutschland 1957 und 1961', *Sozialprodktsberrechnungen der Länder*, Gemeinschaftsveroffentlichung der Statistischen Landesämter, Weisbaden.

KÖTTER, H., 1955, 'Der Einfluss der socialen und wirtschaftlichen Differenzierung der Landbevölkerung auf die Landbewirtschaftung', *Berichte über Landwirtschaft*, Sonderheft 162: 23–57.

——, 1960, 'Das Betriebsgrössenproblem in seiner Abhängigkeit von der gesellschaftlichen und gesamtwirtschaftlichen Entwicklung', Sonderdruck aus der Vortragsreihe der 14 Hochschultagung der Landwirtschaftlichen Fakultat der Universitat Bonn vom 4 und 5 Oktober 1960.

KÖTTER, H. and VAN DEENEN, B., 1961, *Materialien zum Problem der Westdeutschen Agrarstruktur*, München.

KUHNEN, F., 1954, *Die soziale Struktur und der Lebensstandard der Familien in typischen Landgemeinden Baden-Württemberg*, 20, Forschungsgesellschaft für Agrarpolitik und Agrarsoziologie e.V. Bonn.

——, 1959, 'Harmonische Raumgestaltung durch Industrieansiedlung in ländlichen Gebieten', *Agrarwirtschaft*, 8, 3: 82–8.

——, 1961, 'Die Verbreitung nichtlandwirtschaftlicher Einkünfte bei landbewirtschaftenden Familien in der Bundesrepublik Deutschland', *Papers and Discussion of the Second Congress of the European Society for Rural Sociology*, Oslo, 1960, pp. 439–53.

LANGER, M. W., 1964, 'La politique du gouvernement fédéral en matière de structure régionale', *La politique régionale dans la Communauté Économique Européenne*, Brussels.

Materialien zur regionalen Wirtschaftentwicklung in Mittelgebirgslagen der Bundesrepublik Deutschland, herausgegeben der Forschungsgesellschaft für Agrarpolitik und Agrarsoziologie e.V. Bonn:

CRAMER, H., 1964, 'Eifel-Hunsruck', Text- und Kartenband, 150

KÜTTNER, H., 1965, 'Rhon-Vogelsberg', Text- und Kartenband, 151.

LEFFER, C., and SCHALL, S., 1964, 'Bayerischer und Oberpfalzer Wald', Text- und Kartenband, 152.

MÜLLER, J. O., 1964, *Die Einstellung zur Landarbeit in Bauerlichen Familienbetrieben*, 155, Forschungsgesellschaft für Agrarpolitik und Agrarsoziologie e.V. Bonn.

MÜLLER, G. and KÖTTER, H., 1956, 'Wirtschaftlichen und Soziale Bestimmungsgründe der Lage der westdeutschen Landwirtschaft', *Berichte über Landwirtschaft*, 34, 4: 393–414.

NIEHAUS, H., 1954, 'Lage und Aussichten der Kleinbauern in der gegenwartigen Wirtschafts und Gesellschaftsordnung', *Berichte über Landwirtschaft*, Sonderheft 160: 40–59.

PRIEBE, H., 1954, *Wer Wird Die Scheunen Füllen*, Düsseldorf.

——, 1961, 'Begriff und Abgrenzung der landwirtschaftlichen Betriebsgrösse', *Agrarwirtschaft*-Sonderheft 13: 53–65.

RÖHM, H., 1956, 'Die Auswirkungen der Industrialisierung auf die Siedlungsstruktur und die Verteilung der landwirtschaftlichen Betriebsgrössen in Sudwestdeutschland', Sonderdruck aus *Deutsche Siedlungs-und Wohnungspolitik*, Köln-Braunsfeld.

RÖHM, H., 1957 (A), 'Das Problem einer sozialökonomischen Klassifikation der landbesitzenden Familien', *Berichte über Landwirtschaft*, 35, I: 1–40.

——, 1957 (B), 'Die Vererbung des landwirtschaftlichen Grundeigentums in Baden-Württemberg', 102, *Forschungen zur Deutschen Landeskunde*, Remagen.

——, 1959A, 'Stellung und Bedeutung des bodenverbundenen Industriearbeiters in Vergangenheit und Gegenwart', *Berichte über Landwirtschaft*, 37, I: 1–19.

——, 1959B, 'Die Landpacht im südwestdeutschen Raum', *Berichte über Landwirtschaft*, 37, 4: 806–33.

——, 1961, 'Soziale Bestimmungsgründe für die Entwicklung der landwirtschaftlichen Betriebsgrössen und der ländlichen Arbeitsverfassung', *Agrarwirtschaft*-Sonderheft 13: 92–113.

ROLFES, M., 1954, 'Betriebsstruktur und wirtschaftliche Lage in kleinbäuerlichen Dorfen', *Berichte über Landwirtschaft*, Sonderheft 160: 14–22.

——, 1955, 'Die wirtschaftlichen Verhältnisse landwirtschaftlicher Nebenerwerbsbetriebe in verschiedenen Landschaften des Bundesgebietes', *Berichte über Landwirtschaft*, 33, 2: 319–76.

SCHOLZ, H., 1960, 'Betriebsgrösse und Betriebseinkommen in der Landwirtschaft' and 'Ursachen der Einkommenestreuung in landwirtschaftlichen Betrieben', *Berichte über Landwirtschaft*, Vol. 38, Heft 1 & 4, 110–18 and 659–65.

Statistisches Landesamt Baden-Württemberg, *Statistik von Baden-Württemberg*, 1958, Band 48, 'Die Wirtschaftskraft des Landes Baden-Württemberg und seiner Stadt-und Landkreise'.

1964, Band 90, 'Gemeindestatisttik Baden-Württemberg. 1960/61' five parts.

STOCKMANN, G., 1934, 'Die Verbindung von Landwirtschaft und Gewerbe in Baden-Württemberg', *Schmollers Jahrbuch*, 58 Zweiter Halbband 4–6: 551–68 and 675–708.

WAGENER, H., 1958, *Untersuchung Landwirtschaftlichner Betriebstypen in* Württemberg, 80 Forschungsgesellschaft für Agrarpolitik und Agrarsoziologie e.V. Bonn.

CHAPTER 3

BONTRON, J-C., and MATHIEU, N., 1966, 'La population agricole, évolution au cours du V.e Plan', *Paysans*, 60, 23–32.

CUISENIER, J., 1966, 'Fonctions économiques des organisations et des administrations agricoles en France', *Études Rurales*, 21, Avril-Juin, 5–71

DEBATISSE, M., 1963, *La révolution silencieuse*, Paris.

DE LAUWE, J. C., 1946, *Bretagne et Pays de la Garonne*, Paris.

DE VAISSIÈRE, J., 1966, 'Reflexions sur une politique des structures d'exploitations agricoles en France', *Revue Française de l'Agriculture* Printempts, 12–22.

DE VIRIEU, F-H., 1967, *La fin d'une agriculture*, Paris.

DUMANT, M., 1962, *Ce que vaut la terre en France*, Paris.

DUMONT, R., 1956, *Voyages en France d'un Agronome*, 2nd Edit, Paris.

FAUVET, J. and MENDRAS, H., 1958, *Les Paysans et la Politique*, Paris.

FLATRÈS, P., 1963, 'La deuxieme "Révolution agricole" en Finistère', *Études Rurales*, 8, Janvier-Mars, 5–55.

France de Demain, Paris, eight volumes of which:
2. La région du Nord et du Nord-Est.
3. Les régions de l'Est.
6. La région du Sud-Ouest.
7. La région de l'Ouest.
8. La région du Centre.

GERVAIS, M., SERVOLIN, C. and WEIL, J., 1965, *Une France sans paysans*, Paris.

KLATZMAN, J., 1962, 'Monographie de la grande région agricole C.E.E. No. 17 (France)', *Études agricoles régionales à l'échelle de la Communauté Economique Européenne*, 5, Brussels.

LAFON, T., 1967, 'Questions aux agriculteurs associés dans des formules de groupe', *Paysans*, 65, 25–32.

LAMOUR, M. PH., 1964 'Les principes de la politique suivie en France en matière de développement économique', *La politique régionale dans la C.E.E.* 92-108, Paris.

LE BALLE, Y., 1958, *L'ouvrier paysan en Lorraine mosellane, Paris.*

'L'économie agricole', Annual, *Revue d'Economie Politique.*

LERAT, S., 1961, 'L'introduction du mais hybride dans les pays de l'Adour', *Revue Géographique des Pyrénées et du Sud-Ouest*, 32, 97–117.

LEROY, L., 1958, *Exode ou mise en valeur des campagnes*, Paris.

LIVET, R., 1965, *L'avenir des régions agricoles*, Paris.

MALLET, S., 1962, *Les Paysans contre le passé*, Paris.

MENDRAS, H., 1956, 'Structure ecologiques et sociales des régions considérées', *Economie Rurale*, Juli.

MENDRAS, H. and TAVERNIER, Y., 1962, 'Les manifestations de juin 1961', *Revue Française de Science Politique*, XII, No. 3, Septembre: 647–71.

O.E.C.D., 1964, Low Incomes in Agriculture – Problems and Policies Paris.

PHILIPPONNEAU, M., 1957, *Le problème breton et le programme d'action régionale*, Paris.

——, 1963, 'La Bretagne, une expérience de rénovation regionale', *Tendances*, 22, Avril: 153–83

PINEDE, C., 1960, 'L'immigration bretonne en Aquitania', *Revue Géographique des Pyrénées et du Sud-Ouest*, 31, 5–43 and 181–96.

'Politique agricole française' (no date), *Revue Française de l'Agriculture.*

'Politique agricole de groupe', 1965, *Revue Française de l'Agriculture.*

'Premiers résultats de l'enquête au 1/10e pour les structures agricoles en 1963' (The one in ten survey)', 1965, *Statistique agricole*, Ministère de l'Agriculture, Vols. I and II.

QUIERS-VALETTE, S., 1963, 'Les causes économiques du mécontentement des agricultures français en 1961', *Revue Française de Science Politique*, XII, No. 3, Septembre, 555–98.

RIMAREIX, G. and TAVERNIER, Y., 1963, 'L'Elaboration et le Vote de la Loi Complémentaire à la Loi d'Orientation Agricole', *Revue Française de Science Politique*, XIII, No. 2, Juin, 389–425.

Statistique Agricole, annual, Ministère de l'Agriculture, Paris.

'Tableaux de l'Agriculture Française', 1966, *Paysans*, 61.

TAVERNIER, Y., 1962, 'Le syndicalisme paysan et la politique agricole du

gouvernement (juin 1958-avril 1962)', *Revue Française de Science Politique*, XII, No. 3, Septembre, 599–646.
——, 1966, 'Le syndicalisme paysan et la Cinquième Republique (1962–1965)', *Revue Française de Science Politique*, XVI, No. 5, Octobre, 869–912.
VIAU, P., 1963, *Révolution agricole et propriété foncière*, Paris.
WRIGHT, G., 1964, *Rural Revolution in France*, London.

CHAPTER 4

BANDINI, M., 1957 (A) *Cento Anni Di Storia Italiana*, Rome.
——, 1957 (B) 'Six Years of Italian Land Reform', *Banca Nazionale del Lavoro Quarterly Review* 41, June: 5–47.
BARBERO, G., 1961, *Land Reform in Italy, Achievements and Perspectives*, Rome.
CAIZZI, B., 1962, *Nuova Antologia della Questione Meridionale*, Milan.
CAMPLONGO, A., 1962, 'Le Dimensioni Globali del Problema Economico del Mezzogiorno', *Economia Internazionale*, XV, 55–78.
CAMPUS, F., 1965, 'La dinamica delle strutture e della utilizzazione del suolo', *Rivesta di Economica Agraria*, XX, 1 and 2, pp. 249–334.
Cassa per il Mezzogiorno:
1953, *Problemi dell'Agricoltura Meridionale*, Studi e Testi No. 2, Naples.
1955, 'I Problemi della Montagna nell'Italia Meridionale', *Atti del Secondo Convegno Tecnico*, Cosenza, September 1954, Rome.
1956, *Economia delle Transformazioni Fondiarie*, Vol. I, Studi e Testi No. 5, Naples.
1962, Dodice anni 1950–62, Vols. 1 and 2, Bari.
1965, *Rapporto sui Problemi dello Sviluppo Agricolo del Mezzogiorno*, cyclostyled.
CASSIN, E., 1959, *San Nicandro*, London.
Comitato dei Ministri per il Mezzogiorno:
1965, 'Studi su alcuni aspetti demografici economice e sociali del Mezzogiorno', Vol. II, *Relazione sulla Attivita di Coordinamento*, Rome.
1966 (A), *Relazione sulla Attivita di Coordinamento*, Rome.
1966 (B), *Studi Monografici sul Mezzogiorno*, Rome.
1966 (C), *Piano di Coordinamento degli interventi publici Mezzogiorno*, Rome.
COLAMONICO, C., 1960, *Memoria Illustrativa della Carta Utilizzazione del Suolo della Puglia*, Rome.
DE LEEUW, A. and VICINELLI, P., 1963, 'Les certains aspects de l'amélioration des structures agraires en Italie', *Les Structures Agricoles Dans La C.E.E.*, Informations Internes, Brussels.
DELL'ANGELO, G. G., 1960, *Note sulla Sottoccupazione nelle Aziende Contadine*, SVIMEZ, Rome.
DOLCI, D., 1960, *Spreco*, Turin. Published in England as *Waste*.
DICKINSON, R. E., 1955, *The Population Problem of Southern Italy*, Syracuse.
ENTE MAREMMA, 1955, *La Riforma Fondiaria in Maremma 1951–1954*, Rome; issued in English, 1959, as *The Land Reform on the Maremma*.
Ente Puglia-Lucania, *The Agrarian Reform in Puglia, Lucania and Molise*, various dates, Bari.

FRANKLIN, S. H., 1961, 'Social Structure and Land Reform in Southern Italy', *The Sociological Review*, 9, 3: 323–49.

INEA. *Annuario dell'Agricoltura Italiana*, Rome.

Risulti Economici di Aziende Agrarie, for all Regions commencing with the results for 1962, and published annually, Rome.

MEDICI, G., 1952, *Land, Property and Land Tenure in Italy*, Bologna.

——, 1958, *Carta dei Tipi d'Impresa nell'Agricoltura Italiana*, Rome.

MEYRIAT, J. (Ed.), 1960, *La Calabre*, Paris.

MILONE, F., 1955, *L'Italia nell'economia delle sue regioni*, Turin.

——, 1956, *Memoria Illustrativa della Carta della Utilizzazione del Suolo della Calabria*, Naples.

Ministero dell'Agricoltura e delle Foreste, no date, 'Strutture e Servizi per lo Sviluppo Produttivistico delle Campagne', 9, *Quaderni di Studio ed'Informazione*, Rome.

MOSCHINI, F. N., 1958, *La Riforma Fondiaria Agraria in Maremma*, Florence.

ROCHEFORT, R., 1961, *Le Travail en Sicilie*, Paris.

ROSSI-DORIA, M., 1956, *Riforma Agraria e Azione Meridionalista*, 2nd Edn. Bologna.

——, 1958, *Dieci Anni di Politica Agraria nel Mezzogiorno*, Bari.

——, 1962, 'Agricultural Development in the Mezzogiorno', *The Statist*, 6, April; 47–50.

——, 1963, *Memoria Illustrativa della Carta dell Utilizzazione del Suolo della Basilicata*, Rome.

SERPIERI, A., 1947, *La Struttura Sociale dell'Agricoltura Italiana*, Rome.

SVIMEZ, *Informazione SVIMEZ*, Rome. (Weekly.)

——, (1961), *Un Secolo di Statistiche Italiane: Nord e Sud 1861–1961.*

VINCINELLI, P., 1964, 'Rural Areas Development Programme in Italy', *Regional Rural Development Programmes*, OECD Documentation in Agriculture and Food, 66: 235–46.

VILLARI, R., 1961, *Mezzogiorno e Contadini nell'Eta Moderna*, Bari.

VOCHTING, F., 1955, *La Questione Meridionale*, Naples.

CHAPTER 5

BRUNING, K. (Ed.), 1959, 'Die Landwirtschaft in der Europäischen Wirtschaftsgemeinschaft', Parts 1 and 2. Band XI, *Raum und Landwirtschaft* 2, Akademie für Raumforschung und Landesplanning, Hannover, Bremen-Horn.

CLERC, F., 1965, *Le Marché Commun Agricole*, Paris.

E.E.C. Commission, Brussels:

Agrarstatistik (at least eight issues per year), published by the Statistisches Amt der Europäischen Gemeinschaften.

Informations Internes (cyclostyled and with restricted circulation), a series of monographs issuing from the Directorate General for Agriculture.

Newsletter on the Common Agricultural Policy published by the Division for Agricultural Information in collaboration with the Directorate General for Agriculture. (Cyclostyled.)

Recueil des Documents de la Conférence Agricole (des États membres de la C.E.E.) Stresa, 3–12 July 1958.

Studies in the Agricultural Series (various dates).

I.L.O. 1960, *Why Labour Leaves the Land*, Geneva.

NIEHAUS, H., 1958, 'Effects of European Common Market on Employment and Social Conditions in Agriculture', *International Labour Review*, 77, 289–312.

O.E.C.D. (O.E.E.C.)
Documentation in Agriculture and Food, Paris.
1960, *Agricultural Regions in the European Economic Community*, No. 27.
1964, *Regional rural development programmes with special emphasis on depressed agricultural areas, including mountain regions*. No. 66.
Problems of manpower in agriculture, No. 67
1965, *Geographic and occupational mobility of rural manpower*, No. 75.
Agricultural Policy Reports, Paris.
1964, *Low Incomes in Agriculture – Problems and Policies.*

OURY, B., 1959, *L'Agriculture au seuil du Marché Commun*, Paris.

CHAPTER 6

YUGOSLAVIA

ILYIN, M., 1965, 'Co-operation in the Countryside', *Medunarodna Politika No. 7*, Belgrade.

KARDELJ, E., 1962, *Problems of Socialist Policy in the Countryside*, London.

MARKOVIC, P., 1963, 'Socio-Economic Movements in the Countryside', *Yugoslav Survey*, Vo. IV, No. 12, 1711–30.

Popis Poljopriviede, 1960, *Agricultural Census* 1960, Belgrade 1964.

Popis Stanovništva, 1961, *Census of Population* 1961, Belgrade, various dates.

Statistički Bilteni, Belgrade, of which the following are particularly useful:
101 Dnevna Migracija Zaposlenog Osoblja (Daily Migration of Employed Workers) 1957.
263 Popis Poljoprivrede 1960 (Census of Agriculture) 1963.
271 Društvena Poljoprivredna Gazdinstva 1959–61. (Social Agricultural Holdings 1959–61), 1963. Also Bilten 393 for the year 1964.
370 Popis Poljoprivrede 1960, Rezultati Uzorka u Okviru Popisa (Census of Agriculture 1960. Sample Results within the Census Framework) 1965.
387 Anketa o Seljačkim Gazdinstivnna 1964 (Survey of Peasant Holdings in 1964) 1966. An annual survey is available for all the years since 1954/5.
424 Promet Poljoprivrednih Proizvoda 1965 (Otkup i Prodaja) (Turnover of Agricultural Products 1965 (Authorized Purchase and Sale) 1966.

Statistički Godišnjak SFRJ (Statistical Yearbook of the Socialist Federal Republic of Yugoslavia) Annual, Belgrade.

WARRINER, D., 1959, 'Urban Thinkers and Peasant Policy in Jugoslavia 1918–59', *The Slavonic and East European Review*, Vol. XXXVIII, No. 90, 59–81.

POLAND

CHILCZUK, M., 1962, *Rozwój I Rozmieszczenie Przemysłu Rolno-Spozywczego w Województwie Białostockim* (Food Industry of the Białystok Voivodship), Prace Geograficzne Nr. 137, Instytut Geograpfii, Polska Akademia Nauk, Warsaw.

CZERNIEWSKA, M., 1963, Budzety Domowe Rodzin Chłopskich, Warsaw.

DOBROWOLSKA. M., 1961, 'The Influence of Industrialization on the Formation of Regions', *Problems of Economic Regions*, Geographical Studies No. 27, Institute of Geography, Polish Academy of Sciences, pp. 243–55, Warsaw.

DZIEWICKA, M., 1963, 'Chlopi-Robotnicy', Warsaw.

GALESKI, B., 1964 (A), 'From peasant to farmer', *The Polish Sociological Bulletin No. 2*, 1964.

——, 1964 (B), 'Sociology of the Village', *Polish Perspectives*, Vol. VII, No. 12, 25–34.

——, 1966, Zimary Społeczono-Ekonomicznej Struktury Wsi 1957–62. Studia i Materialy, Zeszyt 122, Instytut Ekonomiki Rolnej, Warsaw.

Główny Urzad Statystyczny (G.U.S.) 1966, *Rolniczy Rocznik Statystyczny 1945–1965*, Warsaw.

Rocznik Statystyczny (Yearbook) Annual, Warsaw.

Geographica Polonica, 1965, *Land Utilization in East-Central Europe, Case Studies*, No. 5, Institute of Geography, Polish Academy of Sciences, Warsaw.

GOLACHOWSKI, S., 1967, 'Semi-Urbanization?', *Polish Perspectives*, Vol. X, No. 4, 22–30.

GOLFIN, J., 1961, 'La tâche du développement est elle d'ordre moral?', *Développement et Civilisations*, Avril-Juin, 34–44.

HUNEK, T., 1963, 'New Trends in Agricultural Policy', *Polish Perspectives*, Vol. VI, No. 1, 7–16.

Instytut Ekonokiki Rolnej (I.E.R.) 1966, *Wyniki Rachunkowosci Rolnej Gospodarstw Indywidualnych 1964/65*, Warsaw.

KORBONSKI, A., 1965, *Politics of Socialist Agriculture in Poland: 1945–1960*, New York and London.

MAŃKOWSKA, S., 1961, 'Der Pendelverkehr in der Wojewodschaft Krakow als Element der Ökonomisch-Geographischen Rayonierung', *Problems of Economic Regions*, Geographical Studies No. 27, Institute of Geography, Polish Academy of Sciences, pp. 211–21, Warsaw.

SZEMBERG, A., 1962, *Przemiany struktury agrarnej gospodarstw chłopskich w latach 1952–1960*, Warsaw.

——, 1963, 'Changes in Agrarian Structure', *Polish Perspectives*, Vol. VI, No. 10, 6–12.

——, 1965, 'Farming 1957–62', *Polish Perspectives*, Vol. VIII, No. 4, 24–9.

TEPICHT, J., 1966, 'Agricultural Circles in the Light of the General Problems of Agriculture', *Eastern European Economics*, Vol. IV, No. 4, 29–49.

TUROWSKI, J., 1964, 'Przemiany Wsi pod Wpływan Zakładu Przemysłowego – Studium rejonu Milejowa' (Transformation of the Village under the Influence of an Industrial Plant, the Milejowa region, Lublin), Tom VIII, Studia *Komitet Przestrzennego Zagospodarowania Kraju*, Polsak Akademia Nauk, Warsaw.

GLOSSARY

Ackernährung: the acreage which by local custom, in Germany, is considered adequate to support a family farm.

A.M.P.R.A.: Association pour les mutations professionnelles en agriculture. Established in 1964 and financed from F.A.S.A.S.A. the scheme assists farmers who wish to quit agriculture and acquire new professional qualifications.

Anerbrecht: a German term used in the text in not the strictest sense to refer to the practice of non-partible inheritance. Another term with a similar meaning is: geschlossene Vererbung.

A.M.N.E.R.: Association nationale de migrations et d'établissement rural. Established in 1949 to co-ordinate the activities of organizations assisting the migration of farmers from over populated to less populated regions.

Arbeiter-Bauer: worker-peasant.

Arbeitseinkommen: an accounting device used in the 'Green Report' representing the amount of income left to remunerate labour and management (family and non family) after costs, including a charge for capital, have been subtracted from gross income.

Aufstockung: the increase in area of holdings.

Aussiedlung: the extraction of farm houses and buildings from the congested centres of villages and towns and their re-establishment beyond the built up areas.

basse-cour: poultry yard, farmyard.

Braccianti: hired agricultural labourers.

Cassa per il Mezzogiorno: The Fund for the South, a largely autonomous public body concerned with the financing and planning of economic and social development in the South of Italy.

C.E.A.: Comités économiques agricoles: established by the loi complémentaire agricole of 1962, the task of these committees organized on a regional basis is to harmonize and discipline the production and sale of specific products. It is possible to oblige all producers within a region to adhere. The committees have a national federation.

C.E.N.A.G.: Centre des chefs d'entreprises agricoles. Founded in 1964 by members drawn from the Centre de jeunes patrons, the Mouvement familial rural and C.E.T.A., representative of the economically viable farming interests.

C.E.N.E.C.A.: Centre national des expositions et concours agricoles: a public organization for the promotion of sales of agricultural produce, particularly through the organization of agricultural fairs.

C.E.T.A.: Centres des études techniques agricoles.

C.G.A.: Centre de gestion agricoles.

C.N.A.S.E.A.: Centre national d'aménagement des structures d'exploitations agricoles, established by decree, 1966.

C.N.J.A.: Centre nationale des jeunes agriculteurs, originally founded in 1957 as the Cercle nationale des jeunes agriculteurs in accord with the F.N.S.E.A., this organization attracted many of the activists from the J.A.C. (Jeunesse agricole catholique). Under the leadership of its secretary-general Michel Debatisse – subsequently debarred from that position by an age limit – it became the most vocal and inventive promoter of the young and small peasant interests. The limited success of the structural policies during the '60s cast something of a shadow over its activities. More recently its vigour has been renewed and it has adopted a position on rural matters which coincides with neither that of the government or F.N.S.E.A. Raoul Seriey is the secretary general at present.

CO.F.R.E.D.A.: Compagnie pour favoriser la récherche et l'élargissement des débouches agricoles, a public marketing organization designed to take advantage of the favourable conditions created by the activities of SO.P.EX.A.

Colonia parziaria appoderato: share tenancy where the tenant works a self-contained farm.

Colonia parziaria non appoderato: share tenancy where the tenant is entrusted with the cultivation of land and crops but they do not constitute a self-contained farm.

Comité de Guéret: Founded in 1953 with Roland Viel and Philippe Lamour, the former secretary general of the C.G.A. (Confédération Générale d'Agriculture, defunct after 1953) as principal instigators, the Comité was responsible for barricading the roads in the Auvergne as a protest against government policy in October 1953, three months after the first use of tractors as road blocks in the Midi.

Commassazione: field consolidation.

Compartecipazione: a most precarious form of share cropping where the share cropper performs only part of the work required during the agricultural year. The contract has generally a duration of less than one year.

Comprensorio di bonifica: a co-ordinating authority for land improvement within a circumscribed area.

C.U.M.A.: Coopératives pour l'utilisation des machines agricoles.

E.R.A.S.: Ente per la Reforma Agraria in Sicilia.

Exploitation: in full, exploitation agricole; the unit of operation, composed of contiguous or non-contiguous fields, held in freehold or on lease, or in part freehold and leasehold, that may be part of a larger property.

F.A.S.A.S.A.: Fonds d'action sociale pour l'aménagement des structures agricoles. Created in 1962 for a period of twelve years to finance structural change by the Loi complémentaire agricole (the Pisani Law).

F.E.O.G.A.: Fonds Européen d'Orientation et de Garantie Agricole; in English: E.A.G.G.F. European Agricultural Guidance and Guarantee Fund.

F.I.A.T.: Fonds d'intervention pour l'aménagement du territoire.

Flurbereinigung: field consolidation.

F.N.S.E.A.: Fédération nationale des syndicats d'exploitants agricoles. Founded in 1946–7, the Fédération has become the most powerful exponent of the peasant and capitalist farmers' case. Since the beginning of 1968 M. Michel Debatisse has been the secretary-general. M. de Cafarelli is the president.

F.O.R.M.A.: Fonds d'orientation et de régularisation des marchés agricoles. Established in 1960 to regularise the markets for agricultural produce and to improve the commercialization of the products. It acts also through the mediation of other marketing organizations such as S.I.B.E.V. and Interlait.

G.A.E.C.: Groupements agricoles d'exploitation en commun. A form of co-operative farming which seeks to obtain conditions comparable with those of the family farm, legislated for in the Loi complémentaire agricole (Pisani Law).

G.N.I.B.C.: Groupement national interprofessionnel de la betterave, de la canne et des industries productrices de sucre et d'alcool.

Green Report and Green Plan: an annual report (Bericht der Bundesregierung über die Lage der Landwirtschaft – Grüner Bericht) prepared by the Ministry of Agriculture, which contains plans for the expenditure of agricultural appropriations (Massnahmen der Bundesregierung – Grüner Plan).

I.N.S.E.E.: Institut national de la statistique et des études économiques.

Interlait: Société interprofessionelle du lait et des ses derivés: producer regulatory marketing organization for dairy products.

I.V.D.: Indemnité viagère de depart: an annual sum paid to farmers over 65 who quit their land in favour of the young; the intention being that in the process a concentration of holdings will be favoured. The scheme is financed by F.A.S.A.S.A. The farmer receives between 1.200 and 2.000 francs in addition to the old age pension of 2,500 F. At the beginning of 1968, 107,390 persons had participated in the scheme, which is currently under revision.

Loi complémentaire agricole: the 'Pisani' Law of 8 August 1962.

Loi d'orientation agricole: the 'Debré' Law of 5 August 1960. Jointly the two laws have provided the legislative basis for the structural reform of French farming and the reorganization of marketing.

Mezzadria: strictly a type of labour contract which in fact takes the form of share tenancy in which the tenant retains considerable entrepreneurial responsibilities; most common in Tuscany, Umbria, the Abruzzi and the Marches.

Mezzogiorno: the southern part of peninsular Italy including Sicily and Sardinia.

Milliard: one thousand million.

M.O.D.E.F.: Mouvement de défense des exploitations familiales. Held first national congress in 1965, receives the support of the Communist Party.

N.E.A.: Nouvelle enterprise agricole.

O.N.C.: Opera Nazionale per i Combattenti, a land settlement and reclamation scheme for war veterans to encourage family-sized holdings which became prominent in the Mussolini era. Most of the work was performed in the Pontine Marshes, the lower Volturno district and the Tavoliere.

O.N.I.C.: Office national interprofessionnel des céréales, a state cereal regulatory marketing organization.

O.Z.Z.: Opšte Zemljoradničke Zadruge – the Yugoslav general agricultural co-operative.

Pendler: German for a commuter, hence Pendlewanderung: commuting; Aus and Ein – pendler, i.e. with respect to a given locality an Auspendler is one who commutes out to his place of work, an Einpendler is one who commutes in; a Fernpendler is one who commutes over a considerable distance. The French term is: navette.

P.K.D.F.: Poljoprivredni Kombinati, Dobra i Farme: the Yugoslav state farm.

Podere: a farm, used in the Italian land reform schemes to denote a full-time family as opposed to a part-time (quota) holding.

Polyculture: a farming system, autarkic in content, that ensures a high degree of self sufficiency by combining a wide range of crops with some livestock raising.

Quota: a part-time Italian land reform holding, see podere.

Raumordnung: areal planning, equivalent to town and country planning.

Realteilung: a German term referring to the practice of partible inheritance; alternatively one may use the term Freiteilbarkeit.

Remembrement: field consolidation.
German: Flurbereinigung; Italian: commassazione.

Roheinkommen: an accounting device used in the 'Green Report' representing the amount of income left to remunerate the labour and management of the family after all other costs, including those for hired labour, have been deducted from gross income.

S.A.F.E.R.: Sociétés d'aménagement foncier et d'établissement rural:
Established by decree under the 1960 (Debré) Loi d'orientation agricole and subsequently granted the right of pre-emption in 1962, these 'Land Banks' represent one of the most original and effective mechanisms for structural reform.

S.A.I.F.: Sociétés agricoles d'investissement foncier:
A still-born government project aimed to relieve the farm operator of the burden of capital charges.

S.I.B.E.V.: Société interprofessionnelle du bétail et viandes: a producer meat regulatory marketing organization.

S.I.C.A.: Sociétés d'intérêt collectif agricole: a decree of 1961 now permits these societies that originated in 1919 to accept industrial and commercial members provided the farmers retain a half share of the votes.

S.I.LIN.: Société interprofessionnelle des graines et huiles de lin, a producer regulatory marketing organization for flax products.

S.I.O.F.A.: Société interprofessionnelle des oléagineux fluides alimentaires, a producer regulatory marketing organization for oils.

S.L.U.: standard labour units, an anglicization of European terms which mean the same thing though based upon different methods of calculation;
Vollarbeitskraften (V.A.K.); Unité-travailleur-homme (U.T.H.) and Personne-année-travail (P.A.T.); Unita lavoratrici.

S.N.I.P.O.T.: Société nationale interprofessionnelle de la pomme de terre, a producer potato regulatory marketing organization.

S.O.D.E.C.C.O.: Société pour le développement économique du Centre et Centre-Ouest.

S.O.M.I.V.A.L.: Société pour la mise en valeur de l'Auvergne et du Limousin.

SO.P.EX.A.: Société pour la promotion de l'exportation des produits agricoles, a state information organization to promote sales of agricultural produce in France and overseas.

Sozialebrache: agricultural land left fallow for social rather than agronomic reasons.

S.R.Z.: Seljacke radne zadruge: the unpopular Yugoslav collective.

Structure: in full, structure agraire, agrarian structure; but the French usage produces some unavoidable Gallicisms: structural policy, and restructuration.

S.V.I.M.E.Z.: Associazione per lo sviluppo dell'industria nel Mezzogiorno. A semi-public body concerned with publicizing and encouraging the economic development South, providing information upon and courses dealing with economic growth in the South.

Vergleichslohn: a level of return to farmers for labour and management that is regarded as comparable with industrial wages for a similar level of skill. In short: parity wage or parity income.

Vulgarisation: agricultural extension work.

Index